D1557525

The Sash Canada Wore

The Sash Canada Wore:
A Historical Geography of
the Orange Order
in Canada

CECIL J. HOUSTON
WILLIAM J. SMYTH

UNIVERSITY OF TORONTO PRESS

Toronto Buffalo London

© University of Toronto Press 1980
Toronto Buffalo London
Printed in Canada

ISBN 0-8020-5493-5

Canadian Cataloguing in Publication Data

Houston, Cecil J., 1943–

The sash Canada wore
Bibliography: p.
Includes index.
ISBN 0-8020-5493-5

1. Loyal Orange Association of British America – History.
2. Orangemen – History.
I. Smyth, William J., 1949–   II. Title.
HSI547.074H68   971   C80-094224-8

This book has been published with the help of a grant from the Social Science Federation of Canada, using funds provided by the Social Sciences and Humanities Research Council of Canada, and a grant from the Andrew W. Mellon Foundation to the University of Toronto Press.

The authors wish to acknowledge permission granted by the following for use of copyright material: Academic Press (Inc.) London Ltd. for table 1 and figures 2 and 3 from Cecil Houston and William J. Smyth, 'The Orange Order and the expansion of the frontier in Ontario, 1830–1900,' in *Journal of Historical Geography* 4, no. 3 (1978): 251–64; the governing council of the University of Toronto for figure 1 from Cecil Houston and William Smyth, 'The Ulster Legacy' in *Multiculturalism* 1, no. 4 (1978): 9–12.

To Natasha and Rosemary

Preface

This work explores the role of the Orange Order in the unfolding settlement geography of Canada. Orangeism as an ideology of protestantism and loyalty and the Orange lodge as a focus for social interaction are studied within a wider perspective aimed at elucidating some elements in the social and cultural life of Canada as that country progressed from British colonial status to an ethnically complex and industrially advanced modern nation.

Although a distinctly Irish creation, the Orange Order, early in its development, was inserted into a British North America being opened to British settlers. Protestant Irish soldiers and emigrants, largely Ulster-born, introduced the organization into New Brunswick, Quebec, and Ontario within the first decade of the nineteenth century. For the next forty years, successive waves of Ulster emigrants extended the Orange ideals and the order's institutional superstructure to the settlement frontier. However, by the mid-nineteenth century it was evident that the order was no longer a purely ethnic association. The Canadian-born sons, not only of Ulstermen but of the English, Scots, and even Germans and native Indians, were increasingly represented in the lodges. The organization began to assume a Canadian identity and it was as a Canadian institution that it played a central role in the continuing development of the new country.

Because the Orange Order emerged as a recognizable ingredient in the Canadian mosaic and ceased to be a purely immigrant phenomenon, its study posed several methodological problems. The resultant work drew upon the approaches employed by cultural geographers and folklorists interested in transatlantic diffusions and blended these with methods of analysis most commonly ascribed to social historians. Overall a historical geographical perspective was maintained through the writers' interest in the geographical processes exhibited by the spread of the order throughout Canada and by our perception of Orangeism as critical to emerging Canadian regionalism. In pursuit of our aims we collected and examined somewhat unorthodox, and previously unexamined, source materials, and this archival work was supported, and indeed extended, by intensive field investigations.

Initial interest in the topic was prompted by a shared desire to probe the implications of an Ulster link in Canada's development. Both authors were born in Ulster – counties Derry and Armagh respectively – and both subsequently emigrated to Canada where they met as teaching colleagues in the Department of Geography, Erindale College, University of Toronto, in 1973. Personal interest was sustained by a more formal commitment to the cultural and historical geography of Canada and it was as geographers rather than as émigré Ulstermen that the topic was approached. The first exploratory step was made by interviewing a county Fermanagh Orangeman who had been resident in Ontario since 1926, and from his home on St Clair Ave, Toronto, the research path led us to the national Orange headquarters in Toronto and subsequently to all the provincial grand lodges throughout Canada. Archival research was supplemented by fieldwork in Ontario, Quebec, New Brunswick, Nova Scotia, Prince Edward Island, Newfoundland, and British Columbia, whereby we built up a more extensive body of documentary data and acquired a rich knowledge of local Orange tradition and an appreciation for Orange landscapes in Canada.

The project was a thoroughly pleasant experience but it was made all the more agreeable by the kindness and friendliness which greeted our searches. Several people made the project possible. Norman Ritchie, grand secretary, and David Griffin, grand treasurer, of the Loyal Orange Association of British America; James Book, provincial Orange grand secretary, Ontario East; David Worden, provincial Orange grand secretary, Ontario West; and Arnold Slaney, provincial Orange grand secretary, New Brunswick, deserve a special vote of thanks for their cooperation in making data available to us. Howard Andrews, dean of social sciences, Erindale College, and Jacob Spelt, chairman, Department of Geography, University of Toronto, provided encouragement and access to research support. The Canada Council provided funds for travel to Newfoundland. Support and critical advice were provided by our colleagues in geography and history. We owe a special debt to John Mannion for his perceptive criticisms. Patricia Whitehead, Alan Wallace, and Walter Schneider worked as research assistants for short periods. Geoff Matthews and Jenny Wilcox produced the maps. Gayle Dykeman,

Bonnie Stiff, and Jean Watts typed a scribbled manuscript at short notice with speed and good humour. Bonnie also arranged our first contact with Orangemen.

Above all others, our wives, Natasha and Rosemary, provided encouragement, occasionally research assistance, and tolerance – especially when the authors would disappear at short notice for what was known as an Orange lodge hunt.

Toronto, Canada
Maynooth, Ireland

December 1979

Contents

The Sash Canada Wore:
A Historical Geography of
the Orange Order
in Canada

THE SASH

Chorus
It is old and it is beautiful
And the colours they are fine
It was worn at Derry,
Aughrim, Enniskillen and the Boyne.
My father wore it when a youth
In bygone days of yore
And it's on the Twelfth I love to wear
The sash my father wore.

Verses
Here am I a loyal Orangeman
Just come across the sea.
For singing and for dancing
I'm sure that I'll please thee.
I'll sing and dance with any man
As I did in days of yore
And on the Twelfth I'll proudly wear
The sash my father wore.

Now you look after me, old boy
And I'll look after you.
And we'll keep the old flag flying,
The old red, white and blue.
Our cry was, No Surrender,
No republic we will join.
And it will always be as now
Derry, Aughrim and the Boyne.

Oh, it's now I'm going to leave you
Good luck to you, I'll say
And when I'm on the ocean
I hope for me you'll pray.
I'm going to my native land
To a place they call Dromore
Where on the Twelfth, I'll proudly wear
The sash my father wore.

Traditional song of Orangemen around the world.

1

Introduction

This book examines the role of the resolutely protestant and loyalist Orange Order in the development of Canada. It traces the fraternal organization from its birth in 1795 in a rural village of Ulster, through its rapid transfer overseas, to its culmination as a major social and political force in the colonies of British North America (present-day Canada). Geographically, the order's domain eventually embraced every Canadian province, although its power and influence were greatest in Ontario, New Brunswick, and Newfoundland. All adult male protestants were eligible to join and in Canada toward the end of the nineteenth century as many as one in every three was reckoned to be a member[1]: through contact with Orange fathers, brothers, husbands, friends, and neighbours the order was known by an even larger population. Until recently, it formed an integral part of Canadian life. From its platforms and through its activities it expressed and sustained a vision of the destiny of the new country on whose frontiers and settled parts alike it performed the role of garrison of protestantism and Britishness. It was not, as it is often portrayed today, an anachronism, an unwanted extreme, solely a source of anti-catholicism and social divisiveness. It was rather a bulwark of colonial protestantism.

A politico-religious society, the Orange Order holds as its aims the defence of protestantism, and the twinned insistence of loyalty to the British monarchy and maintenance of Canada's constitutional arrangements with Britain. King William III, Prince of Orange, is its central symbol, his defeat of James II at the Battle of the Boyne River in Ireland on 12 July 1690, its central myth – the victory of combined protestantism and constitutional monarchy. Annually, on the 'Twelfth' of July Orangemen throughout the world parade in commemoration of the events of 1690. The qualifications for becoming an Orangeman, first published in Ireland in 1798, emphasized the religious nature of the fraternity.

He should have a sincere love and veneration for his Almighty Maker, productive of those lively and happy fruits, righteousness – and obedience to His commands. A firm and steady faith in the Saviour of the World; convinced that He is the only Mediator between a sinful creature and an offended Creator. Without these he can be no Christian. Of a humane and compassionate disposition, and a courteous and affable behaviour. He should be an utter enemy to savage brutality and unchristian-like cruelty. Let him be a lover of society and improving company, and have a laudable regard for the Protestant Religion, and a sincere endeavour to propagate its precepts – zealous of promoting the honour of his King and Country, and a hearty desire for victory and success, but convinced and assured that GOD alone can grant it.

A hatred for cursing and swearing, and taking the name of GOD in vain, (a shameful practice) taking all opportunities to discourage it among his brethren. Wisdom and prudence should guide his actions, honesty and integrity influence his conduct, and honour and glory be the motive of his endeavours.

Lastly – he must pay the strictest attention to a religious observance of the Sabbath, and also of temperance sobriety.[2]

Demanding brotherhood and high standards of private and public morality, these principles implied also a political and anti-catholic dimension. In the Orangemen's view, they could be secured only under a British and protestant monarch. The tenets and structure of catholicism were threats, seen as the epitome of disloyalty and moral laxity. Today, almost two centuries later and on the other side of the Atlantic the same attitudes 'toward God, toward Queen and Country, and toward Mankind,' and the same assertive tone are maintained by Canadian Orangemen.[3] For them, in the full meaning of the words of 'The Sash,' there has been 'No Surrender.'

As an unyielding proponent of protestantism and loyalty, Orangeism has acquired a rather negative image replete with tales of community conflict and religious discrimination. In Canada, Orangemen have been judged an unattractive part of the cultural mosaic. References to them appear often in the context of explosive past events – the Riel rebellions of 1870 and 1885, the Manitoba separate schools issue of 1890–96, and the conscription crises of the twentieth century. Other references dwell on Orange-catholic riots which were an all too common occurrence in the nineteenth century. Most serious historical studies focus on the order's political activities and have built a view of the order as a solely Irish fraternity, bent on introducing Old World conflicts into the political setting of the New. Orange alliances and thwarted agreements, personalities, electioneering, and power balances have been the principal interests.[4] Few writers have come forward to alter significantly that

The basic principles of Canadian Orangeism were outlined in this pamphlet issued by the Loyal Orange Association of British America in 1977. The equestrian represents William III (King Billy) crossing the Boyne River in Ireland on 12 July 1690.

emphasis. Casual comments by some indicate an awareness of the order's 'more peaceful and non-political activities'[5] but the dimensions of that role have yet to be explored. It is our intent to broaden the interpretation of Canadian Orangeism through a study of its geography and its role as a bond for protestant communities in a developing nation. The order's rise during the nineteenth century, its demise during the twentieth, and its condition in the 1970s will be analysed.

Orangeism was carried from Ireland after 1795 to most British colonies,[6] but nowhere outside of Ulster did it find as widespread acceptance as in Canada. It was introduced and initially supported there by the large numbers of Ulster immigrants and it eventually achieved a position of such power and respectability that it was able to attract thousands of non-Irish into its ranks. Protestantism and loyalty to the British connection were not values peculiar to protestant Ireland and on that basis,

Orangeism, once established, was able to appeal to a wide cross-section of the Canadian population. The ultra-loyalism and ultra-protestantism of the Orange Order offered a philosophy differing in degree, not in kind, from that held by the mass of Canadian protestants. They were comfortably accommodated within the framework of a protestant, British, and tory Canada which had been separated deliberately from the United States and joined deliberately to a French Catholic realm. The order found in the country a politico-religious atmosphere conducive to its growth for in the nineteenth century religion and politics were inseparable.[7] The accusation was often made that catholics, because of their supposed temporal allegiance to the pope, were incapable of being loyal subjects of a protestant state, a view not confined to Orangemen. The stance of the order was not exceptional and it claimed neither exclusive loyalty nor exclusive protestantism but would 'accept as a member no man whose principles are not loyal, and whose creed is not protestant.'[8]

In its new home the order provided for protestants, both immigrant and native-born, both Irish and non-Irish, a familiar anchorage and source of fraternal aid. From the farming, mining, and urban industrial frontiers of Canada to the isolated fishing outports of Newfoundland, Orangeism served essential community needs. The primary function of the order in Canada was expressed at a local level through the social activities and ritual glamour of individual lodges. Anything from a convivial forum for local affairs to service as a surrogate church could be provided within a lodge. From this essentially social base, the order, through a hierarchical network of district, county, provincial, and national lodges, and by virtue of its ideology and numerical strength, was able to acquire political importance. The order's development was intimately bound up with that of Canada and as the country progressed towards nationhood the fortunes of the order waned.

Our interpretation of the nature of Canadian Orangeism will be developed in the context of the establishment and demise of a colonial frame of mind, not in terms of ethnic cultural retention and eventual acculturation. By virtue of its variety of membership and its persistence for more than a century the order emerged as something more than yet another ethnic organization. The principal focus of this work is a transplanted institution and the role it assumed in a new setting.[9] The principal perspectives are those of historical geography, and they are ideally suited to the study of an institution that grew as Canada's frontiers unfolded, transcending the marked regionalism of the country. Because of the clear association of particular ideas and the institution, study of the temporal and geographical development of the Orange Order reveals the strength and persistence of the Orange ideology. Through analysis of the order, the place of loyalty, protestantism, anti-catholicism, and ethnicity in the development of the nation – elements that have contributed to Canada's 'limited identities'[10] – can be probed. At the outset the order represented an ethnic and immigrant institution, but while retaining its principles it came to be much more. It grew as Canada grew and became an integral part of what might be called the Canadian colonial identity.

2

The Irish, British, and Canadian Beginnings

Here am I a loyal Orangeman
Just come across the sea

Orangeism was a distinctly protestant Irish creation which through the migration of its sympathizers was carried to England and Scotland, British North America, and subsequently throughout the British colonial empire, notably to Australia and New Zealand. Its transfer to those areas was extremely rapid, and once established, the order attracted and grew through the inclusion of groups other than its Irish founders. Orange principles proved remarkably adaptable to a great variety of social and economic milieus. From the rising industrial cities of northern England and Scotland to the logging camps, pioneering agricultural communities, mining towns and fishing villages of British North America, and similarly to the new societies of the antipodes, the rhetoric, songs, and public displays of Orangeism were witnessed. Few cultural phenomena have been transferred so widely and quickly and so successfully implanted and sustained as the ideology and organization of that peculiarly ultra-protestant and loyalist fraternity, first instituted in an insignificant rural village of late eighteenth-century Ireland.

Irish origins

Within Irish social and economic historiography there is insufficient evidence to indicate the precise circumstances that gave rise to the creation and widespread diffusion of Orangeism in the protestant community. There are enough general indicators to suggest that it was bred in an atmosphere of distrust and conflict among protestant and catholic groups undergoing severe economic disruption in the northern province of Ulster. In Ireland, a clear distinction was drawn between the power and privileges of catholics and the protestant ascendancy. The protestants dominated Ireland, a product of England's colonization of the island during the sixteenth and seventeenth centuries. Throughout the colonial society secular power was placed in their hands and especially in those of the English whose Church of Ireland was state established and supported by tithes from Dissenters and catholics alike. The Dissenters, representing approximately half of the protestant population, were the descendants of Scottish Presbyterian settlers. Their position in the ascendancy was secondary, and during the eighteenth century many of them, prompted by their political and growing economic insecurity, made their way to America. By the end of the century, however, their position in Ireland had improved and they were becoming officially acknowledged as part of the 'Protestant Nation.'[1]

Catholics, descendants of native Irish, were excluded from power. From 1690, their religious practices and political and economic opportunities had been constrained by the operation of the punitive Penal Laws. In the latter decades of the 1700s the rights of catholics emerged as the fundamental issue in Irish politics.[2] Some restrictions were removed at that time, and in 1793 catholics were given the right to vote in parliamentary elections. It was not until the Emancipation Act of 1829, however, that they were permitted to sit in parliament. Within Irish society politics and religion were closely intertwined and in many respects the ability of a man to exert power in the community was as much a function of his church affiliation as it was of his personal wealth. As Professor J.C. Beckett, the Irish historian, recently noted:

for Irishmen religion was more than the expression of theological belief. Protestant and Roman Catholic were separated by a gulf deeper than that between the Thirty-nine Articles and the Creed of Pope Pius IV. They formed, in fact, two communities, to some extent intermingled and interdependent, but consciously different; and between them lay the memory of conquest and confiscation, massacre and pillage, conspiracy and persecution. In this long struggle religion had determined the side on which a man stood; but the struggle had been one for land and power, and religion had been a badge of difference rather than the main issue in dispute.[3]

The politico-religious alignment of society had its ramifications not only at the national level of government but also at the local community scale, especially in Ulster. There, the general model of a catholic Ireland ruled by an ascendancy of protestant landlords was further complicated by the presence of a protestant majority at all levels of the social spectrum. In Ulster, the potential for sectarian conflict was greatest. In parts of the province such as north Armagh, catholic and protestant townlands were interspersed and relations between the two groups were often less than neighbourly. At the lower levels of society, as among the elite, power was defined in terms of access to land and both catholics and protestants competed fiercely for it. Farms were labelled protestant or catholic and leases were jealously guarded. Even among the supposedly landless weavers competition for an acre or less of rented potato ground was keen. A rapidly increasing population and a stagnating rural economy[4] in the latter years of the eighteenth century brought the socio-economic competition to a violent and sectarian head. Against this background of conflict and rivalry numerous secretive factions and interest groups had been called into being.

The oath-bound societies, found on both sides of the religious divide and composed mainly of small tenant-farmers and labourers, were essentially defensive, but they engaged frequently in assaults on the property and persons of the more prosperous classes. Rival catholic and protestant societies also clashed with each other. They were purely local in both interest and organization and did not constitute a nationally coordinated force. In county Armagh opposing groups were known as the Defenders (catholics) and the Peep o'Day Boys (protestants), and both had sworn that 'we'll deal with none but our own sort.'[5] In 1795 after one notoriously bloody clash between these two factions, the Orange society was founded in the village of Loughgall to better coordinate local protestant defences. An accident of history and a degree of good organization thrust this society out of otherwise local obscurity to the prominence of a national and ultimately international phenomenon.

As yet no detailed analysis exists of the social and economic character of the incipient Orange movement. Hereward Senior has clarified the linkages within the early leadership,[6] and sociologist Peter Gibbon has attempted to place the rise of the Orange phenomenon in the context of a group designed to defend working-class interests.[7] However, the sources available have not permitted an analysis equal to that which is proposed in this study of the Canadian order. More evidence is required not only on the class background of early Orangemen in Ireland but also on the geography of those networks through which the fraternity diffused with such ease. It is known however that the three founders of the secret Orange society in mid Ulster were local innkeepers, Dan Winter, James Sloan, and a James Wilson, all active Freemasons.[8] It was hardly surprising that the masonic concept of a cellular organization of lodges, together with an internal ranking system of degrees should have served as the model for the new society. The ritual, passwords, and secret signs of middle-class masonry were blended with the more belligerent and lower-class nature of the Peep o'Day Boys. It was from those Boys that the majority of the first Orangemen were recruited and the activities of the Orange society during its first year differed little from those of its predecessor. The wrecking and burning of catholic homes and linen looms, beatings and shootings, summarized by the authorities as the 'Armagh outrages,' forced many catholic families to quit the area.

These activities clashed with the ideals of a respectable fraternity and created tensions among those leaders wishing to cultivate a more disciplined image. None the less, the cult of respectability permitted the association of some gentry with the predominantly popular organization. Two of the earliest such members were the Trinity College students William Blacker and Thomas Verner, sons of county Armagh landlord families. However, events external to the order proved crucial to a much greater involvement of a powerful section of the Irish landed gentry. By 1796, the Defenders and the United Irishmen, Wolfe Tone's doctrinaire republicans, had joined forces, and there appeared a real possibility of an assault on the power and authority of the privileged classes, following the example of the French revolution. The government, to resist the potential uprising and also to guard against a threatened French invasion, authorized the gentry in August 1796 to arm a yeomanry. William Blacker was one of those appointed to command and recruit the new force, a task which he quickly fulfilled 'by taking into council a number of Orange leaders' and recruiting directly from among the Orange lodges.[9] In this way Orangeism came to be identified with defence of the status quo. Its leadership also became increasingly aristocratic. Early in 1797 a ritual degree or rank of marksman was instituted and served to define within the order an exclusive band of reputable men.[10] In June 1797 Thomas Verner, on returning to Dublin from Armagh, founded in the capital Loyal Orange Lodge (LOL) 176, which quickly became known as the Gentlemen's Lodge, drawing many of its members from Trinity College students.[11] The registration number of the Gentlemen's Lodge, 176, indicates that in the short span of twenty-one months following the fight at Loughgall 175 lodges had been established. A critical mass had been reached and on 12 July 1797 a provincial grand lodge for Ulster was created. The Loughgall men, Sloan, Winter, and Wilson, had convened the organizational meeting but stepped aside in favour of the leadership of a group of Ulster gentry, foremost among whom were Blacker and Verner.[12] Under their direction a national grand lodge was formed in Dublin in April 1798. A hierarchical system of local, district, and county lodges, all ultimately responsible to the Irish Grand Lodge, and a standardized set of rules and ritual were designed. The secret society of a small Armagh village had become national.

The strength of the organization in 1798 was readily apparent in the role which the Orange yeomanry played in quelling the United Irishmen's rebellion. An Orange membership of 170,000 was claimed in Ulster at the time, and although that figure was undoubtedly greatly exaggerated,[13] there can be no denying the significance of the Orange involvement. For Orangemen, the rebellion was a reminder of the fragility of their position within a catholic society perceived to be continually subversive and they took up defence of the government with a vengeance. Through its actions the order achieved within the government a reputation of credence and respectability, among the protestant community the position of vigilant defender, but in the eyes of catholics and republicans a notorious image of butchery. Its role in the rebellion thrust the order clearly into the forefront of Irish affairs. An effective national organization had been established and the subsequent spread of its network through the country was rapid. Numerous military lodges extended the order to many parts where it proved attractive to the siege mentality of the 'Protestant Nation.' Landlords, eager to ally with or, more often, harness the movement, encouraged the formation of lodges among a tenantry already well disposed to its principles and thus abetted the process of diffusion. By 1800 lodges had been organized in every county in Ulster, and many of the small and scattered protestant settlements throughout the rest of the country had been drawn into the growing orbit of Orangeism.

The fundamental explanation for the expansion of the order rests with the suitability and appeal of Orangeism to the protestant Irish psyche. 'Orangeism' was simply a term, a convenient label for the established views of a protestant and planted minority perceiving itself perpetually besieged by a catholic majority. A distinction between religion and politics was impossible, nor could religion and politics be extricated from the British and monarchial tradition. In the mixture was a particularly colonial and defensive frame of mind and the protestant Irishman, fearful of any weakening of support from the British and protestant homeland, redoubled his declarations of loyalty while increasingly turning towards the internal security offered by his own community. Self-reliant but socially conservative, the protestant Irish, at home and later abroad, were characterized by intransigent attitudes to catholics and to Britain. In the last five years of the eighteenth century the message of Orangeism was already old, only the ritual and structured organization were new. The order simply provided a fraternal framework for a protestant and loyalist Irish mentality.

While acting as an ideological garrison the order also played an essential role as a focus for life in protestant communities at a time when few opportunities for formal social interaction existed outside the church.

In the heartlands of protestant Ireland, almost every village and hamlet could boast an Orange lodge. The lodges embraced an assortment of small tenant farmers, agricultural labourers, and domestic linen workers.[14] Their meeting places, whether public houses or halls, were centres where everyday matters and political crises could be discussed equally well amid a convivial atmosphere redolent with tobacco smoke and drink. A community supper, the advancement of a member to a higher degree, or the planning of retaliation against some imagined catholic aggression might all form part of the same agenda. The lodge's business was local business.

The local role of the lodge and its preoccupation with the mundane matters of rural Ireland have been neglected by historians in favour of the order's more national political escapades, escapades in which the aristocracy featured and which accordingly generated much comment. To be sure, aristocrats had been central in the order from the beginning, but as the decades after the Act of Union (1800) unfolded in relative tranquility, the interest of the elite waned. Only in the years immediately preceding the 1829 Emancipation Act did they again assume a prominent role in an effort to mobilize the latent power of the mass association. No clearer evidence of this renewed interest can be found than in the appointment of the Duke of Cumberland, the king's brother, as grand master in 1828. The interest was ephemeral, and after a parliamentary investigation of excesses committed in the name of the order, the grand lodge went into voluntary abeyance and the gentry again faded from prominence. However, despite the fluctuating fortunes of the grand lodge, the local community functions continued to sustain the movement.

Widespread inclusion of a middle class within the order was not realized until the last third of the nineteenth century. Initially, the larger farmers of Down, Antrim, and north Derry ignored the organization. Not until the disestablishment of the Church of Ireland in 1870 did Presbyterian ministers and the middle-class elements of their congregations assume prominence in the movement. Thenceforth Orangeism and protestantism became almost synonymous in an organization whose early tone had been set by low church Anglicans. The entry of middle-class groups was further prompted by a wider set of political and economic forces. After more than half a century of rapid industrialization a solid industrial and commercial class had emerged in Ulster which saw its interests as being intimately linked with those of Britain. In the anxiety generated by proposed home rule for Ireland the industrial middle class threw its lot in with the Orangemen. 'By joining the Orange order and linking it to their party, by exploiting the tension between Protestant and Catholic slum-dwellers in Belfast, by stirring up memories of the ancient conflict between settler and native, and by claiming that Home Rule would mean domination by the Catholic Church, the Unionists – as the alliance of Tories and renegade Liberals was now called – were able to mobilise the mass of the Protestant population behind them.'[15] That coalition has constituted political protestantism in Ireland to the present day.

Transfer to Britain

The organizational structure of the order facilitated the diffusion of Orangeism into new areas while retaining sufficient controls to ensure that the offspring would be an authentic replica of the Irish parent. Lodges could be formed only on the authority of a warrant issued by the Irish Grand Lodge. Each new lodge conformed in its ritual and mode of business to a fixed schedule of laws and regulations. These could be supplemented, but not replaced, by the local lodge's own set of by-laws. Individuals, upon initiation, swore a common oath and received a certificate from the lodge master, signifying that the holder was a true and respectable Orangeman in good standing with the order. Orange certificates and lodge warrants, initially at least, were as mobile as their bearers, and given the degree of emigration from Ireland and the movement of army regiments to stations at home and in the colonies it was hardly surprising that the Orange Order should have been carried beyond Ireland in an unchanged form.

The mobility of the government forces, containing numerous military lodges within their ranks, was a major factor in the spread of Orangeism into Britain, and, until 1835, the fortunes of the order there were inextricably bound up with this military link. A regiment of the Lancashire militia carried warrant no. 220 to Manchester in 1798 and thus created the first Orange foothold in England.[16] Sustained by the addition of a few more military lodges and the creation of some civilian units, Lancashire emerged as the initial Orange heartland across the Irish Sea. The bulk of the membership of these early English lodges was composed of both Irishmen recruited by the army in Ireland and recent Irish immigrants.[17] Within their new setting the lodges served as a ready means of preserving protestant Irish culture while at the same time distinguishing the members from the greater mass of catholic Irish immigrants. The fledgling lodges also operated within the British context of a whole host of contemporary working-class self-help and friendly societies, Lancashire being especially noted for this kind of early industrial social welfare. It is quite possible that the character and business of Orange lodges was influenced by the example of the indigenous voluntary societies. Certainly, some of the lodges did incorporate mutual benefit functions, but this arrangement arose from local initiative and was not an integral part of the wider scheme of Orangeism.[18] Unlike other voluntary societies however, the Orange lodges were distinguished by their anti-catholicism and obvious ultra-tory political orientation.

The British version of Orangeism emerged as a purely urban phenomenon. The bulk of its adherents were drawn from the textile factories of Liverpool, Manchester, Oldham, Stockport, and Rochdale and from such Scottish centres as Glasgow, Dundee, and Edinburgh. In London, however, its power base remained relatively weak during the first quarter of the nineteenth century, and despite subsequent growth there the order continued to be largely northern industrial. The geography of Orangeism in England was the geography of protestant Irish immigration. As had been the case in Ireland, the plebian base was soon overlain by a veneer of English tory gentry. Aristocrats were instrumental in founding in Manchester in 1808 an English grand lodge which recalled the warrants brought from Ireland and replaced them with a series of its own. In 1813 a lodge for gentlemen was established in London by lords Kenyon and Yarmouth, and a royal touch was subsequently added to this elite group by the initiations of the dukes of York and Cumberland.[19] The somewhat incongruous alliance of aristocracy and working class in an organization founded only a few years earlier amid the poverty of rural Ireland had all the appearance of a marriage of convenience. To be sure, the Orange tenets of protestantism and loyalty to the monarchy were ideologically appealing to the ultra-tory elite but social compatibility within the movement was scarely feasible. The hope that the London lodge could successfully repeat the performance of its Dublin counterpart in engineering mass political support when necessary, was not to be realized. England was politically much different from Ireland and the anti-catholicism of Orangemen, affected by their own status as immigrants, did not offer a base sufficiently strong for power. Nevertheless, Orangeism survived as a minor element of working-class culture in industrial centres of northwest England and northern Scotland, where immigrants from Ulster and their descendants formed significant communities. Today these regions still boast Orange halls and Twelfth of July parades and regularly send contingents to the Twelfth celebrations in Belfast. Despite its longevity, the order in England was a pale reflection of its counterpart in Canada where Orangeism and Orangemen were able to assume a role central to the society.

Transfer to British North America

The same mechanism that had permitted the extension of Orangeism into England also facilitated its transatlantic transfer. Orange principles and, occasionally, warrants authorizing lodges were carried across the Atlantic to colonial outposts in British North America by both military and civilians. As early as 1799 a military lodge may have been in operation in Halifax[20] and evidence that one did function in Montreal in 1800 has been recorded.[21] Lodges in overseas garrisons were ephemeral, however, dependent upon regimental postings and, often as not, officers' goodwill. Many soldiers, after being demobilized, settled in the new country and they together with the mass of Irish immigrants established the solid foundation of the Canadian order. Orangeism in Canada grew with the country, developing along lines dictated by the unfolding settlement geography of a new society. It assumed a rural and small town character. Protestant Irish immigrants, the largest group moving to that essentially empty land,[22] not only brought Orangeism with them as part of their cultural baggage but insured by their numerical preponderance that their Orange institution would not go unnoticed. Neither could it be suffocated by preexisting political and social alignments.

Frontier lodges were spontaneous creations around one or two settlers who brought with them a certificate of initiation, perhaps a warrant, but more likely only knowledge of Orange ritual and principles. In the pioneering areas there was no one to challenge the right to create such lodges and no organization to direct and regulate their activities. Seldom too was there anyone to record the event and most of the earliest history of Canadian Orangeism has been passed on orally. The early movement of Orangemen up the Saint John River valley in New Brunswick is well known but impossible to document. An important hearth for the order in maritime Canada was created by members of that first incursion. A second major hearth developed equally early in central Canada in the St Lawrence and Ottawa river valleys and along the Lake Ontario shore. One family history illustrates well the desultory beginnings and the persistence of the Orange tradition in central Canada. In 1803 John Murphy and son, both recently released from the Irish yeomanry took up their service allotment of land in the Clarendon district on the Quebec side of the Ottawa Valley.[23] They came to the area from Ulster via Liverpool and the Canadian Maritimes. Lumbering, land clearance, and subsistence agriculture characterized the family's first years on the frontier. Together with their neighbours, the Armstrongs and McCords, the Murphys recreated on the margins of catholic Quebec a new Ulster, a colonial outpost, an implanted enclave. It remains today within and yet separate from the province as a settlement whose heritage, distinguished by Anglican churches and Orange lodges, is strikingly recognizable. A descendant of John Murphy now serves as master of the Quebec Grand Lodge.

Countrymen of the Murphys arriving in the main immigration wave after the Napoleonic Wars followed the same route up the St Lawrence.

Transfer certificate of Joseph Farrell, LOL 115, Bellaghy, Ireland, 1832. This document was found among lodge records in Toronto.

Some settled in Montreal and the nearby Laurentian foothills; however, the majority continued upriver to lands being surveyed in Upper Canada (Ontario). In the eastern areas of the province, around Perth and the Rideau canal, identifiable Orange communities were founded by 1820 and lodges were formed by a number of lesser gentry and former tenant farmers. Around 1825 Arthur Hopper, a past grand master of Tipperary, obtained through the Irish Grand Lodge a special warrant entitling him to oversee the creation of several lodges in the district.[24] To the west, Orange settlements also had appeared in the bush townships of Cavan and Monaghan, north of Lake Ontario, and in Peel County, west of York (Toronto). A Fermanagh man, John Rutledge, had been directed to Toronto Township from New York by the British consul, an Orange-man,[25] who perhaps saw in his Orange brothers loyal subjects. Rutledge and his brothers acquired three lots in 1819 and almost immediately undertook the organization of a lodge among his neighbours. 'A tattered old warrant brought out from Ireland ... was offered as charter of the new lodge. It was accepted. The lodge declared itself to be in existence, and officers were duly elected.'[26] Some years later, Rutledge deeded a parcel of his land for an Orange hall and granted another nearby plot for his town's Anglican church and cemetery. The connections between settlement, church, and lodge, epitomized in the person of Rutledge, were notable but hardly unique in Peel County, an area renowned for its strong Orange tone.

In nearby York a Twelfth parade was held as early as 1818[27] and four years later the Reverend John Strachan, a member of the colonial elite and later Church of England bishop of Toronto, delivered a post-parade sermon to a gathering of about one hundred Orangemen from the town and surrounding townships.[28] Strachan was present also at the Twelfth in 1823 and although he was not a member of the fraternity he maintained close interest in its affairs. Years later, he appointed a Scot, the Reverend G.J. McGeorge to the Peel County parish of Streetsville, home of the Rutledges. On that occasion Strachan wrote to an official in London: 'I shall place him [McGeorge] at Streetsville a village distant from Toronto from 22 to 24 miles. The village and neighbourhood contains a great number of church people, many of them Orangemen recently from Ireland, a class with which Mr. McG. has been in the habit of dealing in Glasgow.'[29] McGeorge served his parish as writer, editor, politician, cleric, and Orangeman and rose within the order to the chair of the grand chaplain. His mission among the Orangemen appears not to have affected a career that eventually saw him return to Scotland as the dean of Oban.[30]

From the beginning, Orangeism in Canada had been able to attract non-Irish and persons of some standing in society. From Perth one critic

C.W. Jefferys' image (ca 1935) of the Twelfth of July walk from Grahamsville (Peel County, Ontario) to York (Toronto) around 1820. (Public Archives of Canada)

reported in 1827 that the local lodge was gaining strength and that 'several members joined it who have no connection with Ireland, and a few of them not even subjects, one in particular, a labouring man, lately from the United States.'[31] The same writer had ventured previously that 'persons of respectability were supporting the lodges.'[32] Despite this ability of the lodge to attract non-Irish it failed to find many recruits among the established colonial elite, the Family Compact. Strachan, although a leading member of that group, did not provide through his dealings with the Orange community the stamp of approval necessary for their acceptance in the closely knit colonial administration. From the outset there were those who regarded the Orange intrusion with suspicion and dread. As might be expected, objections were raised by the few catholic clergy. In addition, many of the first families, English high church and tory, perceived a threat to their political position in the Orange amalgam of low church and low tory Irish immigrants.

Despite such opposition Orangeism attained a firm foothold in the colonies of British North America. Two distinct core regions were evident by the 1820s – New Brunswick and Ontario – and in both areas the order was sustained by the continuing immigration of large numbers of protestant Irish. In Ontario in particular the protestant Irish were the largest single group coming to settle. The diffusion of Orangeism had been attendant upon the migration of these people and represented a spontaneous consequence of their presence in the New World. Although there were a few key organizational figures at isolated places in the colonies, there was no plan to spread from Ireland the doctrines of the organization. That diffusion was the result of a series of individual personal decisions taken by rather ordinary immigrants in their new settlements. All the lodges operated largely in isolation, and unlike the situation in Ireland and England at the time, no central administration existed to oversee their activities. Many gatherings of Orange immigrants were held throughout protestant Irish settlement areas without even the formal authority of a warrant. Not until the arrival of Ogle Robert Gowan late in 1829 were efforts undertaken to create a grand lodge in British North America. The success of that venture was permitted by the seeds sown by earlier Irish settlers.

3

Orangeism and the Settlement Geography of Central Canada 1830–1920

The British and largely protestant colony of Ontario offered a realm conducive to the growth of Orangeism. Settlement of the province had been initiated by the movement of United Empire Loyalists rejecting the new American republic. They contributed a monarchical and British tone to a territory subsequently separated from catholic French Quebec by the colonial administration. The founding principles they provided were augmented by the ideologies of succeeding waves of emigrants from Britain and Ireland. Ontario remained throughout the nineteenth century a British, protestant and tory place, despite massive social and economic modernization. From its initial position as a pioneering agricultural outpost the province developed into a commercial-industrial and colonizing society, but throughout all these changes it retained its British connection. Orangemen, numerous among the immigrants, perceived their new land not as a mere colony but as an extension of Britain itself, a reservoir of protestant and loyalist traditions within which their own principles could be accommodated easily. Their institution, the Orange Order, would prove itself capable of adjusting to the emphatic changes transforming life in the province. From its desultory beginnings the order grew steadily throughout the nineteenth century to achieve a position of prominence in the social and political affairs of Ontarian society.

Establishment of the Grand Lodge

In 1829 Ogle R. Gowan, the son of a county Wexford landlord, sold his property and, together with his family and two servants, set sail for British North America. His father, a founding member of the Irish Grand Lodge, had named the son in honour of another early and prominent

Orangeman, the Rt. Hon. George Ogle, MP. Born and raised in an aristocratic and Orange environment the young Gowan had joined the order in 1818 at the young age of fifteen years. He was to show a talent for organization and administration within the fraternity, and within a few years he became the copublisher of an Orange newspaper in Dublin. Following disbandment of the Irish Grand Lodge in 1825 the young Gowan transferred his interests to the 'Benevolent and Religious Orange Institution' which had been established to provide a charitable and less politically oriented alternative to the then defunct grand lodge. When he decided to emigrate he sought and obtained authority to organize Orangemen in the Canadas. Two others had received similar dispensations earlier in the decade but neither managed to effect any significant consolidation of the spontaneous Orange associations. A critical mass had been achieved well before Gowan's arrival and although poor communications within the colony may have hampered the forging of a formal Orange institution it was principally lack of leadership that had kept Orangemen unorganized until Gowan arrived.[1]

Gowan began his career immediately on disembarking at Brockville in Ontario. The town at the time contained over one thousand people and was the first large town west of Montreal and the fifth largest in the province. It was home to a large number of Irish immigrants. In the 'rich back country of Perth and other settlements,'[2] Irishmen were numerous and the effects of local Orange sentiment were already apparent. The newly arrived Wexford gentleman quickly perceived the beachhead that Orangeism had established and set out to extend it. Within a few months, and the shortness of the period indicates a great deal about his conviction, his ability, and the local potential, Gowan had summoned to Brockville a number of prominent gentry and social equals, men who had been involved with lodges in the Canadas. Three individuals came from Montreal and the rest were from Perth, Brockville, and other nearby settlements. They met at the courthouse on 1 January 1830, debated, discussed, and constituted the Grand Lodge of British North America, a mechanism for the centralized administration of existing lodges and the promoting of new ones.[3]

As in Ireland, well-to-do and educated gentry had assumed direction of a movement that had been developing spontaneously. The Irish organizational model was also applied. The grand lodge delegated authority through a hierarchy of territorial jurisdictions, Orange counties were presided over by county grand lodges which in turn oversaw the operation of district lodges and ultimately individual local lodges. The order's territorial hierarchy replicated the administrative subdivision of the new colony. Orange counties were conterminous with the existing county political and electoral units; Orange districts were defined territorially as townships. In effect, a scheme was created for the orderly expansion of the organization. A complementary set of rules and regulations for the behaviour and operation of the various levels of the administrative hierarchy was drawn up and published. Gowan was elected deputy grand master, the title of grand master was retained for the Duke of Cumberland, grand master of the empire.[4] Gowan began at once to issue warrants although it was not until April 1832 that the new grand lodge was officially acknowledged by Cumberland as a separate jurisdiction. This recognition was token. The British American order had been fashioned without supervision from the old country and was to develop independently thereafter.

Under the new administration lodges were authorized by warrants obtained from the grand master. Warrants could be issued on the basis of support expressed at a public meeting or if five certified Orangemen petitioned for a warrant through a local district master who, in turn, forwarded the request through the county master to Gowan. A warrant, numbered according to its place on the central registry, would then be issued. By these means, the expansion and development of Orangeism could be controlled. Expansion of the organization however would be greatly dependent upon interest at the lower levels of the hierarchy. There was scope for district masters and higher officials to promote the order by encouraging applications from local settlements, but ultimately success would be determined by the extent to which sympathy for Orange principles already existed among the settlers. The system also allowed for the founding of lodges in areas remote from established Orange districts. Orangemen going to pioneering settlements could obtain from officers of the order in the older centres dispensation to organize men at their final destination. A warrant would be issued upon receipt of proof that the holder of the dispensation had managed to gather together a number of bona fide Orangemen. The group, once warranted, could then build a membership through initiating non-Orangemen or accepting new arrivals who already held an Orange member's certificate. It is indicative of the community support that existed for Orangeism that many new lodges initiated upwards of twenty members at their inaugural meeting. In many cases during the early decades, lodges were formed without the requisite document of the British American Grand Lodge, perhaps on the basis of an old military warrant from Ireland or England, an Irish member's certificate, or simply the voluntary association of Orange pioneers from the old country. A few lodges established in these ways operated without warrants from the grand lodge into the late nineteenth century and their existence highlights the importance of local enthusiasm. The grand lodge's organizational system provided the possibility of tapping and marshalling enthusiasm at many levels. The Orange warrant represented the grand lodge's success.

The number of warrants issued each year in Canada (including Newfoundland and excluding New Brunswick) since 1830 is illustrated in figure 1.[5] These data provide an index for gauging the rate and dimensions of the spread of Orange ideals. It indicates to a great extent the consequences of territorial expansion of the Canadian settlement frontier because lodges were more likely to be created in new rather than established Orange areas. The effects of population growth are also reflected in the index, but to a lesser degree. A rural lodge generally served twenty to forty men, and in towns and cities much larger memberships were possible because of greater population densities. Increases in local membership resulting from either heightened Orange fervour or population growth could be absorbed to some extent within an established lodge, but at a certain point a new lodge would have to be created. Lack of space in a meeting place, distances some members had to travel to lodge meetings, the problems of keeping track of a large membership, or the natural inclination of identifiable sub-groups within the lodge to keep to their own social network are all factors which could have led to the creation of a new lodge in an established Orange centre. The issue of warrants, despite the problem in sorting out the contributory factors, affords a measure that can be used to outline the temporal and geographical advance of the fraternity.

Warrants were issued every year until the mid 1960s[6] but, as illustrated, the temporal variability was considerable. Irregular progress through the 1830s and early 1840s was followed by six years of apparent organizational inactivity during which only forty-eight lodges were formed. The subsequent period of 1854–60, however, witnessed unparalleled growth in the order. Almost one-third of the lodges established during the nineteenth century were created during this period, and practically all of them were in Ontario. Ontario was to remain the core of Canadian Orangeism throughout the century and a half represented; only in the 1870s did the effects of developments outside the central province significantly offset its early dominance.

The creation of lodges outside Ontario took place earliest in New Brunswick and Quebec. Quebec's warrants, like those of Ontario, were issued by the Grand Lodge of British North America, but in the old colony of New Brunswick Orangemen enjoyed a unique arrangement whereby they were entitled to issue their own warrants. During the 1860s additional lodges were established in Nova Scotia but it was not until after 1870 that pronounced development of the order took place outside the

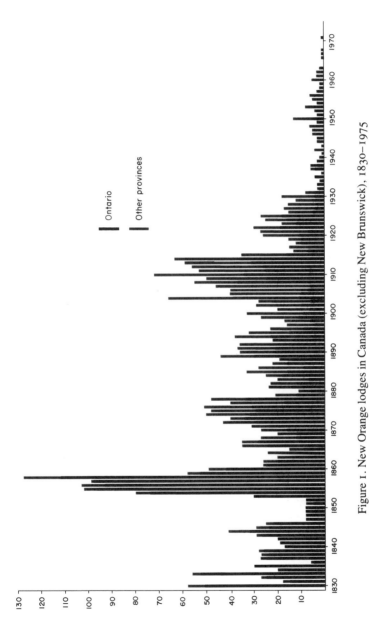

Figure 1. New Orange lodges in Canada (excluding New Brunswick), 1830–1975

early Orange hearths. In 1870 the first prairie lodge was established at Fort Garry (Winnipeg) but growth in Manitoba was hesitant until the decade of the 1880s and the construction of the Canadian Pacific Railway (CPR). Further development of the Manitoban base continued during the 1890s and in the following decade the movement spilled over into Saskatchewan, Alberta, and British Columbia. On the eastern side of the country growth was greatest in Nova Scotia in the 1890s. Newfoundland, which acquired its first lodge as early as 1863, emerged as a major centre of Orangeism during the first two decades of the twentieth century. The temporal and spatial dimensions of the Orange advance testify to a phenomenon powered by two contrasting forces – in the west territorial inclusion and the creation of new settlements, in the east diffusion into already settled communities. Amid these advances, however, Ontario remained the heartland and guiding centre and was itself affected by those same factors which stimulated the advance elsewhere in the country.

Growth in Ontario

In Ontario, lodge formation oscillated from year to year and the periodicity illustrated in figure 1 reflects the effects of coincidental anti-catholicism and the province's unfolding settlement frontier. Historians have argued on the basis of newspaper reports and a discrete series of grand lodge proceedings that Canadian Orangeism was powered by anti-catholic sentiment and usually exhibited its greatest vigour during political crises pertinent to the order. However, analysis of the development illustrated on the graph reveals little to substantiate this claim. Early peaks are exaggerated and represent the initial organizational rush both to include within the new grand lodge already existing local lodges and also to dispense warrants to potential Orange areas. The 1837 rebellion brought many Orangemen into the government forces but had little apparent effect in promoting new lodges. Nor did the failure of the colonial authorities to give Gowan a government post in recognition of the Orangemen's contribution in 1837 spur the issue of new warrants. That slight severely upset the order, particularly as it aggravated the sensitivity aroused by an earlier disapprobation of the fraternity. In 1823 the Upper Canadian House of Assembly had attempted to proscribe Orangeism. Relations with the colonial administration steadily deteriorated until 1840 when the subject of a union of Upper and Lower Canada was officially publicized. In their own view, the Orangemen were

about to be united to a numerical majority of persons [French Canadians] disaffected to Her Majesty's Government ... [the Orangemen had also been] assured

Orange certificate of William Cooper, LOL 328, Toronto, 1853

from the pen of the Lieutenant Governor himself that, the order for our extermina-
tion as a body, has only been delayed, because there was not sufficient power
found to ensure its execution. [At the Grand Lodge Meeting of June 1840 they
resolved] like Britons and like men, to use every exertion that human energy
places within our reach, to ward off the meditated stroke, and to place our great
and glorious cause on such an eminence that it may defy the combined efforts of
the unnatural coalition, so ungratefully formed for our extinction.[7]

The resolve was not translated into any significant increase in the issuing
of warrants, nor was there any effect when the Act of Union came into
force in 1841. Two years later Orangemen were again outraged at the
proscriptive intent of two bills on secret societies and party processions
tabled in the legislature. The rise in the graph for 1843–4 may reflect a
combative response but it may just as well reflect a coincident administrative reorganization of the order. Paper warrants were recalled and replaced by parchment documents in 1844 and in the shuffle the accuracy of
the record suffered. A rise in protestant fears, tensions, and uncertainty
resulting from the influx of destitute catholic Irish in 1847 was not
reflected in any increase in lodge formation. New lodges could be
authorized in a matter of weeks, but there is no indication in figure 1 of
much activity before 1853.

Weak leadership and a developing rift within the upper echelons of the
order inhibited development of the organization between 1846 and 1853.
In 1846 Gowan had retired after sixteen years as grand master. He was
replaced by George Benjamin whose period of tenure until 1853 was
marked by virtually no expansion of the order. Because of his lesser
ability and different philosophy, Benjamin was a much less effective
leader than his predecessor. In 1853 the two men clashed and the order
split. Two rival grand lodges, one representing the views of Gowan, the
other supporting Benjamin, vied for the support of local lodges until a
rapprochement was effected in 1856. Growth of the order was nevertheless rapid during the period of schism because, although the quality of
leadership was undoubtedly a factor in how well the order harnessed
Orange support, the effects of events external to the administration were
crucial.

The great surge during the 1850s coincided with a decade of growing
international anti-catholicism, stimulated by Garibaldi's attack on the
Papal States in 1848 and Pius IX's appointment of bishops to titular sees in
England – events which received widespread coverage in North America.
In Canada the anti-catholic mood of the period was intensified by the
rantings of the ex-priest Alessandro Gavazzi and the tensions inherent
under the political union of French catholics and English protestants.

Some of the turbulence of this period may have stimulated the expansion of the order as indeed may have later crises such as the Fenian invasions of 1866, the Riel rebellion of 1870, the murder of a Montreal Orangeman named Hackett in 1877, the Jesuits' Estates Act of 1889, and the Manitoba schools controversy of the mid 1890s, all of which correlate with peaks in the graph.[8] Caution, however, must be exercised in equating Orange growth with politico-religious crises as the apparent historical correlations might well be spurious; the influence of geography has to be considered. Temporal variation in the development of Orangeism correlates just as well with extension of the settled area and population growth. Orangeism, sustained not merely by a series of transient crises but by a set of deep-seated beliefs, was an integral part of the philosophy of many Ontarians and was carried with them as settlement proceeded. The importance of the order and the reasons for its growth in protestant Ontario are clearly indicated by its geography.

Geographical spread through Ontario

After formation of the grand lodge in 1830, Orangeism spread from the scattered bases established informally among the Irish settlements of the province. Formal incorporation of pre-1830 lodges into the order was accomplished quickly. Undoubtedly, the grand lodge officers were instrumental in the rapid take-off of the organization. In the first three years ninety-one warrants were issued, half of them to areas represented by the infant organization's principal officers (figure 2). The Irish gentry and half-pay officers of Lanark and Leeds were most prominent in the directorate, although there were representatives from other towns in the early settled sections along the lakeshore. Of the forty-one leaders in 1833, nine were accorded an 'esquire' after their name, fifteen a rank or profession before theirs, and seventeen were untitled.[9] The committee constituted an elite prominent in efforts to mold a political force from immigrants in the older districts. However, the order's constituency in Ontario was much more extensive than that from which its leadership was drawn. Men of more common lineage were establishing local lodges flung far from the Brockville threshold.

The geographical distribution of lodges (figure 2) indicates that the order was planted in every major and many minor protestant Irish settlement district. In the newer Irish areas, from Peterborough in the east to Mono Township northwest of Toronto, and even along the remote shore of Lake Huron, local lodges had been constituted. Irish settlers, to get to these areas, necessarily passed through and may have been encouraged to take warrants from the older centres of known Orange sentiment. But

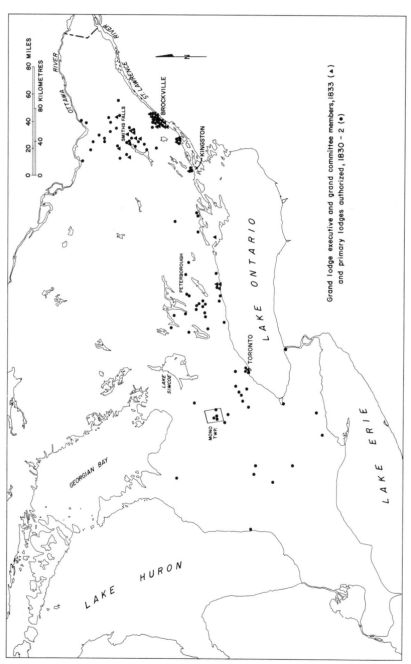

Figure 2. Early Orange lodges and grand lodge members, 1833

Grand lodge executive and grand committee members, 1833 (▲)
and primary lodges authorized, 1830 – 2 (•)

likely as not, encouragement to take a warrant was not needed, for the Irishman heading inland, like his more established immigrant brethren, was firmly convinced of the fraternity's importance. Lodges were established as soon as the possibility arose, whether in the isolated pockets of Irishmen southwest of Toronto or among the larger communities around Peterborough and Mono Township. The hilly lands of Mono, pioneered first by Ulstermen in the late 1820s, had within a few years become an almost exclusively protestant Irish area. The Church of England pastor of Orangeville (no connection to Orangeism) reported: 'On Friday, 12th July 1833, I preached in Mono to about four hundred people and baptised the children. The Orangemen who are so numerous in that part of the country attended and it was on account of their meeting that day that so many people assembled.'[10] Such Orange strength was not uncommon.

Orange control of certain districts during the 1830s contributed to distinctly segregated settlement patterns. The strong Orange presence in Mono deflected catholics from the township and they created their own enclave in neighbouring Adjala. In other areas deliberate actions were taken to exclude catholics from Orange territories. In John Rutledge's district, attempts by catholics to settle were challenged by a gang called the Town Line Blazers.[11] Through intimidation and occasional burning of property the protestant, and presumably Orange, blazers kept catholics away. In Cavan Township near Peterborough the local blazers carried out an irregular campaign against any semblance of encroachment from neighbouring catholic settlements. Their bullying tactics were replaced in later decades by more sophisticated economic, political, and social devices, as was the case elsewhere. Although decried by moderates, the Cavan night raiders never were rebuffed by their own communities: 'no man could be found to complain of them and no magistrate with sufficient courage to issue a warrant for their arrest.'[12] Such groups were reminiscent of the secretive factions out of which the Irish order arose in 1795. Their tactics were similar to those employed in land-hungry Ireland, but the New World context was much different. In Canada in the early nineteenth century the Irish land-labour ratio had been inverted. Only feelings of sectional bigotry remained.

In the 1830s the advance of Orangeism encompassed a great margin of territory along the north shore of Lake Ontario and the St Lawrence River (figure 3). Northward extensions into every township with a protestant Irish settlement had occurred from Bytown (Ottawa) in the east to Peterborough and Peel-Simcoe-Dufferin counties in the west. In the latter area the protestant Irish formed concentrations around such centres as Derry West, Tullamore, Violet Hill, and Enniskillen. The pattern of spread comprises those areas where Orangeism had developed spontaneously before Gowan arrived and also those areas pioneered in the 1830s. Just as remarkable as the areas to which warrants had been issued is the distribution of older townships without a lodge. The absence of lodges in the northern half of York County represents the ethnically mixed character of a territory in which the protestant Irish were few and usually isolated. The Irish generally had avoided upper York. To the east, the axis of the Canadian Shield across the St Lawrence interrupted the pattern of settlement. Beyond it, in the Glengarry-Prescott region, catholics, either Highland Scots and Irish or later French, predominated and many communities there never received a lodge during the nineteenth century, or the twentieth for that matter. Along the Lake Ontario shore the loyalist stronghold of Prince Edward County also disrupted the extension of Orangeism and although individual loyalists were prominent in the early Orange administration the order did not obtain many recruits from this group. A greater impediment was offered by the already well-established American and English communities along the Lake Erie shore. There, protestant Irish were prominent only in a few scattered townships of the Talbot settlement, and the order was unable to replicate the intensity and cohesion of its geographical development in the east of the province. The key to the distribution of lodges in the 1830s is clearly the geography of protestant Irish settlement. Subsequent areal extension of Orangeism continued to follow the trend of settlement in the province.

During the 1840s the most significant inroads were made in the northwest. Although it cannot be verified, it may be suggested that this again represents the arrival of sizable numbers of protestant Irish in the districts. Further penetration along Lake Huron, up the Ottawa River, and into the third tier of townships bordering the Shield in the central sector was most definitely coincident with the arrival of Irish settlers, loggers, and miners. In the main the geographical changes of the 1840s helped to smooth the rough edges of the core sectors from Peel to Carleton counties, and continued the development of the patchwork pattern of the southwest. This diffusion of the order through the migration of settlers was augmented to a minor extent by a missionary drive organized by the grand lodge in 1840.

The appointment of the order's chaplain as a paid field organizer confirmed the seriousness of the Orangemen's expansionist aims. The missionary 'by personal intercourse with the members at large was directed to promote, extend and perpetuate the Orange cause in every corner of this portion of our Colonial Empire.'[13] Gowan's final instructions limited the field of operations to the Home District, an area around Toronto and comprising the counties of Peel, York, and Ontario.[14] The success of the mission is difficult to determine. The appointee, the

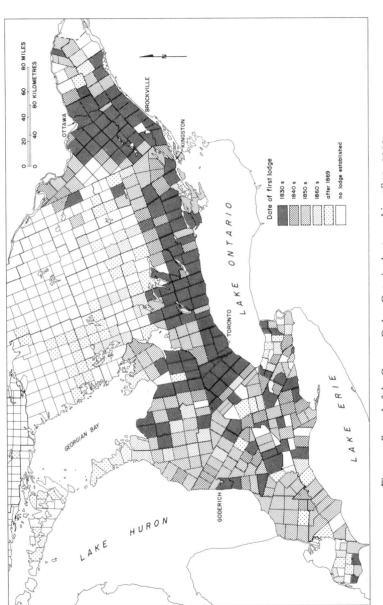

Figure 3. Spread of the Orange Order, Ontario, by township, 1830–1900

Reverend Montgomery West, had a poor record in a previous venture. In 1825 the British Grand Lodge had given him authority to organize lodges in British North America but West managed only to form a second lodge at Kingston in 1828.[15] As an Englishman he may have had difficulty in dealing with the immigrant Irish. In addition, at the time of his 1840 appointment 'several slanderous reports' raised questions about his character and suitability for the task.[16] Whatever West may have attempted as missionary, only two of the forty-six lodges created in Ontario during 1842 and 1843 were located in his missionary district. In later years others were appointed to organize the brethren, but the main force in effecting the introduction and spread of Orangeism continued to be the large number of Orangemen going to settle in new areas and taking with them lodge warrants.

In 1846 when Gowan stepped down as grand master, the order's networks could serve most settled districts, and even if his successor, Benjamin, had been an excellent organizer, he could not have maintained the earlier pace of organization. The Orange presence was already well established, and consequently growth during the late 1840s was bound to be small. It would require more than the influx of catholics and protestants fleeing famine-ridden Ireland to stimulate again development of the organization. Ontarian Orangemen were interested that their brethren leaving Ireland at the time should come to the colony. They resolved at the grand lodge meeting of 1848 'that Canada West offers a safe and quiet retreat for our Brethern at home; and that much better opportunities would be afforded them were they to emigrate to this colony, than is afforded by any other colony under the British Crown.'[17] It is impossible to measure how active a role the order played in attracting protestant Irish to Canada but its potential as an immigration agency was certainly there. The order had reached this position of strength during the 1840s largely through its affinity with the traditions of protestant Irish immigrants and its ability to adapt to a growing region. During the 1850s it continued to demonstrate these characteristics but also showed a much wider relevance to Ontario for it made significant roads into non-Irish communities.

The order experienced the most expansion in its history during the 1850s when more than 550 lodges were formed, one-third of all lodges established during the century. New lodges were created both in established communities and in those portions of the Lake Huron uplands in Grey, Bruce, and Perth counties which were then being settled. Orangemen and the agricultural frontier in the latter region advanced simultaneously, as had been the case in eastern Ontario earlier. That can be inferred from the coincidences at the township level of no settled population in 1851, a lodge or lodges at mid decade, and a protestant population of one to two hundred in 1861. For example, Wallace Township was settled in 1855 by Canadian-born Orangemen who had come from the cleared farmlands of Simcoe to repeat in Perth County the experience of their Orange fathers.[18] Henry Richardson formed the first lodge on the township's third concession within a few weeks of his arrival there, and inside a year other lodges had sprung up among the neighbouring settlements of Gore, Whitfield, Orange Bank, and also on the ninth and tenth concessions. A similar coincidence between the arrival of settlement and Orangeism occurred on other northern margins. The events of the 1850s which created a new region characterized by native-born Orangemen drastically changed the geography of the order's realm.

The territorial expansion of the decade reflected growing population pressure within the older settled parts of the province. Ontario's population, sustained by both natural increase and continuing immigration, was growing at a rate of 4 per cent per annum. The sons of the Irish immigration of the period 1825–35 were coming of age, preparing to start their own families and farms, and eligible for the first time to join the order. They provided the potential for at least one or two new recruits for every Orangeman in the lodges of the early 1830s, and whether they moved to new areas on the frontier or remained behind in the older neighbourhoods they were bound to augment the order's strength. The salutary effect on the order of the maturing of Canadian-born protestant Irish was supplemented by a preponderance of protestants in the continuing trickle of Irish immigrants during the 1850s.

The order was ideally suited to an expanding frontier where population was scattered thinly and without the community benefits of established institutions. A local lodge could perform as a surrogate neighbourhood. It provided an easily organized forum where men could get away from the humdrum burdens of breaking land and return momentarily to a realm of certain myth and familiar tradition. It served such a function more naturally than would a church; the lodge allowed men of all protestant denominations to mix in a para-religious setting at a time when population densities were not sufficient to support a formal church. A lodge did not require an 'ordained' leader. The fact too that the lodge was primarily a social rather than religious organization gave it distinct advantages over a church. Men could escape from their families for an evening at lodge with the implied suggestion that their activities away would be honourable and orderly. Yet they themselves knew the great difference between the imposed sobriety of church surroundings and the conviviality of lodge attendance. The lodge, with its veil of secrecy, its ritual, social gossip, and perhaps drink, better served the young pioneer's demand. Conviviality in the bush was a valued commodity, and the lodge could provide a setting for it long before the church ever could, and often before a tavern or other settled commercial establishment took root.

In addition to the growth on the frontier during the 1850s and in the by then traditional Orange and Irish areas, new lodges were created in areas not known for their Irishness: upper York County, Prince Edward County, and the tip of the province east of Prescott, all areas settled for over thirty years but hitherto without lodges. Lodges were established in the settlements of Barb, McCrimmon, and Caledonia in the eastern end of the province. Their founders and members were of Scottish origin. In Prince Edward County, Orange lodges were begun among a population heavily marked by loyalist and English traditions and with few catholics. Similar traditions prevailed in upper York. In these areas, Orangeism could not be explained simply in terms of the transferred bigotry of the protestant Irish, but in the wider context of the order's increasing respectability contingent upon both its growing non-immigrant character and its association with the Conservative party of John A. Macdonald. The Orange principles of protestantism and loyalty remained unaltered. It was society's perception of Orangemen that had changed.

In York County two lodges, LOL 548 and LOL 644, were organized in 1854 and 1855 respectively by the Button brothers, John and William.[19] A third brother later became master of another local lodge. The Buttons were a well-respected family in a community which valued highly its traditions of British loyalty and protestantism. Their grandfather had come from Connecticut in 1798 with his wife and two children and settled on two hundred acres of bush in Markham Township. Although a cooper by trade, the first Button did well as a farmer *cum* land speculator and quickly rose to become an important political figure in the area. During the 1837 rebellion he captained a troop of militia and was commended by the colonial government.[20] The reasons for his grandsons' involvement in the Orange Order remain unknown; they could not have derived from the family's English and loyalist background. The need for conviviality and social intercourse which motivated men on the frontier in places such as Wallace Township would also not have been a factor for the well-to-do and socially established Buttons. Likely as not the growing Canadian identity of Orangeism and its potential as a vehicle for political leverage attracted political aspirants such as the Buttons, as well as the Oslers and Strachans of York County, all established non-Irish families.[21]

In the mid 1850s it was apparent that the order through its ability to bring in second generation Irish and others of longer and non-Irish Canadian traditions had passed from its early stage of official distrust to one of growing public acceptability. The metamorphosis of the immigrant Irish-based organization had been underway essentially since the fraternity's arrival in British America. Even before 1830 there had been a report of non-Irish members[22] and the consequent indication that Orangeism's appeal could be more than ethnic. In the mid 1840s in Stratford, 'the two brothers, James and Peter Woods, another Englishman named Hines, Jackson and others of the English contingent, became Orangemen. There were no rainbow variations in Stratford then – the bow bore but two colours, a man was either orange or green.'[23] Such conditions were not isolated anomalies, and even some of the province's elite found a ready place among the immigrant Orangemen. By the early 1840s in Toronto, William H. Boulton, third generation member of the Family Compact, grandson of Chief Justice D'Arcy Boulton and nephew of Sir John Beverley Robinson, had joined the order. Boulton's home, the Grange, was a genteel social centre and his position in privileged Toronto society was not endangered by his staunch protestantism and membership in an immigrant 'secret society.' His public acknowledgment of his Orangeism was one important indicator of how far the Orangemen of British North America had come by the 1840s. Throughout the province the order was being recognized and less attention was being given to its early identification as a mere immigrant fraternity. By the sheer weight of its numbers, its vociferous rhetoric, and the territorial extent of its constituency, Orangeism was beginning to blend with much of Canadian society.

The rate of extension of the order dropped dramatically during the 1860s. The geographical pattern was mainly of filling in the established areas and no new significant territories were added to the order's domain. Little scope for such inclusion existed. Ontario's settlement frontier had stabilized along the northern margins of the agricultural zone at the edge of the Canadian Shield. There had been, however, some attempts to promote settlement in pockets of agricultural land at the edge of the Shield by building colonization roads northwest from established areas. Two such roads, the Bobcaygeon and Hastings, leading from old Orange districts near Peterborough, were corridors for the order's northward development. The alignment of these roads is apparent in figure 3 since the townships along them all received lodges as an adjunct of the settlement effort. By 1870 Orangeism had reached all but twenty-five of the more than four hundred settled townships in the province and within those twenty-five the potential for diffusion of Orangeism was minimal given their ethno-religious character. The acquisition of major new territories for the order would have to await a greater thrust of settlement northwest in search of timber and mineral resources. By 1870 an essential stage in Ontario's economic development had been completed. The best farm land had been settled. Resource districts in the Ontarian north were being intruded upon, migration from Ontario to the northwest was beginning, and rapid industrialization was to be encouraged by the Conservative party's National Policy. Eighteen hundred and seventy is also the first year for which a reasonably accurate map of Orangeism can be drafted (see figure 4).

In 1870 about 930 lodges operated in Ontario, 300 fewer than the number of warrants issued before then. Many lodges had been short-lived, and reasons for closing varied from the personal incompatibility of members to the impersonal forces that affected population redistribution and reflected the turmoil of the whole settlement process. Lodges were by no means ubiquitous in the province. Toronto, dubbed by Orangemen the Belfast of Canada, and Kingston, the Derry, formed the two largest concentrations. Ottawa, Hamilton, and London also had several lodges. Although the major urban centres are recognizable on the map, the overriding features of the pattern are its extent and rurality. South of a line extending westwards from Toronto the Orange presence was sporadic with only a few lodges operating along the Lake Erie shore and an almost total absence in the largely German area northwest of Hamilton.[24] A dearth of lodges also is evident in the eastern end of the province and across the north. Overall, the strongest expression of Orangeism and its greatest retention were to be found in the order's initial cores along the Rideau Canal and the Lake Ontario shore and in those counties of western Ontario settled after 1850.

The geographical pattern of lodges in 1870 coincides quite closely with the distribution of protestant Irish at the time. Maps of the distribution of lodges (figure 4) and the proportionate strength of the protestant Irish[25] (figure 5) demonstrate an extremely similar geographical variability. Figure 5 indicates that the protestant Irish were present to some extent in all the settled townships of the province and in the majority of the townships they constituted more than 20 per cent of the population – a simple reflection of their primary place among Ontarians. Their early arrival in large numbers had permitted them to establish in many townships distinct communities which through succeeding migrations and natural demographic growth, stood in 1871 as marked regional concentrations of population – along the Rideau axis, north of Lake Ontario, and northwest of Toronto – also regions of noticeable Orangeism. The greatest concentrations of protestant Irish in 1871 are clearly related to the densest groupings of lodges. Conversely, the smaller protestant Irish populations are related to the lowest densities and absences of lodges – the unsettled north, the German area northwest of Hamilton, the French and American areas of the extreme southwest, and the French and Scottish catholic areas of the extreme east. In the Lake

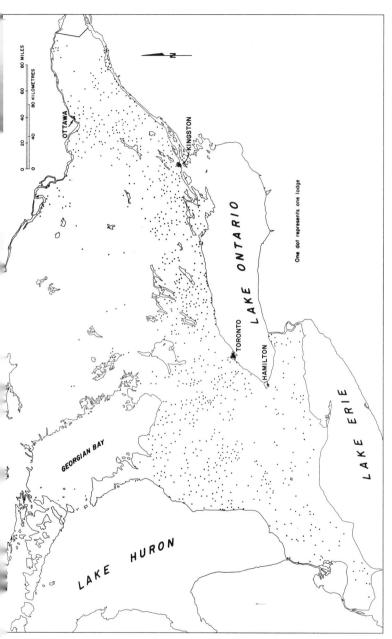

Figure 4. Orange lodges, Ontario, 1870

Erie plain as well, the Irish presence and the Orange Order were weak. Distance from the St Lawrence entry points was undoubtedly a factor in the inability of the Irish to establish a strong presence along Lake Erie, but the opportunities were also much reduced by the earlier American and English settlement there. The scattered nature of protestant Irish settlement and the submergence of Irish traditions in the wider protestant community contributed to the weakness of Orangeism in the Lake Erie plain. Nowhere else in the English-speaking protestant areas of the province did the order fail to develop a sound base.

Despite the apparent and expected links between the Irish and the order, non-Irish communities and groups had been enclosed within the movement. As will be demonstrated in chapter v, individuals from the non-Irish groups also had joined in the order's march through the more Ulster regions of the province and above all second and third generation Canadians had made their presence felt. The role of Canadians was particularly important in the later frontier areas where new communities tended to be more mixed than those established in the first three decades of the nineteenth century. Although Irish immigrants had provided the initial impetus, and Irish Canadians had maintained the core of the organization, the order's advance in its first half century and its geographical dimensions in 1870 are indicative of a much wider constituency.

The situation in 1870 also does little to sustain a view held by some that 'the essential elements for the success of the Orange Order in a community were religious tensions and religious balance.'[26] The order was not necessarily strongest in zones where catholics and protestants were numerically equal. Ideologically, Orangeism was born of the perceived threat of catholicism in general. It did not require local catholics to stimulate it. Indeed, in areas where the population was exclusively protestant, the order was at its strongest because it could provide a central social role while having at its disposal a large demographic base for recruits. There were besides few Ontarian communities of protestant and catholic balance. Ontarians of protestant Irish background outnumbered their catholic countrymen in a ratio of 2 to 1.[27] In the 400 or so townships, the catholic Irish almost equalled the protestants in only 55, significantly surpassed them in numbers in another 40, and were soundly outnumbered by them in over 300. The protestant Irish formed the province's major ethnic group – there was little probability of catholic-protestant balance among the Irish. The catholic Irish were generally found in urban centres, particularly the larger ones, and did not impinge strongly upon the rural dominance that the protestants had achieved. Orangeism was strong where the protestant Irish were strong and that strength was not dependent upon the presence of a local catholic community comparable in size.

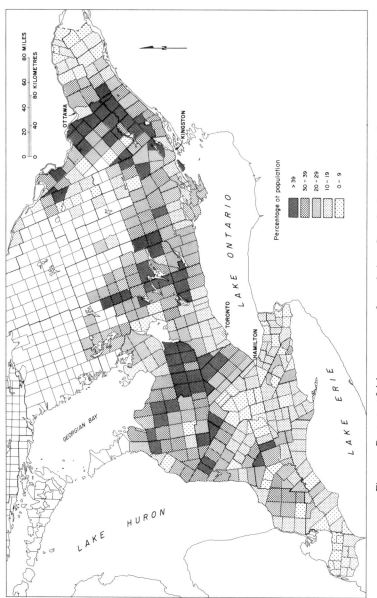

Figure 5. Protestant Irish percentage of population, Ontario, by township, 1871

Geographical expansion and adjustment in Ontario, 1870–1920

After confederation Orangeism continued to advance simultaneously with the spread of settlement onto the Shield. In 1870 the county master of the order in north Simcoe reported that 'the new County of Muskoka [is] the most thoroughly Orange County in Ontario – literally seven out of ten of the settlers in that vast region are Orangemen. Such a phenomenon as a Roman Catholic is hardly to be found.'[28] This description, which is perhaps partisan and exaggerated, does nevertheless impart the close association of protestant settlement and Orangeism. In the adjoining Parry Sound district, 'McKellar Township was incorporated in the spring of 1873, under a special Act of the Ontario Legislature, granting municipal institutions in unorganized districts without connection with any County Council. The first election for Reeve and Councillors was held in the Orange Hall, McKellar Village, on Thursday, the 1st day of May, 1873.'[29] The first white man had come to trap in the area in the summer of 1868 and the first shanty was built that fall. In 1869 the township was surveyed. The pioneers, Patterson, Armstrong, Tully, and Moffatt, had common protestant Irish names. They instituted an Orange lodge in 1870. By 1878 there were one hundred ratepayers in the village, and besides the post office and nine commercial establishments stood a Methodist church, an Orange hall, and a school house. This pattern of church, Orange hall, and school would be repeated in many places throughout new Ontario during the rest of the century.

By 1875 the remote north shore of Lake Superior had been reached by Orangeism. The Grand Lodge of British America met at Sault Ste Marie in 1893, and in 1899 it was suggested that an Orange administrative district might be created for the scattered lodges of Murillo, Schreiber, Port Arthur, and Fort William, all connected by the Canadian Pacific Railway.[30] The advance through Ontario had been virtually completed by 1900 although Cobalt, Sudbury, Kirkland Lake, Iroquois Falls, and other unborn places would receive their lodge in the early twentieth century. In its extension northward the order demonstrated a capability for straddling more than one frontier. Apparently it was as relevant in the new northern resource and transportation centres as it continued to be in the old farm settlements of Cavan and Mono.

Table 1 summarizes the spread of Orangeism to the end of the nineteenth century. The province is subdivided into seven regions defined by the aggregation of townships obtaining their first lodge within the same decade (figure 3). It is evident that the older settled townships of the province which obtained their first Orange lodge before 1850 remained the core area of the order having almost two-thirds of the total number of

TABLE 1
Percentage of Orange warrants issued in Ontario, 1830–1900

Areas in which first lodge was established during	Percentage of lodges established during decade beginning							Total 1830–99
	1830	1840	1850	1860	1870	1880	1890	
1830s	15.0	6.1	15.5	3.9	5.3	2.5	2.9	51.2
1840s		3.7	5.2	1.0	1.3	0.5	0.4	12.1
1850s			14.0	3.9	3.5	2.2	2.0	25.6
1860s				2.1	0.8	0.4	0.3	3.6
1870s					3.0	0.7	0.5	4.2
1880s						1.6	0.3	1.9
1890s							1.4	1.4
Total	15.0	9.8	34.7	10.9	13.9	7.9	7.8	100.0

lodges formed during the century. In the post-1850 period all new areas received their greatest number of lodges during the decade of the initial appearance of Orangeism. As measured by lodge establishment, development of the order was greatest at the edge of its expanding frontier and the geographical pattern is one of an institution moving with that frontier, buoyed along by the migration of those most familiar with and sympathetic to its principles. The vitality in new areas is further emphasized by the fact of the 575 lodges created during the peak decade of the 1850s some 40 per cent were located in townships previously without a lodge. The expansion so evident in figure 1 is therefore a function of both intensified anti-catholic sentiment and the greater ongoing process of settlement and territorial inclusion. Some 60 per cent of the new lodges created during the 1850s were located in the old Orange core within which a heightened anti-catholic mood may have provided a stimulant. But there too changes in demographic structure were having their effect through the provision of initiates to the order. Throughout the century the dynamics of population growth and the wider settlement processes in the province continued to be reflected in the order's own development, but during the last decades that development was affected also by the redistribution of population in the older regions.

An overall impression of decline in the order is conveyed by figure 6 but the map actually belies the vitality of Orangeism in all districts. Rationalization of the existing network of lodges in the older areas, not rejection of the order was the major factor. Marked decreases in the number of lodges occurred throughout most of eastern Ontario especially in the old Orange areas around Peterborough and the Rideau. Both the rural areas and the stagnating towns along the lakeshore were affected by lodge closure. Similarly, to the west in Perth and Huron counties, the order lost some of its local units, but along Lake Erie the pattern of decline was less extreme, almost mirroring the hesitancy of the Orange advance in that region. In the rural strongholds population had either stabilized or declined, a process begun as early as the 1850s in the Rideau area and more apparent in the first settled townships of the lakeshore from 1860 onwards.[31] In eastern Ontario the rural population fell by 10 per cent between 1870 and 1920. Young men were migrating to the larger and growing industrial centres as well as heading northward into the Shield and Manitoba. References to the latter migration and its apparently deleterious effects on local Orange membership were numerous in the annual reports of the Grand Lodge of Ontario East from 1884 to 1886. Improved accessibility and competition from major service centres hastened the decline of many hamlets and villages and led to a restructuring of settlement and a concomitant reorganization of the Orange network. Many lodges closed down and consolidated their membership in fewer and more centrally located lodges. Agricultural retreat from the pockets along the limestone southern edge of the Shield and the exhausting of old localized mineral resources also led to reductions of lodge numbers. The population redistribution also coincided with improved bookkeeping within the order.[32] From the 1870s dormant lodges were more frequently struck from the records, lodges with very small memberships were amalgamated with others where possible, and greater attention was given to scrutinizing arrears and payments of dues. The effect of the improved accounting was to bring about the demise of many lodges in the period 1870–1920, lodges which in actual fact had not functioned for several years before 1870, and thereby contribute to an exaggerated decline in figure 6. Nevertheless, even allowing for discrepancies in the record, that decline was sizable and reflected the fundamental forces of geographical change.

Within the agricultural zone of southern Ontario there were exceptional areas of Orange growth. These were mainly districts which the order had begun to penetrate only in the second half of the nineteenth century. The Bruce Peninsula and Manitoulin Island were settled after 1870, and their acquisition of lodges was an intrinsic part of the ongoing extension of agricultural settlement. However, in the eastern Ontario counties of Prescott, Glengarry, and Stormont growth was a result not of colonization but of continued diffusion of Orange principles among Scottish communities faced with a southward intrusion of French Canadians.

The movement of the order into eastern Ontario (figure 7) is especially significant. Not only was it powered largely by Scots but it also took place in an area of marked religious and linguistic separation. A large part of Glengarry County had been settled initially by catholic Scots and around

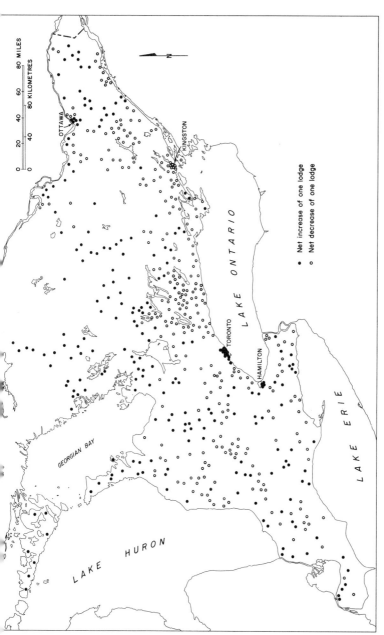

Figure 6. Net changes in Orange lodges by township, southern Ontario, 1870–1920

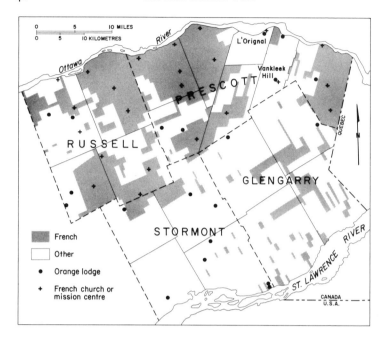

Figure 7. French Canadian settlement and Orange lodges, eastern Ontario, 1885 (French settlement, church, and mission centres after D. Cartwright)

the fringes of their territory were many protestant countrymen and other British protestants. The protestant Irish were not an important component in the local population. To the north, the Ottawa Valley counties of Prescott and Russell had been experiencing, from the 1840s, planned French Canadian colonization and large contiguous sections of those counties were French by 1860. In the next decades further expansion, powered by natural increase and continued migration from Quebec, contributed to a marked French presence in this part of Ontario. The French had made few inroads into protestant Stormont County by 1885 but they were apparently more successful in establishing a foothold in Glengarry County.

The French colonization venture in Prescott and Russell counties had been led by priests delegated for the task by the Quebec hierarchy. As leaders in the secular as well as religious life of the community the priests were responsible for selecting localities suitable for settlement and recruiting settlers in Quebec. The preferred locations were marked by the placement of a cross and they subsequently developed into mission and church centres and acted as the foci for the new French settlements.[33]

Today, many of these locations are still marked by crosses, thereby contributing to a distinctive cultural landscape. The role of the catholic church in this area was one of an institution leading and directing settlement; by contrast the Orange Order grew within settled English-speaking communities. It is probable that the development of the Orange institution in this region, especially after 1870, may represent a defensive expression of protestant insecurity. Figure 7 illustrates the respective distributions of Orange lodges and French mission centres and churches. Only in Vankleek Hill and L'Orignal do lodges and catholic churches coincide. Elsewhere the lodges are found within the heart of solely protestant territories and abutting the perimeter of the French district. They are virtually absent in the protestant southern end of Stormont County and, as one might expect, completely absent from the catholic settlements of Glengarry.

The cultural conflict that developed in this part of the province found its clearest expression in the landscape through the locations of churches, crosses, and lodges. Politically, it was passionately articulated in a protracted debate over the use of French in Ontario schools and it led ultimately to Regulation 17, a 1912 measure designed to stop the use of French as a language of instruction after grade two. The language question was heightened by the anti-catholic mood of Ontario, and a book widely distributed by the Orange Order at the time insisted that the movement of French colonists into Ontario had been a 'popish plot.' 'The fact of their being diverted from their own province and passing in a steady stream into Ontario confirms the statement that the priests had settled on a plan of campaign to bring that province under their control ... The people of Ontario were slow to realize the purpose of the invasion.'[34] Such sentiments undoubtedly contributed to the formation of the lodges among the Scots in eastern Ontario during the late nineteenth and early twentieth century. However, Orangeism was only a symptom of the sentiment, not its cause.

The greatest geographical extension of the order after 1870 was not promoted by this conflict but by the movement of surplus population to the resource towns of the north. Lodges there had lives as short as the duration of the localized timber and mineral resources that had first attracted settlers. Others on the sandy spillways that provided meagre bases for agriculture have survived to the present day. As in the agricultural south they were organized to serve the essential need for conviviality, familiar social forms, and religious expression, but in the twentieth-century towns of the north they took their place alongside trade union locals. Given the geography of the north, Orangeism naturally assumed an urban character there, but that character was emphasized by the growth

Orangemen, Rainy River, Ontario. Upper 1907, lower 1905. (Archives of Ontario)

of the order in the rapidly developing cities of the south, and nowhere more apparent than in the metropolitan centre, Toronto.

In Toronto the increase in the number of Orange lodges, from seventeen in 1870 to fifty-nine in 1920, reflected the population growth of the protestant city. After 1860 Irish immigration had been an insignificant factor in the city's development. Orange recruits were drawn primarily from the native-born Torontonians and the thousands of rural-urban migrants. The same process of rural-urban migration which was effecting changes in the distribution of rural lodges was supplying Toronto with young men familiar with Orange traditions. They had come to a city renowned for its Orangeism. The order was a powerful force in the city's administration and the sense of its power and its control of patronage made its strength self-perpetuating. Many of the newcomers were attracted to the fraternity by both an appreciation of its principles and motives of opportunism.

By 1920, after a century of development, Ontario was the leading province in the order's Canadian realm with 54 per cent of all lodges. In the contiguous agricultural settlement zone, the non-contiguous resource settlements of the north, and in the metropolitan centre of Toronto, Orangeism had established a pervasive presence. The Orange community was not restricted territorially, and in its geographical extent it reflected a dynamism whose dimensions were not determined by transient political crises and the directions of great men. Its widespread acceptance indicates that it could not have been simply an Irish immigrant institution. The forces that powered the organization in the central Canadian province were not unique. They were intrinsic to much of the greater settlement processes and ideologies of a colonial population for whom protestantism and loyalty were ingrained truths.

Quebec

Quebec too was infiltrated by the protestant fraternity, and the Orange developments east of the Ottawa River represented to a large degree an echo from the Ontarian core. But without a position of strength as in Ontario, the order in Quebec was but a facsimile. Quebec was largely French and catholic and the arrival of protestant Irish immigrants relatively late in the colony's history limited the possibilities of the order's establishing a dominating geographical presence. For the protestant Irish as for most English-speaking immigrants in the nineteenth century, Quebec was only the corridor to the Ontarian destination, and only handfuls of protestants remained in Quebec to form pockets of settle-

ment. Nevertheless, although scattered through a few areas, the Orangemen of Quebec did manage to build a local tradition which, taken with
their brethren's activities elsewhere in Canada, left an indelible image
with many Québécois. The order's reputation was created not by its role
as a functioning community organization but through its association with
episodes such as the violence of the Gavazzi riots in the 1850s, its
reaction to the murder of the Orangeman Hackett in 1878, and most
damnably by its attitude to Louis Riel. As the nineteenth century progressed the French catholics of Quebec found it increasingly difficult to
distinguish Orangeism from protestantism and Britishness. To them *les
orangistes* came to embody not only Orangemen or even protestant Irish
but a much more inclusive group of intransigent protestant, loyalist, and
English-speaking Canadians who adopted a general anti-French stance on
national cultural issues.

In the first decade of the Canadian grand lodge's history twenty
warrants were issued to Quebec (figure 8) in comparison to over two
hundred issued to Ontario. The beginnings in Quebec were meagre but
significant, given that the province received only a small fraction of the
immigration coming up the St Lawrence. In following decades this
differential would remain, and although the number of warrants issued to
Quebec was extremely small the temporal pattern of lodge creation in the
nineteenth century followed in step with that of Ontario. The short
intermittent peaks of development, particularly during the 1850s and
1870s were reflections of the larger trend in the English-speaking province. The order's growth in both provinces was shaped by the same
forces of settlement, demographic expansion, and resettlement. Similarly, the periods of especially heated protestant-catholic conflict were not
notable periods in the Quebec order's expansion.

The relative weakness of the order in Quebec is summarized well in
figure 9 which depicts the distribution of lodges in the St Lawrence and
Ottawa valleys in 1878. With the exception of a small base that would be
created during the First World War in the Gaspé, an area neighbouring
New Brunswick, the order had reached its greatest extent by the late
1870s. From then it experienced an imperceptible but nevertheless sure
attrition and decline. Even in 1878 the order's areal base was minor
particularly in comparison to the breadth and density of Orange territory
in Ontario. The lodges of Quebec were confined to small cores of English
speakers – the larger cities of Montreal and Quebec, rural settlements of
the Eastern Townships (south of the St Lawrence), and in two farming
areas north of the Ottawa River. The St Lawrence Valley lands of French
Quebec were expectedly void of an Orange presence.

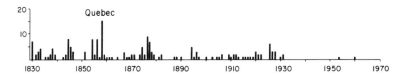

Figure 8. New Orange lodges, Quebec, 1830–1975

Montreal received one of the first military lodges brought to North America around 1800, and from these garrison beginnings the order was augmented in subsequent years by the desultory immigration of protestant Irishmen. During the 1820s a significant thrust of Ulstermen into Montreal was occasioned by the same Irish emigration that was then flooding to Ontario. In 1825 the Montreal Irish numbered 3,000 in a population of 25,000[35] and, given the general patterns of immigration at the time, probably more than half would have been protestant. Civilian lodges were created and in 1830 three Irishmen from Montreal were instrumental in the founding of the grand lodge at Brockville. By 1850 about half a dozen lodges were operating in the city and for the rest of the nineteenth century the number of lodges there fluctuated between eight and twelve. No late century increase in Orange strength comparable to that which took place in Toronto occurred in Montreal. It did not have a protestant let alone Orange hinterland approaching that of its Ontarian rival, and rural-urban migration was more likely to be non-Orange or French speaking. The townships south of the St Lawrence were only weakly Orange and many of the out-migrants from that area headed south to New England and New York. There, they may have joined their brethren from the Canadian Maritimes at lodges in industrial towns between Everett, Massachusetts, and Yonkers, New York. In addition, protestant Quebeckers further west in the Ottawa Valley were drawn to the mining districts and later the pulp mills of Ontatio's north. Ontario's frontier was also theirs. Under such circumstances Montreal Orangeism was destined to be a minor element of that city's identity.

In Quebec City the weaknesses of Orangeism were even clearer. An old military lodge functioned there well into the 1830s,[36] but not until

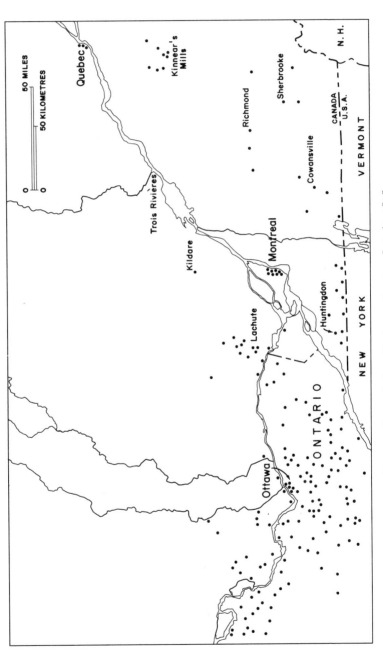

Figure 9 Orange lodges, Quebec and eastern Ontario, 1878

1843 was a civilian lodge opened. Others followed, but the capital, even more French and Roman Catholic than Montreal, was ill suited to the Orange fraternity. In 1871, Quebec's population was 59,700, protestants numbered only 7,400 and the number of Irish among the latter could have been little more than 1,000.[37] Given the number of protestant Irish in the city it is surprising that there were even three lodges in 1878. It also suggests that non-Irishmen were probably involved in the lodges. Regardless, the order's base was weak and during the 1870s and 1880s it was weakened even more. Protestants were drawn from the economically stagnating city towards Montreal and Ontario and by the 1880s Quebec was largely a French-speaking city. In 1886 the grand lodge of Quebec was 'informed by Bro. Porter, an old member of one of the Quebec lodges, and now residing in Montreal, that the lodges in Quebec were at present in a dormant state, and suggested that this Grand Lodge should appoint some brother to go to Quebec to look after the warrants and other lodge property.'[38] There would not again be a lodge in Quebec City. The order failed to recognize the significance of migration trends. In his annual review, the Canadian grand master noted in a familiar litany, 'I am happy to say everywhere is progress reported, with the exception of the Province of Quebec. There our brethren have popery in all its forms to contend with. There popery, has by its withering influence, sought to suppress and destroy the liberty which Orangemen hold so sacred.'[39]

Behind Montreal, the Lachute and Kildare areas of the Laurentian foothills had also been among the order's first bases in Quebec. A number of warrants were issued to both areas in the early 1830s, but in the Kildare area the small numbers of protestant Irish and the transiency of a population in a marginal agricultural region prevented development of a strong Orange foothold. The community too had a large catholic Irish population which later facilitated its absorption by the inland movement of land-hungry French Canadians back from the St Lawrence. Conditions in the Lachute district differed in that the Orange section of the community was enmeshed within a much larger and more cohesive protestant enclave. Orange success was easier to obtain there.

To the west of Ottawa, the Gatineau-Pontiac area also received lodge warrants early in the 1830s. Protestant Irish came in search of land or work on the canal projects and in the growing lumber trade. Many of them remained to augment the small population that had been established there by people like the Murphys of Clarendon soon after 1800. The Gatineau-Pontiac region quickly became an important Irish and Orange district. It formed the biggest rural core of the Quebec order during the 1830s and 1840s and remained a significant Orange area throughout the nineteenth century. Minor expansion of settlement northward along the Gatineau

River during the 1860s and 1870s also saw the creation of Orange lodges at the northern limits of the English-speaking frontier. Later in the century the German community at Ladysmith and Schwartz would become associated with the Orange Order. In all, the Gatineau-Pontiac showed many of the characteristics of Orange Ontario. In fact, it was closely related through its Irish settlement and its Orangeism to the townships on the Ontarian side of the Ottawa River (figure 9) and was very much an extension of English Ontario into French Quebec. As such it paralleled the later French extension across the Ottawa River into Prescott and Russell counties of Ontario.

The presence of lodges in the protestant Irish areas of the Eastern Townships also dated from the 1830s and except for the core around Kinnear's Mills the broad outline of the pattern illustrated in figure 9 was set in that decade. Lodges in the Kinnear's Mills area were not created until the 1850s, although why they should have been established so late is unknown since this area did have an Irish protestant population from an earlier date. This area also had a large Scottish component, but it is not possible to determine whether, as was the case in Ontario at the same time, the Scots were adopting the order. At any rate, the Eastern Townships communities represented by lodges were in all cases overwhelmingly English-speaking and protestant. Although there were neighbouring French-speaking and Irish Roman Catholic settlements there was definitely nothing in the geographical dimensions of the order to suggest that protestant-catholic balance was a factor contributing to the cause. If anything the geography of the Eastern Townships operated against the Orange movement. Lodge dormancy rates were high in the district. The Irish were dispersed through the British, loyalist, and American settlements which themselves were generally separated by the foothills' topography of the Appalachians. There was not the opportunity for widespread geographical dominance as was enjoyed by the protestant Irish in Ontario. In the Eastern Townships too, the movement of French Canadians into the area during the mid and late nineteenth century further added to the discontinuity of the pattern. The Eastern Townships were in many respects similar to the Lake Erie plain of Ontario. Early arrival of Yankees and English left little space for the protestant Irish and their fraternity.

The geographical extent of the order in Quebec was arrived at through the efforts of the same agents that operated in Ontario – immigrant Irishmen coming together to form local lodges in their new homeland. Lodges were created on the frontiers of British settlement in Quebec and remained to serve those communities as they matured and prospered. In later decades they also sprang up further inland on the secondary extensions of agriculture into the poverty of the Shield. Unlike Ontario, where the latter movement was noted easily because of the vast territory involved, in Quebec the Shield frontiers were only ten- and fifteen-mile extensions from initial heartlands. The geography of Quebec did not permit the apparent flowering of the order on later frontiers among second and third generation Canadians as it did in Ontario. As a consequence the order's geography in Quebec was completed essentially by the 1870s and there were only a few changes until 1920. Quebec City was vacated and the number of lodges south of Montreal began to decline in response to the out-migration and loss of sympathetic population there. The only advances occurred in the second decade of the twentieth century. In 1911 a lodge was opened in Trois-Rivières and in 1912 another in Albert Mines. The long-settled Gaspé received its first lodge in 1915 in the non-Irish settlement of Escuminac Flats and before the end of the First World War lodges were opened in nearby New Carlisle and Hopetown, places settled by Channel Islanders and demonstrating once again Orangeism's ability to extend beyond its Irish identity. Establishment of these lodges also coincides with a period of extreme protestant agitation over French as the language of instruction in catholic separate schools in Ontario and doubts of French Canadian loyalty during the war. However strong the temporal coincidence may be, it is impossible to make the connection between protestant passions and the Orange advance. More likely, as was the case elsewhere in Canada, they appeared as spontaneous expressions of purely local motivation and conviction.

The order could never have approximated in Quebec the strength achieved in Ontario. The make-up and geography of Quebec society were against it. For one, the scale of Irish immigration to Quebec was a great deal smaller and had virtually ceased by the mid 1850s. By then Ontario had established an overwhelming grip on Ulster immigration to Canada – a grip it has not let go. The absence of a Quebec frontier other than in industrial Montreal to which second generation British Quebeckers could go was also instrumental in constraining the order's growth. Orangeism was unable to grow with its society because that society itself had only limited opportunities for expansion. It had been grafted onto an established and foreign society and its resultant geography was marked by a set of isolated enclaves. Split into widely separated footholds the Quebec order like the larger British community had great problems maintaining internal unity. Communications were difficult and interregional squabbles common. All these weaknesses showed in the linkage and power differential between the Quebec and Ontario wings of the organization.

Although Montreal Orangemen had played a significant role in 1830, the contribution of Quebec Orangemen to the national movement and conversely the national order's support of the Quebec brethren were faint. A provincial grand lodge had been established in 1849 but it maintained cool relations with the British American organization. It was particularly difficult for Quebec Orangemen to understand how some of their political leaders in Ontario could fraternize with French Canadian politicians. In 1858 their peculiar position was fully shown when they objected to being subordinated to grand lodge policies and almost left the order.[40] In 1878 they were humiliated when Ontarian Orangemen, after months of blustering and posturing their anger over the death of Hackett, failed to show, as promised, for the 12 July parade in Montreal. A group of Quebec Orangemen also attempted to hive off five counties from the territory of the Grand Lodge of Ontario East during the 1880s, probably with the view of consolidating some strength.[41] All in all, Quebec Orangeism was a weak movement although it contributed the word *orangiste* which is still enunciated with bitter contempt by older French Canadians.

4

West and East

Like Ontario and Quebec, the other regions of British North America sustained the Orange Order within their protestant and British communities. However, unlike the central Canadian provinces and New Brunswick, Orangeism was introduced to the other regions by Canadians, not Irishmen, and rose without an immigrant base. In New Brunswick the order's roots had been established by Irish immigrants early in the nineteenth century as had been the case in Ontario and Quebec, but elsewhere in the Atlantic region development of the order came later. In general, Orangeism in the east diffused from New Brunswick and was grafted onto long-established and largely non-Irish communities. In Nova Scotia and Prince Edward Island it was mainly Scots who supported the organization, while in Newfoundland it was entirely dependent on those of English descent. In the Canadian west, on the other hand, the process of expansion was akin to that of Ontario after 1850 and Ontarians were primarily responsible for its success. In the prairies, Orangeism was buoyed along on waves of new Canadian settlement.

Manitoba

Manitoba was incorporated in 1871 as a province of the Dominion of Canada. Its population at the time was only 11,400, of which more than half were French speaking, catholic, and born in the territory.[1] Given the general balance of English and French population, the possibility existed for the new province to become the embodiment of those principles of cultural dualism which marked the Canadian confederation. Events were to prove otherwise and within a decade 'the solid British-Ontario core of rural Manitoba had been formed.'[2] By 1881 the more than 19,000

Ontarians in Manitoba constituted 51 per cent of the population, the largest single group in the province.[3] French speakers numbered less than ten thousand. The total English-speaking population outweighed the French in a ratio of approximately 4 to 1. Continuing migration of a new generation from the depopulating areas of rural Ontario would widen the differential between the two and end any hope of the dual identity of the nation being achieved in Manitoba. The settlement of the area had been the focus of much of Ontario's imperialist sentiments since the 1850s and the hope of realizing that aspiration coupled with the possibility of acquiring farm land propelled a spillover of Ontarian migration. As had been the case in the central Canadian province before 1870, agricultural settlement would serve as the primary vehicle for the diffusion of Orangeism. The carriers however would be Ontarian, not Irish.

The initial stimulus for the spread of the order into Manitoba was the execution in 1870 of an Orangeman, Thomas Scott, by Louis Riel's insurrectionary forces in the Red River Colony. Scott, a native of Madoc, Ontario, had been captured during an attempt to rescue the local politician, J.C. Schultz, another Orangeman.[4] Scott's execution after a court martial provided a cause célèbre for the protestants of Ontario for whom the unmistakable hand of disloyal catholicism had again been bared and, even worse, bloodied. In reacting to this episode the Orangemen were no more strident than the mass of protestant Ontarians through whose agitation the national government was forced to muster an expedition against Riel. Among the volunteers sent to the Red River Colony was private Thomas Hickey of the first Ontario Rifles and the bearer of Orange warrant no 1307, the first formal warrant on the prairies. LOL 1307, was organized 18 September 1870 on board the steamship Jessie McKenney anchored offshore at Fort Garry.[5] At the inaugural meeting Hickey was elected master by a membership drawn exclusively from Ontario (table 2).

LOL 1307 soon secured a firm role in the new colony. It reported to the grand lodge in Toronto in February 1871:

Already we are accomplishing a great amount of good for some of our Brethren from Ontario coming here, as we procured for them employment and pointed out for them the best lands and provided relief for others when penniless. We have surprised a great number of our Brethren coming here who never dreamed of such a thing as an Orange lodge in this priest-ridden country, but when they came and found sometimes a hundred members in our Lodge room it cheered their Orange hearts.[6]

It was also reported that the lodge roll included 'one hundred and ten members – good men and true,'[7] an impressive strength in a settlement

TABLE 2
Names and origins of first members of LOL 1307, Fort Garry, Manitoba, 18
September 1870

| Name | Origin | | |
	LOL	Settlement	Orange province
William Hickey	65	Centreton	Ontario East
Albert Vanderwoort	233	[South Lake]	Ontario East
Johnston Cooper	136	Toronto	Western Ontario
Robert Hinton	272	Oakville	Western Ontario
R.B. Albertson	272	Oakville	Western Ontario
W.D. Derry	11	Kingston	Ontario East
William Fargey	102	Roslin	Ontario East
William McKee	811	Picton	Ontario East
Robert Culham	1111	Millbridge	Ontario East
Stewart Mulvey	839	Hagersville	Western Ontario

SOURCE: *Proceedings of the Provincial Grand Orange Lodge of Manitoba*,
1935, 84.

whose population was little more than five hundred. The bulk of the
membership was comprised of soldiers, local functionaries, merchants,
and tradesmen, but there were also four members of parliament and one
member of the Legislative Council.[8] Not all members had come to the
new colony as Orangemen but conditions apparently encouraged enlistment in the order. The large numbers of men wishing to join the Fort
Garry lodge in the first months of operation forced the lodge to carry out
initiations twice a week.[9] In the next year, 1872, the new town of
Winnipeg witnessed its first 12 July parade at which some 250 attended.[10]
   In the aftermath of the rebellion, immigration to the new territories
became the object of national policy and a cause for Orange extension. At
the 1871 meetings of the Grand Lodge of Ontario East the future of the
new colony was a major subject of discussion and the grand master
asserted that 'it seems to me a thing to be hoped for and wished for that a
large Protestant emigration from Ontario may pour into that country, and
that of the emigrants, Orangemen shall not form the least proportion.'[11]
Migration to the new territory would not be easy. The most direct route
was across the upper Great Lakes by boat to Fort William and thence by
the tortuous Dawson road to Fort Garry. A less direct but certainly more
feasible alternative was the American route through Minnesota and
thence down the Red River to Selkirk's old settlement. It required the
arrival of the transcontinental railroad in 1883 to create an effective
all-Canadian route to the northwest and open the gates to a flood of
settlers from Ontario. Despite the early inaccessibility of the Manitoban
settlement, many Ontarians were enticed by the prospects of the new
land. Among the first to go west were farmers from Huron, Bruce, and

Grey counties, areas which had been opened less than two decades
earlier.[12]

Settlement of the new province of Manitoba proceeded haltingly during the 1870s and the creation of Orange lodges was similarly slow and
uneven (figure 10). In the first half of the decade pioneers were confined
to the prairie and parklands of the Red and lower Assiniboine rivers. In
1872 the old Red River parishes of Kildonan and St Andrews between
Winnipeg and Selkirk, received their first lodges. A lodge was also
organized at the western edge of settlement in Portage la Prairie and
another at Headingley, the northern end of the trail leading south to the
Missouri River. In 1875 a warrant was issued to Orangemen at Emerson,
the dispersal centre on the Minnesota border for settlers arriving via the
United States. By the second half of the 1870s settlements had begun to
develop westward along the Assiniboine River and south from that river
into the open prairies. A lodge sprang up at the southern edge of this
movement in 1877, and in the same year further Orange intrusions were
made into the Lisgar region north of Winnipeg. By the end of the decade
twenty lodges had been formed in the new province and their geography
(figure 11) illustrated an advance coincident with the initial steps of
Ontarian settlement. In Manitoba the order progressed as an essential
accompaniment of the protestant vanguard that secured the North-West
for the dominion.

In the creation of Manitoba the Orangemen from Ontario played an
active and prominent part and in more than one instance were involved in
clashes with the French-speaking population. Near the junction of
Rivière aux Isles de Bois and the Headingley trail to the Missouri a group
of protestant Ontarians squatted on Metis land. The Metis were away on
their annual hunt at the time and when they returned to find their home
land usurped a dispute arose. Neither party would give way and the issue
was presented for arbitration to the lieutenant governor who subsequently
decided in favour of the Ontarians. To commemorate their victory the
Ontarians renamed the upper course of the Rivière aux Isles de Bois, the
Boyne River.[13] The same name was given to their settlement. An Orange
lodge functioned in that rural district until 1936. Another squatting
incident occurred near the American border in four townships set aside by
the Colonization Society of Manitoba for French Canadians being repatri-
ated from the United States. 'So many Orangemen had settled on its
reserve that in one township there was no room for anyone else, with the
result that sixty French Canadian repatriates were reported to have returned to New England. The Society accused the Orangemen of indulging
in a racial and religious war, in order to disrupt its work of repatriation,
counting on a similar immunity to that granted to other Orangemen who

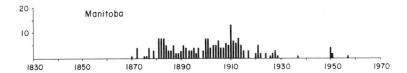

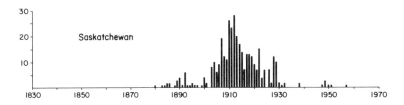

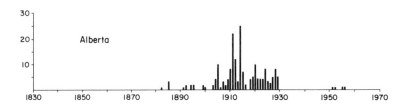

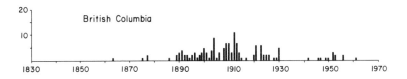

Figure 10. New Orange lodges, western Canada, 1870–1975

had squatted on the Mennonite reserve.'[14] Squatting on French and Metis
land was a characteristic feature of the protestant domination of Manitoba
during the 1870s, it was not in any measure confined to the Orange
fraternity. The events were reflections of generally held protestant attitudes toward those whose French language, Roman Catholic faith, and
dissenting politics set them apart from the incoming protestant groups.

During the 1880s the power of those groups was consolidated and
completion of the national railway opened the way for further settlement.
Territorially, the fraternity's advance continued to trace the early routes
taken by Ontario settlers (figure 11), and those the railroads had begun to
impose upon the prairie cadastre. For example, at Fairview in 1881 a
lodge was instituted just as the railway reached the area and within a year
the Orangemen had built a hall. On alternate Sundays until 1901 the hall
served as a local church.[15] Other lodges were organized as the Canadian
Pacific Railway arrived and still others were formed in the railroad's
wake. Virden, a rough tent and shack settlement on the prairie was
reached simultaneously by the railway and the order in 1883 and although
LOL 1519 did not acquire a building of its own until 1888, the Orange hall
still predated the erection of churches and the arrival of the other fraternal
societies, Oddfellows, Freemasons, and Foresters.[16] Away to the north
from the CPR, Birtle, Rapid City, Oak River, and Minnedosa lodges
preceded the railroads. To the south at Clearwater, Pilot Mound, and
Cartwright, lodges were again established some five years before the
railroad. Both the immediate effect of the railroads in creating settlement
and the reaction of settlers anticipating the eventual direction of rail are
reflected in the distribution of Orange lodges during the 1880s (figure 11).

As the order advanced through Manitoba consolidation of its position
in the earlier settled areas around Winnipeg, Portage la Prairie, and
Emerson continued. By 1890 there were fifty lodges operating in the
province and in Winnipeg a fund to erect an edifice in memory of Thomas
Scott had managed to acquire donations from many parts of the dominion. Orangeism was well established in the province and prepared for the
coming national fracas over Manitoba's abrogation of rights to school
instruction in French. The order was weak or absent only in those older
districts where the French and Metis were dominant and in the new
districts set aside for the group settlements of Mennonites in the south and
Icelanders along the west shore of Lake Winnipeg. The order generally
failed to penetrate non-British communities and was confined mainly to
areas where protestant Ontarians settled. This was the case too after 1897
when Manitoba's last agricultural frontier was opened by the arrival of
the railway in the northern regions of Dauphin and Swan River. Again,
the order arrived with the new settlers, many of whom came from earlier
Ontarian strongholds in the southern portion of the province.

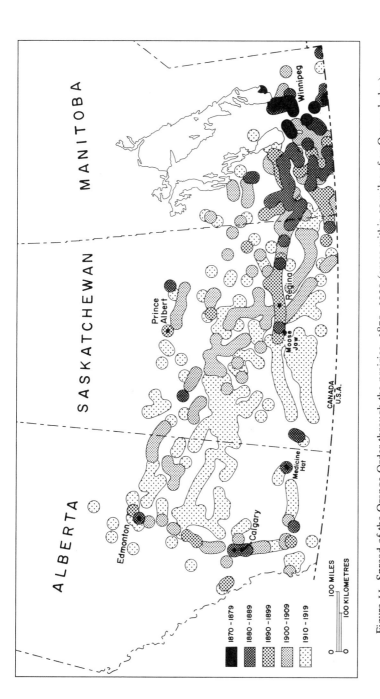

Figure 11. Spread of the Orange Order through the prairies, 1870–1920 (areas within 10 miles of an Orange lodge)

Saskatchewan and Alberta

Penetration of Saskatchewan and Alberta proceeded from the extensive beachhead secured in Manitoba and took on a significant dimension only after 1905 when migration to the prairies swelled (figure 10). Along the route of the CPR, lodges had been created early in the 1880s as far west as Medicine Hat and Lethbridge (figure 11). At the same time, well beyond the CPR, the outlying Saskatchewan settlements of Carnduff in the southwest, the territorial capital of Battleford in the north, and Princepeth in the northern Carrot River District became early centres of Orangeism. In 1885 Riel's rebellion brought troops, many of them Orangemen from central Canada, to northern Saskatchewan. In the aftermath of the battle at Batoche, Orangemen from the Midland battalion stole the bell from the local catholic church, carried it back to Ontario and mounted it as a war trophy in the firehall at Millbrook, Cavan Township. Only after considerable pressure had been applied by the national government was the bell returned to the western settlement.[17] Among civilians, the Ontario Orange connection was also paramount. Samuel Gray, born in Peel County, Ontario, helped to organize LOL 1608 at Regina in 1891.[18] In 1892 William Kernaghan, born in Colborne, Ontario, formed LOL 1688 in the isolated northern centre of Prince Albert[19] whose most illustrious residents, the Diefenbakers, arrived many years later from Ontario's Bruce County. However, growth of the order was discontinuous and reflected the fact that although there had been considerable railroad development throughout the region, only a small fraction of the agricultural land had been settled before the twentieth century.

The configuration of the distribution of lodges created during the period 1890–1905 reflects the basic underlying pattern of railway corridors. Not until the turn of the century were many lodges formed. Along the Soo Line southeast from Moose Jaw lodges appeared in the first years of the 1900s. Extension of the order was effected from the north in Drinkwater, then Milestone, Yellow Grass, Weyburn, and Estevan respectively. Although the railway had been completed in 1893 the greater part of the adjacent lands were held from the market until 1902–3 when demand was sufficient. Americans came north from Montana and the Canadians south from Moose Jaw. The Canadian inflow continued in 1903–4 along a neighbouring parallel line, just completed southeast from Regina. This rapid insertion of lodges heralded the beginning of Orangeism's greatest westward surge.

In 1905 the area west of a diagonal from Battleford southeastward to Estevan in Saskatchewan and extending across Alberta was unoccupied with the exception of lands along both the CPR and the development corridor between Calgary and Edmonton. Within the next fifteen years the greater portion of this territory was settled. The movements of Orangemen in the years 1906–7 effected infilling in the Red Deer and High River areas along the Calgary-Edmonton line (figure 11) and a simultaneous infiltration of settlement along the rail route northward from Regina to Battleford. At the same time rail was laid north from Regina to Nokomis and lodges made an immediate appearance. Orange settlement continued northwest through the Battleford area and into Alberta around Vermilion. By the close of the first decade of the twentieth century a relatively extensive network of lodges had been created through the settled parts of Saskatchewan and Alberta.

The movement continued west of Saskatoon and into Alberta during 1910–12. In the Saskatchewan section Orange lodges formed in communities along the margins of German catholic settlement. By 1912 the movement was diverted into dry lands west and south of Moose Jaw. Settlements along the CPR were the first to receive lodges during 1912 but they were quickly followed by Gravelbourg and neighbouring settlements in the centre of Palliser's Triangle. Lodge establishment in the region continued past the central towns to such cadastral addresses as Section 17, Township 5, Range 26, West of 2nd Meridian, and Sec. 4, Tp. 9, R2, W of 3. By 1915 the movement into the dry lands was spent. New inroads were made in the mining centres of the Rocky Mountains as well as into the northern pioneer fringe from which Orangemen would reach the settlements of Grande Prairie and Peace River in the west's last agricultural frontier.

By the time of the First World War a relatively extensive network of protestant garrisons had been established west of Ontario, although the nature of settlement precluded a distribution as dense as that found in the central Canadian province. In the western half of the prairies in 1911 rural population densities of only five to ten persons per square mile were common and stood in stark contrast to those of twenty to forty in the rural areas of southern Ontario. Sparse settlement was the rule on the prairies, distances between service centres were greater, and the spacing of lodges reflected that geography. Even in heavily protestant districts the potential for lodges was relatively small. Given the density of population and the fact that large tracts were settled by non–English-speaking immigrants, it is not surprising that major gaps existed in the geographical pattern of lodges. In the Mennonite areas and particularly the Slavic regions of eastern Saskatchewan an Orange presence could not be realized in any formal sense except in some regional towns. Among the immigrants that flooded into the prairies after 1905, central and eastern Europeans constituted a major proportion. Considerable fear about the nature of this

Orange parade passing under an arch on the main street of Estevan, Saskatchewan, 12 July 1906. (Public Archives of Canada)

immigration was voiced by grand lodge officers in the 1890s and eventually was enshrined in policy announcements. The grand lodge platform of 1911 impressed the need to offer inducements to stimulate immigration from Britain but the tide of non-British immigration could not be stemmed. On the prairies it remained to those protestants from Orange Ontario and the Maritimes and the occasional sympathizers emigrating from Britain and Ireland to carry the principles of Orangeism into the new society, and in that task they were successful.

British Columbia

In 1863, twenty years before the arrival of the CPR and five years after the first gold rush to the Fraser Valley, an Orange lodge was opened in British Columbia.[20] At the annual grand lodge meeting of 1861 it had been reported that 'a Brother from Kingston being about to emigrate to Vancouver Island is desirous of obtaining either a dispensation or Warrant to enable him to open a Lodge in that region.'[21] The warrant was issued and successfully carried to the Pacific coast where the lodge opened not on Vancouver Island but in New Westminster, the capital of the mainland colony. It had twenty-five members in 1864, a fact proudly recorded by the order: 'It will be gratifying to the brethren to know that this off-shoot from the parent stem already gives fair promise of becoming a goodly tree, whose branches will spread over the entire Pacific Coast, yielding much fruit and affording shelter and protection to the weary, wandering brethren of other lands.'[22] The Orangemen of New Westminster erected a hall in 1866[23] and for many years it was the only such establishment west of the Rockies. In a pattern of spread similar to that of the prairies, the order in British Columbia was carried by Ontarians, and subscribed to by them and the small number of settlers who had come directly from Ireland. By the turn of the century British Columbia had thirty-four active lodges coordinated by a provincial grand lodge established ten years earlier.[24] The initial spurt in the growth of the order there occurred during the late 1880s and 1890s (figure 10) at a time when the Kootenay mining operations were developing and the population was increasing rapidly. During this period lodges were opened in mining towns such as Fernie near the Albertan border and Sandon in the Kootenays but the high turnover in population and the fluctuating fortunes of the towns mitigated against any firm rooting of the order.

In 1900 the order's presence was strongest in Vancouver and the neighbouring towns of Delta, Surrey, and New Westminster. Beyond the lower mainland area Langley and Chilliwack also had lodges as had outlying towns such as Kamloops, Revelstoke, and Golden, all on the CPR. On Vancouver Island, Victoria, Nanaimo, and the Saanich peninsula were important foci.[25] In general, lodges were most numerous in those settlements best able to survive amid the boom and bust economy of the province. Even within the lower mainland, however, frontier conditions were still evident at the turn of the century. The photograph of the Orange parade in Vancouver in 1888 clearly indicates the recency of that settlement.

The formation of the lodge on the west coast in 1863 coincided with the establishment of the first lodge in Newfoundland and marked an important juncture in the Canadian order's history. Those events were hailed by Orangemen as indications of their movement's vitality and its centrality to the realization of a country *a mari usque ad mare*. When the national grand lodge met for the first time in Vancouver in 1906 the grand master proudly declared: 'We meet today in this splendid City of Vancouver, on

First Orange celebration held in Vancouver, 12 July 1888. Marching west on Hastings St, halted on crest of hill between Dunlevy and Jackson Aves. Loyal Orange Lodges of Vancouver, Victoria, and New Westminster. (Courtesy of Vancouver City Archives)

Orangemen parade along Cordova Street, Vancouver's main street, 12 July 1893. The plank street and sidewalks, and the barely visible unfinished church and dead trees of the former forest in the background, clearly indicate the recent emergence of the city. King Billy's stetson further adds to the western quality of the Boyne commemoration. (Courtesy of Vancouver City Archives) the shores of the Golden Pacific. Our gathering marks another step in the onward march of the Orange Association.'[26] Despite its symbolic significance, British Columbia, with only the same number of lodges as tiny Prince Edward Island but a population many times larger, never became a major Orange province. Orangeism had run its course when it reached the Pacific.

The essential weakness of the order in British Columbia was a product of the lateness of its development. Orangeism was an anachronism there. The western province had emerged out of the final maturing phase of nineteenth-century industrialism and the basic polarization in the province was never between catholics and protestants but between workers and their corporate bosses and between oriental and white labour. The trade union, not the Orange lodge, the political ideology of socialism, not the principles of protestantism and loyalism, were more typical of that society.[27] Even Victoria, the urban epitome of Britishness and belief in empire, never provided a power base for the order. British Columbia, with a population which was largely foreign born, and separated from central Canada by time and space offered little sustenance to the order.

New Brunswick

In 1889 the grand secretary of the Orange Order happily reported to the annual general meeting: 'From few in number we have grown to thousands and thousands, from a limited area in the province of Ontario we have spread until today from the Atlantic to the Pacific, throughout the length and breadth of the great Dominion of Canada ... the Grand Lodge is obeyed, respected and acknowledged.'[28] What is not pointed out in the secretary's statement are the early beginnings of Orangeism in the Maritimes where the order had developed quite independently of the Ontario-based grand lodge. In New Brunswick Orangeism had achieved a position of strength early, comparable to that attained by its counterpart in Ontario.

The beginnings of Orangeism in New Brunswick date from the first years of the 1800s, and it is known that a military lodge operated in Saint John continuously between 1818 and 1831.[29] In the latter year, a civilian lodge, Verner LOL 1, was instituted in Saint John by a newly arrived Irish immigrant, James McNichol. He had joined the order in Ireland in 1824 and through his activities in the New World acquired the title of 'Father of Orangeism in Eastern Canada.'[30] In 1838 he organized the forty or fifty lodges operating in the colony into a provincial grand lodge.[31] Six years later his organization was put under the jurisdiction of Gowan's Grand Lodge of British America. The New Brunswick order, however, retained the right to issue its own warrants according to its own numbering system. This degree of independence, accepted by Gowan but opposed by his successor, Benjamin, was one of the contentious items which led to the Orange schism of 1853–6.[32] Nevertheless, New Brunswick retained its privilege and even today its warrants are not recorded in the central Orange register for British America.

The early vitality of the order was maintained and by 1868 a total of 150 warrants had been issued,[33] although it is impossible to estimate how many of them were actually in operation. The Grand Orange Lodge of New Brunswick in 1864 noted: 'Our register gives the number of lodges as one hundred and fifty while fifty may be taken as the extreme or maximum number in working order and paying regular dues.'[34] It is known that in 1880 85 lodges were active, and by 1900 this figure had increased to 119, thereby making New Brunswick the second largest Orange province in Canada.[35] The areal distribution of Orange strength in 1920 (figure 12) reflects the basic division in the cultural geography of the province. Lodges were absent from most of the northern and eastern regions with the exception of a few centres in the lower Miramichi Valley and port towns such as Campbellton, Dalhousie, and Bathurst located on the Baie de Chaleur and linked by the Intercolonial Railway. This pattern illustrates well the separation between the northern and eastern French populations, descendants of the displaced Acadians, and the English-speaking protestant populations of the Saint John River valley and south-eastern portion of the province.

The lodge distribution evident in 1920 was the product of many decades of development and adjustment of Orange districts. Saint John had been the first base of the order and from there it extended upstream into both agricultural and logging areas. Along the valley between Meductic and Aroostook, lodges were located within ten miles of each other at virtually every bridging point and lumbertown. These communities were composed of a mixture of loyalist and protestant Irish settlers. From these early areas of strength the order continued its advance into sympathetic areas such as the lumber towns of the ethnically mixed districts in the lower Miramichi Valley and the English districts of the southeast. The major points of concentration on the map reflect not only this initial rural base but also the effects of subsequent railroad development and industrialization in the last two decades of the nineteenth century. Moncton, the creation of the Intercolonial Railway, boasted a lodge within a few years of its founding, as did other much smaller centres along that transportation corridor. The factory town of Marys-ville, across the river from Fredericton, the provincial capital and itself a

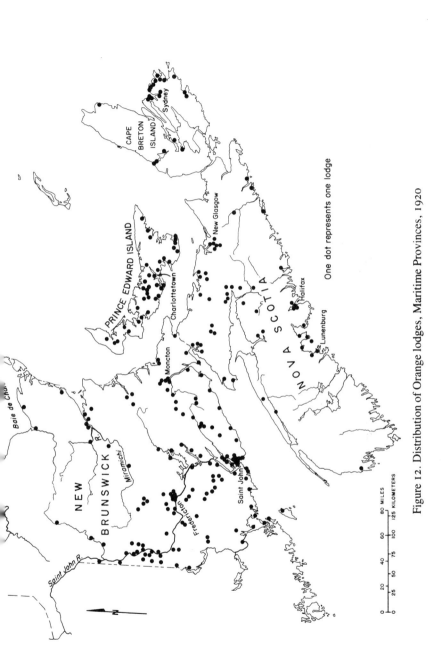

Figure 12. Distribution of Orange lodges, Maritime Provinces, 1920

major Orange centre, was incorporated in 1885 and almost immediately acquired a lodge.[36]

New Brunswick's Orange history, like that of Ontario, is replete with tales of sectarian violence. Riots at Woodstock in 1847 and at Saint John two years later involved conflict with catholic Irish[37] but much of the anti-catholic sentiment of the province's Orangemen was directed against the French-speaking population. The separate school riots involving Orangemen and French Canadians at Caraquet in 1875 is a good case in point.[38] The issue of religious instruction in schools was the focus for much Orange agitation which took place against the background of a growing population imbalance favouring the French and catholic communities. Between 1871 and 1901 the French percentage of the provincial population rose from 15 to 24 and the more inclusive catholic element increased from 33 to 38 per cent. In the political life of New Brunswick, Orangemen represented a decided force articulating the fears of those protestants and staunch loyalists apparently threatened by the demographic reality of their society. It contributed to the legacy of polarization which characterized provincial politics. Yet, as is clearly illustrated by its location in the lumber camps of Miramichi, the old shipbuilding centre of St Martins, and in the newer industrial communities of Moncton and Marysville, the order provided an important social focus and attracted a wide range of the protestant community to its ranks.

Nova Scotia

Although a lodge may have existed in Halifax in 1800 no record of a permanent lodge appears until 1847 when one was formed under a New Brunswick warrant.[39] Other lodges were created under authority from New Brunswick until the mid 1850s when the fraternity in Nova Scotia was placed under the direct jurisdiction of the Canadian grand lodge. By 1859 there were sufficient lodges to justify the creation of a provincial grand lodge. Growth of the order, although pronounced in the mid 1850s (figure 13), was most significant in the post-confederation era when, during the periods 1865–80 and 1890–1915, 180 lodges were created – some 80 per cent of the total warrants issued prior to 1920. The two periods of rapid Orange expansion coincide with major phases in the economic history of the province.

During the periods of rapid growth five regional concentrations of lodges arose – the mining areas of Pictou, central Cumberland, and northern Cape Breton, the city of Halifax, and the marsh settlements of Cobequid Bay (figure 12). Two lesser concentrations were to be found in Lunenburg and Guysborough counties. In other established settlements

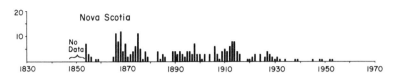

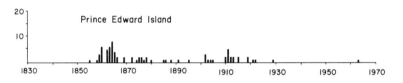

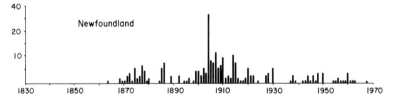

Figure 13. New Orange lodges, Atlantic Canada, 1830–1975

in Kings County, the Annapolis Valley, and western Cape Breton only a handful of lodges were ever formed and few of them lasted more than a decade. In Cape Breton the territorial preponderance of catholic Highland Scots formed an obvious block to the spread of Orangeism. It is more difficult to explain the absence of lodges among the English and loyalist settlers of the Annapolis Valley and Kings County. These groups joined the order in Ontario and New Brunswick but tended to remain aloof from the movement in Nova Scotia. The anomaly is further emphasized by the fact that the order found a relatively strong base in the non-Irish county of Lunenburg, 70 per cent of whose population was of German origin in 1871.[40] A petition to the Nova Scotian government from No Surrender Lodge 26, Mahone Bay, Lunenburg County, in 1893 was signed by twelve members, nine of whom bore clearly non-Irish names, for example, Zwicker, Zink, Smeltzer, Strum, and Buzgozic.[41] Their interest in the Britishness and protestantism of the Orange Order and their presence within it makes the absence of the English even more puzzling.

Elsewhere in the province a clear association between Orangeism and mining communities existed. Both the temporal and geographical dimensions of the order emphasize its links with the developing coal-mining and iron and steel industries. The New Glasgow district of Pictou County got the majority of its lodges in the twenty-year period following 1865, the time of local industrial development.[42] In Cape Breton the arrival of the railway in 1891 stimulated the development of coal mining and laid the basis for the emergence of the iron and steel industry. Cape Breton Orangeism, beginning in 1889 and peaking in the early twentieth century, paralleled the stages of industrialization. The nomenclature of Orange lodges in these areas – Reserve Mine LOL 1857, Acadian Iron Mines LOL 1421, Dominion #1, LOL 3029, and Dominion #6, LOL 2840, the latter two named after the Dominion Iron and Steel Company – testify to the close relationship between the development of resource industries and the emergence of Orangeism. In the colliery districts lodges were an important part of life. It has been suggested by J.M. Cameron, a local historian in Pictou County, that the order was transferred directly to the region by coal miners brought from Scotland by the mining companies.[43] If such is indeed the case it is indicative of the strength of the fraternity in that it would have represented a transfer twice-removed from the order's homeland. Despite the late and direct transatlantic link apparent in this instance, the base of the order in the province was much more indigenous. An Orange organization existed prior to the immigration of miners and its success in both Springhill and Cape Breton was dependent almost exclusively upon native-born Nova Scotians who formed the bulk of the mining population.[44]

Orangeism in the 1860s was bound up with the processes of population displacement and industrialization and it was even intrinsic to the structure of a few company towns. In many towns virtually every facet of life was controlled by the mining company. One such town, Acadia Mines, later called Westville, had been built by the Intercolonial Coal and Acadian Coal companies after coal was discovered there in 1865. Within two years an Orange lodge had been organized.[45] Similarly nearby Albion Mines (later Stellarton) was built by the General Mining Association, and until the late 1870s 'the company owned the land, rented the houses, and hired and fired the employees. No man, professional, tradesmen, shopkeeper, labourer could do business within the town if not approved by the company.'[46] An Orange lodge operated in the town from 1867, presumably with the blessing of the company. Further evidence of the capitalists' approval of the order was demonstrated by the appointment of J. Cumming, a prominent New Glasgow industrialist, as provincial grand master of the order in 1905. A lodge also was named after him in Eureka.[47] The strength of Orangeism within mining communities in Nova Scotia contrasted with its weakness in resource centres of British Columbia. In Nova Scotia, a more paternalistic class of entrepreneur and a largely native-born population provided an environment within which Orangeism was welcome. By the same token, the cultural linkage between northern Ontario and the heartland of Canadian Orangeism to the south permitted the extension of Orangeism into another major mining region. No such conditions existed to foster the order in the western province.

Nova Scotian Orangeism toward the end of the nineteenth century extended beyond the realm of the collieries and the iron and steel mills. In two major areas, metropolitan Halifax and around Cobequid Bay, a district which included rural service towns and the growing industrial centre of Truro, the order's growth was pronounced. In Halifax, population increase may have been a factor. Interestingly, the city's trading links with the Caribbean were illustrated in the fact that Bermuda, which received an Orange lodge in 1865 and another in 1875, was under the jurisdiction of the Nova Scotia Provincial Grand Lodge.[48] The Cobequid Bay district is especially noteworthy as it was originally settled in 1762 by Ulster protestants under the supervision of Alex McNutt.[49] Their arrival in North America predated the formation of the Orange Order in Ireland, but their Irishness was not the sole factor in their acceptance of the order. The timing of lodge formation in the district correlates more strongly with the rise of Truro as a major industrial centre. The links between Orangeism and industrialization were as strong there as elsewhere in the province. The community of Cobequid Bay was one of the few concentrations of protestant Irish in Nova Scotia, and the order in that province was maintained almost exclusively by persons of Scottish descent and Presbyterian denomination.

By 1920 the order had begun to decline in Nova Scotia. During its peak it had been an important part of the mining and industrial communities where it successfully united a preindustrial concept of social division with a fully fledged system of industrial capitalism. Westville, especially, was a protestant and Orange company town and there the order was stronger than the Oddfellows, Freemasons, or Knights of Pythias. July 12 was a civic highlight and the Orangemen were so active in the community that they were able to publish their own weekly newspaper in the late 1890s.[50] Stimulated by the forces of industrial expansion the order was sensitive to changes in the economic well-being of the province. A very high turnover in the workforce, the shattering of the industrial aspirations of many towns, and economic stagnation in the maritime province were reflected in a high rate of closure among the lodges.[51] Out-migration and the rise of trade unions further eroded the Orange foundations so that the map of the lodge distribution in 1920 shows only seventy-one operating in Nova Scotia.

Prince Edward Island

The inhabitants of the 'million acre farm'[52] have often, and with good reason, complained of being ignored in the annals of Canadian history. No good social history of the province has been written and the occasional references which are made to the island rarely suggest anything to imply that Orangeism had any role to play. Yet the order was evident in many of the small communities and infrequently its stand on public issues made headlines. As in most other provinces, religious divisions were marked and took precedence over racial or social splits.[53] Protestant and catholic rivalry characterized much of island life.

As early as 1847 a bloody sectarian fight between protestant Scots and catholic Irish was recorded at an election in Belfast, Queens County.[54] Three men were killed in the foray and although subsequent sectarianism did not reach this level of violence the folk tradition was endowed with an epic to be commemorated by the two communities. Tensions heightened again during the late 1850s when the issue of Bible reading in public schools became a matter of political debate. Lines were drawn between the Liberal party, consisting of catholics and some protestants, and the anti-catholic Conservative party. The Orange Order was prominent in the debate which resulted in the election of an all-protestant Conservative party in 1859.[55] The question of church-state relations in the field of education would continue to involve the Orange Order until the passage of the Public School Act of 1876.

The educational dispute arose out of a context in which the population, almost all of it native born, was radically divided into catholics, mainly Acadian and Irish, forming 40 per cent of the total, and Scottish and English protestants. Protestant Irish were but a small minority and the Orange Order obtained its support primarily from the Scottish population. The first lodge was organized in 1855 and the period of most rapid growth was the decade of the 1860s (figure 13) when thirty-three lodges were established amid the political turmoil over education. During the last third of the century eighteen additional lodges were created and in 1900 a total of thirty-two lodges, with a combined membership of 830, were active.[56] The number of active Orangemen represented approximately 7 per cent of the adult protestant male population, a smaller proportion than in either Ontario or New Brunswick but nevertheless strong enough to make its voice heard. Within some communities a much higher proportion of the population would have been Orangemen.

Regionally, the order was strongest in the central Queens County (figure 12) which had a high proportion of Scots, and weakest in the northwestern Prince County, a distinctly Acadian area. Surprisingly, there were few lodges to the east in Kings County (figure 12) which had a mixture of Scottish and Irish settlers. As with Ontario, the order was strongest not in the zones of religious mixture but in those areas which were most homogeneously protestant. The greatest concentration of lodges was to be found in a district west of Hunter River in the centre of the island where lodge masters with names such as McLeod, McPherson, and McPhee testified to the Scottishness of the organization.[57] Charlotte-town had two lodges but most of the lodges were located in small villages and hamlets. In localities such as Canoe Cove which today consists of only a Presbyterian church, a public school, and an Orange hall, the order was an intrinsic part of the local community.

The minute books for LOL 2298, formed at Brackley Point, Queens County, in 1911, indicate clearly the community role of the local lodge.[58] The first entry in the records notes: 'A public meeting was held in Hawe's Hall on November 6th 1911 for the purpose of organizing an Orange Lodge, after which a lodge was organized to be called King George Lodge No. 2296 [sic]. The night of meeting was fixed on the first and third Fridays of each month.'[59] Of the ten committee members elected at the founding meeting four bore the surname Cudmore, two were called Shaw, and two called MacCallum. Kinship was obviously a factor in recruitment for the lodge. A local protestant minister, it was noted, declined to join on the ground that he 'could do better work for humanity beyond the pale of our society. The Rev. gentleman also thought that Orangemen should be more active in their work in checking the advance of Roman Catholicism.'[60] The Orange Order did not create that feeling of sectarian bitterness. It was, in itself, a by-product of it, and the association's comfortable niche amid the everyday social life of the community indicated that in many Prince Edward Island settlements, as in the rest of Canada, Orangeism was not an unwelcome intrusion.

Newfoundland

Newfoundland represents an enigma within Canadian Orangeism. The island did not receive a lodge until 1863 when a Prince Edward Islander brought a Nova Scotian warrant to St John's.[61] From this late starting point the order rapidly developed into a social and political force of major importance. During the present century that growth has continued, despite declines in Orange strength in all other provinces and Newfoundland is today the second largest Orange jurisdiction in Canada. The persistent strength of the order in Newfoundland is anomalous, but even more anomalous is its exclusively English base. In no other part of British North America was the order able to graft itself so completely and so successfully onto a society in which protestant Irish and Scots were insignificant.

The island was colonized during the eighteenth and early nineteenth centuries by two distinct groups, protestant West Country English and catholic Irish from counties Waterford, Kilkenny, Cork, Wexford, and Tipperary. From these groups alone is descended the bulk of the Newfoundland population. Territorially the two settled and developed in distinct regional patterns. In the populous Avalon Peninsula this was particularly marked. In 1836 the Cape shore of the southern Avalon Peninsula was entirely Irish except for thirty English settlers near Placentia. Even on the more ethnically diverse northern parts of the peninsula the English and Irish tended to be settled in separate blocks.[62] This pattern of segregation remains. The census of 1945, the last before confederation, recorded 265 settlements of more than 50 people on the Avalon Peninsula, 96 were almost entirely protestant and 97 almost entirely catholic. Within the protestant community of Newfoundland as a whole Anglicans and United Churchmen were the main sects and together with Roman Catholics they formed 31, 25, and 33 per cent of the population respectively. The predominance of protestants among the population was expressed in their distribution around the island while Catholics were confined largely to the Avalon Peninsula. The territorial segregation was reinforced by the fragmented topography and isolation of outport settlement.

The pattern of geographical separation was paralleled by a social and political split. Education was organized on denominational lines, Catholics, Methodists, Anglicans, Presbyterians, Congregationalists, and later the Salvation Army, all operated their own schools. Patronage and public employment were also distributed according to church affiliation. In 1909 the island's House of Assembly deemed it fitting to analyse both the number of jobs and the proportion of salaries in the civil service allocated to members of the various religious groups.[63] The final report of this enquiry published the ratio of representation in the civil service to the strength of the denominations in the total population. Religious divisions were publicly recognized and politically catered to in Newfoundland and thus were much more apparent than in any other part of British North America. As a former premier of the province has written, 'the sectarian spirit saturated all society in Newfoundland.'[64]

It has been argued that 'the constituent elements of the new community from the very beginning contained in their respective traditions and memories from the old world the seeds of social conflict in the new.'[65] However, the possibility that the inherent sectarian bitterness would break out into open violence was minimized by the geographical separateness of the two communities. But in mixed areas such as St John's or in the settlements at the head of Conception Bay the potential was great and was in fact realized in a bloody clash between protestants and catholics at Harbour Grace in 1883 when seven people were killed.[66] Into this tradition of divisiveness the Orange Order fitted easily, and with its conviviality and fraternalism it was an attractive social proposition for the outport settlements. Ideologically the ultra-protestant principles of Orangeism were redundant in Newfoundland; the innovations were the structure and ritual of a secret society and the establishment of a formal set of social links between isolated communities and the outside world.

The distribution of Orange lodges may be used to highlight the geographical divisions that existed between catholics and protestants in Newfoundland. Nowhere was this division more evident than on the Avalon Peninsula (figure 14). Forty-eight lodges operated in 1920 on the coastal stretch from St John's to the southwest shore of Trinity Bay, the densest area of lodges on the island. They represented a quarter of the Newfoundland total. Half the lodges were to be found in settlements which were more than 95 per cent protestant; the remainder were found in settlements between 50 and 95 per cent protestant. Over half of all the settlements with a protestant majority had lodges and these could also

serve adjacent outports. Orangemen commonly crossed the coves by boat
to attend meetings in the nearest lodge.[67] The density of lodges and their
location within predominantly protestant settlements is reminiscent of the
Ontarian example. The presence of lodges throughout the exclusively
protestant bays of Newfoundland is also the strongest evidence that
religious balance and religious tension within a settlement were irrelevant
as factors stimulating Orangeism. Locally the Orange Order was not the
symbol of a beseiged minority but a community organization central to
the social activities of local males. Many of the smaller outports could
boast an Orange hall better than the church hall, and christening parties,
wedding receptions, and Christmas fêtes were all held in the LOL hall.

Figure 14 also illustrates the geographical segregation of the Avalon
communities, and from it the broad pattern of a protestant north embracing the outports of Conception and Trinity Bays and a catholic east,
south, and west coast may be discerned. The only major exception is the
catholic enclave in the Harbour Main and Holyrood sections of Conception Bay. Most striking is the string of completely catholic settlements
along the coast between St John's and Long Harbour, north of Placentia.
Of the forty-five settlements in this tract only three had significant
protestant components. The duality of settlement in Newfoundland was
symbolized by the Orange hall, protestant churches and schools on the
one hand, and catholic institutions on the other. The symbolism was
extended further into public life by the fact that the Mondays nearest to 12
July and 17 March have become traditional public holidays on the island.
In no other Canadian province are these dates officially recognized. The
ritual and tenets of Orangeism subscribed to by Newfoundlanders were
identical to those of their brethren in mainland Canada but boat journeys
to lodge meetings and benevolent payments to the widows of fishermen-
members lost at sea added a local character to the organization. The
process by which the order was diffused throughout the island also
reflected that maritime flavour.

The development of the order in Newfoundland was greatest during the
1870s and in the first two decades of the twentieth century (figure 13). In
1870 when the provincial grand lodge was established, eight warrants
already had been issued to Newfoundland, three to St John's and five to
settlements of Conception Bay. During the next decade thirty-three
lodges were established, half of them in Conception Bay, four on the
southern Burin Peninsula, and the remainder scattered from Twillingate
in the north to Port aux Basques and Burgeo in the southwest. Thirty more
lodges were created in the last two decades of the century. The Orange
presence was consolidated in Conception Bay and other concentrations
were created in Trinity, Bonavista, and Notre Dame bays. By 1898 some

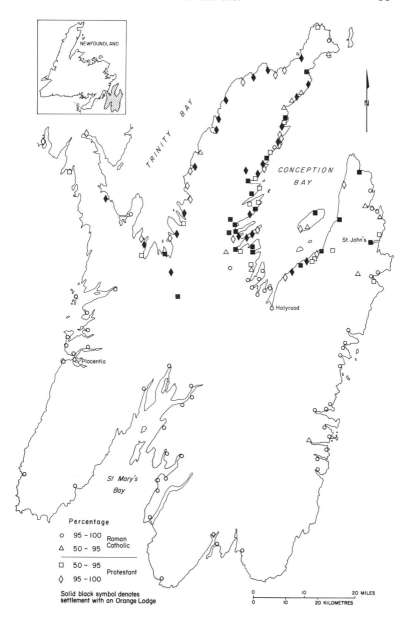

Figure 14. Distribution of settlements (by religion) and Orange lodges, Avalon Peninsula, Newfoundland, 1920

sixty lodges had been formed in Newfoundland and of these only three had ceased to function.[68] No province in Canada even approximated this high retention rate.

The stability of early Orangeism was maintained during the great development period 1900–20 when 134 new lodges were created. The old areas of Conception, Trinity, and Bonavista bays received almost 30 during this period but the main thrust during the first decade was north into Notre Dame Bay, including remote Fogo Island which got its first lodge in 1902. This marked the virtual completion of the spread of Orangeism into protestant northern Newfoundland. During the next decade the southern shore, west of the Burin Peninsula, was the primary centre of development. In 1910 the first lodge in Labrador was established at Red Bay. Settlement in Newfoundland was almost exclusively sea-oriented and the distribution of lodges necessarily reflected that orientation. But in 1905 the Anglo-Newfoundland Development Company acquired timber rights in the northern interior and 'in the next four years a large paper mill was constructed at Grand Falls, and around it a modern town – the first Newfoundland community out of sight and sound of the sea.'[69] Grand Falls got its first Orange lodge in 1907, two years before the production of newsprint began there.

The expansion of Orangeism followed a distinct geographical pattern. The periodicity of the spread into different regions was not just coincidental but it is impossible to discover from the available data the precise mechanism of diffusion. On at least three occasions prominent Orangemen visited parts of the colony to propagate the order. In 1883 Donald Morrison, the grand secretary, visited the northeast.[70] Two years later other officers visited northern outports, most likely in Notre Dame Bay.[71] In 1890 an Orange missionary from the mainland visited the colony.[72] Because there is no record of their itineraries available, the efforts of these organizers cannot be linked to the creation of individual lodges. At best, they could have been responsible for setting up seventeen lodges, less than 10 per cent of the total formed in Newfoundland. The rapid spread of the order among the protestant outports suggests that rather than an organizational effort, some process of contagious diffusion was at work. By the late nineteenth century the settlement pattern of Newfoundland was fixed and although there were both local and long distance migrations between outports, a considerable degree of isolation persisted.

Church administration created links that may have been particularly important in the spread of Orangeism since many of the warrants were issued to clergymen. Another transfer mechanism was provided by the mixing of outport crews in the long distance Labrador fishery, 'a branch of the industry confined entirely to the north-east, to the fishermen of Conception, Trinity, Bonavista and Notre Dame bays.'[73] Professor Noel in explaining the diffusion of another organization, the Fishermen's Protective Union (FPU), in Newfoundland has argued for the effectiveness of the Labrador fishery mechanism. Perhaps a stronger factor was the outport linkages built by the seal fishery. From 1863 the seal fisheries were increasingly dominated by steamers. Originating first in St John's and later in the century from the northern coast of Bonavista Bay, the steamers drew crews from wide hinterlands in northeastern Newfoundland.[74] From 1874 to 1884 many outport fishermen visiting St John's to join the sealing fleet were initiated in the city's Orange lodges.[75] From that juncture and by that process the principles of Orangeism could be spread among the seal fishermen and carried back to the outports. These factors do much to explain why the Orange Order spread so rapidly in the four northern bays and more slowly along the southern coast where the economy was localized in family operated inshore fishing.

It is interesting to note that the FPU, a cooperative and political movement prominent in Newfoundland politics from 1908 to 1923, was strongest and spread most rapidly in the same areas of northeastern Newfoundland as had the Orange Order. The movement formed by William Coaker had its first meeting in the Orange hall in Herring Neck and rapidly spread among the fishermen of Notre Dame Bay.[76] The diffusion of this political group followed closely upon that of Orangeism and may have been facilitated by linkages previously established by the order. 'The FPU consciously adopted some of the characteristics of a fraternal order, with officers' sashes, flags, emblems, annual parades and fetes.'[77] It also of necessity would have included the local community's Orangemen. Indeed the non-sectarian, socialist FPU was unable to shake off its image of being a protestant party, and the catholic population, believing it to be dominated by the Orange Order, refused to lend their support.

The geographical, temporal, and membership correlations between the FPU and Orange Order are striking. Equally striking is the large number of lodges which operated in Newfoundland. By 1920 there were 190 lodges. To some extent this number was a function of the nucleated settlement pattern – each nucleation generally requiring its own lodge. Given the lack of social alternatives in an outport, most males could be attracted to the order and for this reason the largest lodges in the world were to be found on the island. The primary attraction of the order was its fraternalism and conviviality and less important was the involvement in politics at election time.

Orange Membership:
Strength and Composition

The spread and extent of the order's realm and the political power commonly ascribed to the fraternity, especially in Ontario, New Brunswick, and Newfoundland, suggest a movement of considerable strength. Tens of thousands of committed adherents were required to sustain it, but to date no attempt has been made to quantify the dimensions of that Orange support. Neither have serious attempts been made to analyse its ethnic, religious, and social character. Often the assumption has been that Orangemen were Irish and immigrant, Presbyterian, and usually of low social status but the order's geography as outlined here indicates a much larger social base. Men from a wide variety of backgrounds and ethnic groups belonged to the order, and as the nineteenth century progressed immigrants became a minority in an increasingly Canadian organization. Similarly, the order was not the domain of any single protestant denomination. In religion, as in social class and ethnicity, it reflected the composition of the communities in which it operated.

Numerical strength

The first estimate of the number of Orangemen in Canada was presented by Gowan in 1833. According to the grand master there were 11,243 in Ontario,[1] and a year later he placed the membership at 12,853.[2] Given that the province had received 144 of the 154 warrants issued in British North America (exclusive of New Brunswick) up to that time, the total membership of the order in 1834 could not have exceeded fourteen thousand. The figures offered by Gowan in the first years of his administration were the last of such precision until the 1890s. Accurate returns on the condition of the order in the nineteenth century were difficult to obtain and for decades the organization operated with incomplete records. Orangemen, nevertheless, were not deterred from creating and propagating estimates of their numbers. In 1850 it was claimed by John Hillyard Cameron (grand master, 1859–70) that there were 60,000 to 70,000 Orangemen in Canada[3] and by 1860 100,000.[4] In 1864 the number had increased dramatically to some '200,000 loyal and brave'[5] men, a contingent which grew to be 250,000 in 1886.[6] In 1889 a smaller number, 200,000, was offered for Canada and Newfoundland in reports from New Zealand. According to the information from the antipodes 'there [was] scarcely a British colony in which the Orange Society [was] not established,' and the empire could count among its population 995,000 Orangemen.[7]

The estimates of membership in British North America grew out of a projection from Cameron's claim of 60,000 to 70,000 Orangemen made in 1850. Ten years later in a petition to Queen Victoria he argued: 'We wish to inform your majesty that the Orange Association in British America is not merely an Irish Society, but that it numbers in its ranks upwards of one hundred thousand men drawn from all classes, and of various national origin.'[8] Despite that claim of 'upwards of one hundred thousand men' in 1860, Cameron in response to a question on lodge membership posed at the 1861 grand lodge meeting asserted: 'Whether we number 10,000 or 110,000, there is no means of ascertaining.'[9] For Cameron, Orangemen included not only paid-up members of the order but any ex-Orangeman, and perhaps even Orange family member or other protestant sympathetic to Orange principles. Gowan, during the 1850s, also interpreted the strength of the order in the more general protestant rather than specific membership terms. It was politically necessary at that time to present as large an estimate of strength as possible. Representation by population was a major issue and various groups vied for attention, patronage, and effect. Statistics were also fashionable.

The active Orange membership in Canada was much less than that proposed by Orange leaders. Membership varied from lodge to lodge and from year to year but scattered records tend to indicate an average lodge size in the range of twenty-five to forty (figure 15). In 1857 the average membership of a lodge in the city of Toronto was fifty-four but outside Toronto in the rural areas and villages of York County the average was thirty-four.[10] The average membership of Toronto lodges reached a high point of eighty-eight in 1872[11] but had dropped again to only fifty-two by 1880[12] and stood at seventy in 1894.[13] In the densely populated towns and cities large lodges were often found, but the limits imposed by sparse populations and relative inaccessibility in farm areas generally kept rural lodges smaller. From a fairly complete Orange census of eastern Ontario in 1884 the average size was only twenty-seven.[14] On Prince Edward Island, Charlottetown's lodge was larger than those in the province's smaller settlements but again average lodge size was only twenty-five in 1886.[15] The smallest lodges were naturally enough located on the Prairies, the average lodge size being twenty-four in Manitoba and Saskatchewan in 1890,[16] and twenty-two in Saskatchewan and Alberta in 1895.[17] An anomaly was created by the province of Newfoundland, however, where average lodge size approximated that of the city of Toronto and from the 1890s to the 1920s never fell below sixty. In fact the largest lodges were to be found on the island. For example, in 1913 LOL 1327 in Bonavista had 439 paid-up members and the combined active membership of LOLs 1282 and 1285 in St John's was 698.[18]

By 1900 there were about 1,450 active lodges and based on an average of 40 members each, 60,000 Orangemen represents a quite liberal estimate. About 38,000 members or 63 per cent of the total resided in Ontario,[19] a proportion in line with that of the province's share of lodges. There were almost 16,000 members in the Atlantic region and 2,000 in Quebec.[20] On the prairies 3,000 men maintained active connection with the lodges and in British Columbia there were another 1,200.[21] In a total protestant adult male population of about 1 million,[22] 60,000 Orangemen represent no more than a token force, and in the face of the historical image of Orange political strength, the number appears incredibly small. However, the size of the active membership does not adequately impart the full significance of the movement. Turnover in the fraternity was great and for every active member there were several ex-members in any given community.

At the local lodge level Orangemen could almost double or halve their numbers in a single year. For example, LOL 1093 in Petrolia, Ontario, had 53 members in good standing in 1870, but this had increased to 93 in 1871.[23] It was not a unique case. At the provincial grand lodge level changes in local membership were reflected in aggregate. In Ontario east the number of paid-up members increased from 13,364 in 1908[24] to 19,538 in 1919[25] and dropped to 18,007 in 1920.[26] Average lodge size ranged in the same period from 35 to 45. Variability in the order's membership has been assessed by one historian, J.D. Livermore, who has noted that in Kingston, Ontario, during the 1850s, 'economic malaise ... provided fertile ground for the growth and expansion of the Orange Order.'[27] In a similar vein, G.S. Kealey insists that 'on the national level the periods of most rapid growth correspond both to economic disruptions and to the Riel Rebellions.'[28] With respect to the effects of economic disruptions the grand secretary of Western Ontario reported in 1880 that 'the progress of the Order in this Province has not been as rapid this year,

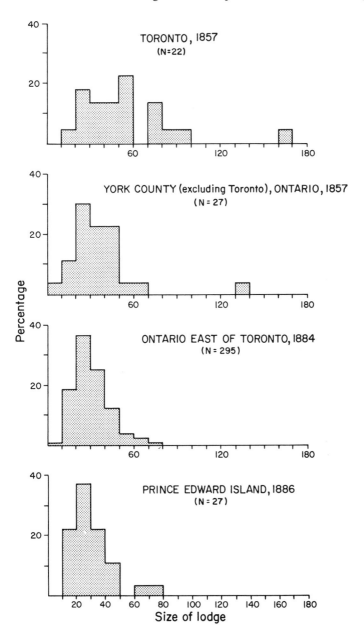

Figure 15. Percentage distributions of lodge size

as in the previous year owing to a great extent to the scarcity of labor and money.'[29] At the following grand lodge session it was noted that 'the return of prosperity may be a means of augmenting our order by bringing back some of those lost because of financial circumstances.'[30] Similar statements about the effects of falling exports, good harvests, and industrial unemployment were made in 1863, 1866, 1882, 1890, 1894, and 1899.[31] Orange membership reacted positively to economic prosperity; in times of economic hardship members, unable to pay their dues, withdrew although some lodges temporarily waived the dues for such brethren.

The growth consequences of the Riel rebellion have already been questioned in the examination of the factors that propelled the geographical extension of the order. By the same token the documents do not support Kealey's other assertion that in Toronto 'the exceptional incidents of violence like the Jubilee riots of 1875, the Rossa riot of 1878 and the O'Brien riot of 1886 all seem to have fueled growth in the Order.'[32] For sixteen Toronto lodges that operated throughout the period 1874–9 the total combined membership declined in each year from a peak of 1,531 in the first year to 983 in the last.[33] That period also included the Montreal Orange crises surrounding the Hackett and Beaudry affairs.[34] Orangeism's strength was not founded on such occasional political crises. The order flourished when times were good and potential members could meet the financial obligation. Exclamations of protest from the grand lodge and Orange press in times of crises were no more than that; they generally did not bring men to the fold.

Orange membership was extremely fluid as a consequence of the voluntary nature of affiliation and the system of personalized certificates which permitted an Orangeman to withdraw from one lodge and enter another anywhere in the world. Although the active lodge membership may have been only sixty thousand in 1900, many thousands more than that had been introduced to the order and passed through it 'on certificate.' Members under suspension, and others voluntarily withdrawing, took back their Orange certificate of initiation from the lodge secretary. For the member voluntarily 'out on certificate,' re-entry to a lodge required only his depositing the document. Suspended members were reinstated on fulfilment of the suspension penalty, which was usually exclusion from the lodge for a time. Many, temporarily removed from the lodge, never returned, and under this system many of those initiated may have had only a brief formal relationship with the order. Being out on certificate effectively removed an Orangeman from lodge discipline, but not from his allegiance to basic principles he had sworn to uphold when accepted into the mysteries of the order.[35]

Turnover of membership is hardly surprising given the high degree of mobility among the population of British North America. Rootedness was the exception not the norm and patterns of migration in Ontario illustrate that clearly. For example, in Peel County at midcentury less than 30 per cent of the population remained for more than ten years in the same locality.[36] In the city of Hamilton, a similar situation existed.[37] Population turnover was high both in urban and rural areas. In the countryside the younger sons of farm families, and sometimes farmers themselves, moved to either new farming frontiers or urban centres where alternative employment was available. Inter-urban mobility, likewise, affected the population. Much of the migration took place over relatively short distances but there were many long distance migrations. Families moved to Toronto and other cities from most parts of the province, thousands more moved into the American midwest, and toward the end of the nineteenth century Ontarians in large numbers went to settle in the Canadian prairies.

Orangemen were no less mobile. In addition, the voluntary nature of their organization permitted any amount of membership turnover. Partial records of four Ontarian lodges indicate that the stability of the membership was relatively low. In Hamilton, LOL 71 had twenty-three members in 1851 but nine years later only three of the original members remained. Similarly LOL 215 outside Toronto lost twenty-one of its original twenty-seven members between 1842 and 1852. Conditions were much different in an isolated rural lodge at Marvelville in eastern Ontario. There between 1856 and 1863 only seven of the initial twenty members had left the lodge. In New Brunswick, LOL 24 in Saint John was organized in 1870 with sixteen members. In 1907 the lodge had a total of fifty-four members, but in the intervening thirty-seven years a total of four hundred members had been initiated into that lodge. In none of these lodges had total membership declined; the loss of out-going members had been compensated for. As long as the individual lodges continued to receive as many as they lost, and new men were initiated into the order the sphere of Orange influence would grow.

Table 3 illustrates the effects of membership turnover for the province of Ontario in 1898, a year of economic depression. A large number were initiated during the year but a net loss of 90 was incurred through deaths and the geographical and inter-lodge redistribution of members 'on certificate.' Suspensions were numerous mainly because of non-payment of dues. In 1896, a better year economically, only 1,206 had been suspended in all of Canada.[38] As a result of the changes of 1898 the active membership of the order in Ontario declined by 90, but in reality 1,737[39] men were added to the reservoir of Ontarian Orangemen at large, not

TABLE 3
Turnover of Orange membership, Ontario, 1898

Initiations	1,913	+1,913
Out on certificate	888	−259
Returned on certificate	629	
Suspensions	1,724	−1,386
Reinstatements	338	
Expulsions	92	−92
Deaths	266	−266
Total net change		−90

SOURCE: GOLBA, *Proceedings*, 1899.

affiliated to any lodge. A further indicator of the effect of turnover is that in Canada in the 1890s alone some 40,000 men were initiated into the order,[40] although the net increase in the number of active men in the ranks may have been only one-tenth of that. In 1903, 6,100 Canadians were initiated and in 1904, 6,800.[41] It was from such men that Orangeism obtained latent strength, men who had passed through the order at some time and whose numbers had accumulated among the protestants of Canada. The high turnover and apparently small active membership are not indicative of weakness. Rather they reflect the intrinsic power of an ideology that could attract perhaps as much as one-third of all protestant adult males.[42]

The strength of Orangeism was based on a large section of the Canadian population, and the organization through its members was capable of expressing a sizeable voice in the community. Through auxiliary organizations, linked directly and indirectly to the order, that voice extended beyond the Orange fraternity. The Orange Young Britons (OYB) acted as a youth wing. First suggested in 1853 as a means of introducing young men to the principles of Orangeism, the OYB did not begin to operate until 1869.[43] Separate rituals and constitutions were designed for this organization and in its early years of development an Orange patron supervised the operation of each local OYB lodge. About three hundred warrants were issued before 1880[44] but the organization operated peripatetically and experienced considerable difficulty in establishing a solid administrative foundation. There were only ninety OYB lodges operating in Canada by the end of the nineteenth century and at least eighty of them were located in central Canada, mainly in the old Orange strongholds east of Toronto.[45] Another wing, the Ladies Orange Benevolent Association, was created in Hamilton, Ontario, in 1889 and had five lodges operating in that city by 1892.[46] The sorority was to become in the twentieth century an extremely important element of Orangeism. Many other groups, the 'Prentice Boys, the Irish and Scotch Black Preceptories, and the Loyal True Blues, were allied with the Orange cause. The presence of these fraternities in Canada, all with Protestant and especially Orange principles, testify to the pervasiveness of Orangeism in Canadian society.

Characteristics of the membership: rural and small town

The order's position in Canada arose in part from the numerical strength of its membership but in greater part from the fact that it constituted a representative spectrum of protestant Canada. The historiography of Orangeism in Canada assumes an overwhelming Irishness supplemented by a view of the fraternity as an immigrant society. Neither characteristic is sufficient to explain the magnitude of the support that the order derived from protestants. To be sure it had been introduced by Irish immigrants but in the spread of the organization through the country the support of many non-Irish groups was enlisted. This facet of the order already exemplified in the discussion of its geographical spread may be demonstrated in greater detail by an analysis of lodge membership in a number of Ontarian and New Brunswick communities. The records represent a considerable sample of communities from rural hamlets to the metropolitan capital of Toronto. Data are presented for the villages of Leslieville and Unionville in York County just outside Toronto and the town of Dunnville located on the Lake Erie plain and well beyond the influence of Toronto. Farm communities are represented by the lodges that met in the neighbouring villages of Udora and Vroomanton in Ontario County and in the village of Kinlough high in the western lands of Bruce County. Marvelville, a crossroads hamlet at the edge of the Scottish settlement southeast of Ottawa, will also be discussed, and other community lodges will be introduced as the analysis proceeds.

Examination of the birthplace of Orangemen reveals that the Irish, preponderant among early lodge memberships, declined in importance during the nineteenth century, a reflection of the general provincial demography. In Vroomanton the Irish born were the largest single component among the founding members of LOL 570 (table 4). John Bolster who obtained the warrant in 1854 had emigrated from Ireland. According to census records he had been in Ontario at least since 1851 when his first child was born. John was joined in the lodge by four sets of brothers, the Brethours, Francises, Gordons, and Shiers, all Irish immigrants except for John Shier who had been born in Quebec. John Hart, Samuel Watts, and William Oliver from England completed the foreign-born contingent. Among the 'Canadian born' was a Nova Scotian, an Ontarian, and

Minutes of the first Meeting of Loyal Orange Lodge. Number 570.

According to appointment of the Worshipful Master the Lodge met at its Room in Vroomanton on the 14th day of September, 1854. The Chair was taken by the Rev. E. Gowan one of the grand Officers: and the deputy chair was filled by the County Master, brother William Stevenson.

Present, Brother Nathaniel Bolster, Master L.O.L. 571
  "   " Christopher Switzer, from   No. 454
  "   " Samuel Mills   "   No.   32
  "   " Philip St. Johnston   "   No. 567
  "   " Peter Baker   "   No. 567

Moved by brother William Stevenson, seconded by brother John Gardiner Bolster that brother Nathaniel Bolster act as secretary, pro. tem. -   Carried.

Proposed by brother William Stevenson, seconded by brother Christopher Switzer, that brother John Gardiner Bolster act as Treasurer, pro. tem. -   Carried.

Brother Arnold Brethour jun. presented a Certificate from L.O.L. Number 208 and was admitted a member of this Lodge.

Page from minutes of first meeting of LOL 570, Vroomanton, Ontario, 1854 the above-mentioned John Shier. In the same year Bolster's bachelor brother Nathaniel obtained a warrant with which he founded LOL 571 in nearby Udora. In 1856, however, Nathaniel left Udora, took up residence with his brother in Vroomanton where he assumed the role of local postmaster, and joined LOL 570. By 1871 the immigrant character of the Vroomanton lodge had been reduced greatly; native born and non-Irish provided the bulk of the membership. The original Irish immigrant members had all disappeared from the lodge's roll book and in their place were the Ontarian-born Bagshaws and Smiths of English parentage, and the Glendinnings and McFaddens of Scottish descent. Canadian sons of Irish parents were also in the lodge but so too were other first generation Ontarians of U.S. background and one William Vrooman, son of the Dutchman after whom the settlement was named. Within a span of seventeen years the lodge's ethnic immigrant composition had been changed and it was to function for another century in the same community among many of the same families.

The neighbouring lodge at Udora may have been much less Irish to begin with. It was definitely not Irish in 1860 (table 4) as the membership then included three English and one Welsh immigrant, although three sons of Irish immigrants were identified among the six Canadian born. In 1871 Irish, English, and one Scot made up the foreign-born group and in the Canadian-born contingent there were five of Irish, six of English, two of German, and one of Scottish background. As in the case of LOL 570, the lodge at Udora represents a much wider constituency than the local Irish community. Members of the Leslieville lodge were mainly Irish in 1850 and in the subsequent changeover to a large Canadian-born fraction in 1871 the sons of Irishmen were presented exclusively. In the other lodges listed in table 5 a wide variety of ethnic communities is represented although in each the Irish are an important component. Marvelville at the edge of the oldest Scottish settlement in Ontario had at least five Scots among its native-born members. At Unionville the lodge was split evenly between Irish and non-Irish, both native and foreign born. At Dunnville and Kinlough the Irish were a clear majority, and although there was a mix of British groups in the local population the lodge appeared not to have been able to draw them in. The Irish were important in varying degrees in all the lodges described above, but an overwhelming presence of Irish in a community was not a necessary condition for the operating of a lodge.

The Irish were the largest single group within the lodges but they were also the largest single group in Ontario's population. In 1851 Irish-born protestants constituted 30 per cent of the foreign born, and in 1871 those of Irish background constituted 35 per cent of the total population and

TABLE 4
Place of birth and denomination of Orangemen, selected lodges, Ontario, 1850–75

Lodge	Location	Date	Place of birth				Denomination						Identified	Total
			Ireland	Britain	Canada	Other	Anglican	Methodist	Presbyterian	Lutheran	Other	Unknown		
215	Vroomanton (Ontario Co.)	1854	16	3	3	–	13	6	3	–	–	–	22	33
		1871	4	2	24	2	15	10	4	–	3	–	32	51
571	Udora (Ontario Co.)	1860	2	4	6	–	8	3	1	–	–	–	12	26
		1871	3	3	14	–	6	7	1	–	3	3	20	31
215	Leslieville (York Co.)	1850	5	1	3	1	8	–	1	–	1	–	10	20
		1871	4	1	5	–	9	–	1	–	1	–	10	27
228	Unionville (York Co.)	1860	3	3	6	–	4	2	1	3	–	1	12	32
428	Dunnville (Haldimand Co.)	1862	8	3	4	1	6	3	5	–	1	1	16	38
706	Marvelville (Russell Co.)	1860	5	2	14	–	4	3	10	0	4	–	21	38
1139	Kinlough (Bruce Co.)	1875	6	4	3	–	5	4	4	–	–	–	13	22

SOURCES: Manuscript records of lodges and censuses.

two-thirds of them were protestant. The ethnic backgrounds of the Orangemen were more representative of the wider protestant community than an Irish immigrant minority. But the wide dispersal of the Irish meant that they would be found in most lodges to one degree or another. There were only a few protestant districts of the province where the Irish were absent, but they were not necessarily a barrier to the extension of the order. It has already been noted how the Mennonite district of Waterloo county and much of the Lake Erie shore were poor breeding grounds for Orangeism, but in respect to the Scottish parts of eastern Ontario it was reported in 1866 that 'we have at least a half a dozen Lodges, in which there are none but Scotchmen.'[47] Lodges had begun to be formed in the protestant Scots settlements of Stormont, Russell, and Glengarry during the 1850s and halls in these areas still stand as reminders of the Orange presence. In the Scottish settlement of Apple Hill for example a new lodge was instituted in 1917 and by the end of 1922 there were sixty-two members on its rolls. All but one was a Presbyterian; all had been born in eastern Ontario, thirty-four in Apple Hill itself.

Lodges operated on several of the province's larger Indian reserves, including LOL 99 near Deseronto, LOL 953 at Oneida, LOL 307 at Ohsweken, and LOL 1131 at Saugeen. Most had a rule that generally excluded whites from membership, and those Indian lodges that still operate continue to do so under that regulation. For example, LOL 99 in the Mohawk reserve of Tyendinaga has had only two white members since it opened in 1848. That community's loyalist and protestant character is summarized by a tablet set above the limestone portals of the reserve's All Saints Anglican Church – Fear God, Honour the Queen. In this community and the settlements of the Scots, Orangeism, as witnessed by its presence and long life, was apparently as attractive to the Canadian non-Irish as it had been to the inhabitants of county Armagh. Canadian Orangemen cannot be equated with Irishmen or immigrants nor can they be seen as members of a peculiarly immigrant society perceived of in opposition to an established community. The Ontarian community was itself an amalgam of immigrants and their sons, the makeup of the Orange Order simply reflected that amalgam.

As might be expected given the ethnic characteristics of the lodges listed in table 4, the Orangemen represented a wide range of protestant denominations. Adherents to the Church of England formed the largest group but the Methodists were also well represented, particularly at Udora and Vroomanton where some of the sons of Anglicans presented themselves as Methodists. The Presbyterians were generally the Scots and, popular assumptions to the contrary notwithstanding, the protestant Irish were most likely to be Anglicans and Methodists. They were not derived solely from the same population as that group known as the Scots-Irish in the United States but included many descendants of English planters. Scots-Irish was a name unknown to them. Lutherans, Baptists, and sundry other denominations made the gamut of protestantism practically complete within the lodges. Orangeism could serve the function of uniting members of diverse protestant sects in a secular institution which nonetheless had a religious character.

The lodges also provided a forum for passing the Orange tradition on to new generations. As they came of age young men entered through the rites of initiation and degrees to take their place alongside established elders. The age distributions (table 5) demonstrate that fact. At Vroomanton the median age of Orangemen remained in the late twenties throughout the nineteenth and early twentieth centuries and there was always an important component of young initiates. It is to be remembered that the Vroomanton lodge wás predominantly Canadian by 1871, and since there was no immigration to the district after that date the lodge had to draw from its own established community. It continued to elicit support from the young. At Udora and Kinlough too the young were well represented, and most of them again were native Canadians. The pattern of older immigrants and younger natives was strongest at Marvelville where in 1860 the five men over forty were also the five foreign-born in the lodge. Apple Hill's initiation records indicate that not only young men but men of all ages joined the new lodge. Orangeism's rural strength was thus based on an active and representative section of Ontario's population not upon immigration or a convinced hard-core legion of old timers. Through the progressive inclusion of members of new generations the order demonstrated the suitability of the Orange ideology to Canadian conditions and its relevance to Ontario's rural communities.

The occupational characteristics of lodge membership reflected elements common to rural society and those unique to individual settlements. Farmers and agricultural labourers comprised the bulk of the membership in rural areas and a professional and clerical element was provided by local small service centres. Table 6 presents occupational data for nine lodges in Ontario over a number of decades. Change through time and from lodge to lodge is evident. The prominence of farmers in the lodges varied significantly from the high proportions at Kinlough and Marvelville to a total absence in the lodge at Dunnville. Kinlough village had only one school, three churches, and a couple of shops from which a non-farming element could have been drawn and the absence of professionals, tradesmen, and others, except for the merchant, cannot be considered unusual. Likewise at Marvelville where the single-room school was the only permanent non-farm building it is not surprising that

TABLE 5
Age structure of Orangemen, selected lodges, Ontario, 1854–1922

Lodge	Location	Date	Age group						Total
			18–19	20–9	30–9	40–9	50–9	60–9	
570	Vroomanton	1854	3	8	7	4			22
		1871	8	10	8	5	1		32
		1913	3	14	11	6			34
571	Udora	1860		4	2	5	1		12
		1871	2	9	5		3		19
1139	Kinlough	1875	2	8	7	4	1		22
228	Unionville	1860		4	7	1			12
428	Dunnville	1862	2	6	5	2	1		16
706	Marvelville	1860	1	10	4	2	2	1	19
2677	Apple Hill (Glengarry Co.) (initiates only)	1917–22	5	15	8	2	5	1	36

SOURCES: Manuscript records of lodges and censuses.

the membership was composed of farmers, labourers, and a carpenter. Dunnville, however, with a population of 1,270 in 1861 was a thriving regional town and the lodge was insulated from the surrounding farm communities, themselves served by local rural lodges. For other lodges described in table 6 that separation did not exist. Vroomanton, Udora, Leslieville, Unionville, Holstein, and Apple Hill were small villages fully integrated to surrounding farm populations and the variety of groups in their lodges typifies the occupational mix of village and farm.

Merchants, like the farmers, were common in the lodges throughout the nineteenth century but the presence of other groups was more variable. Tradesmen were prominent from 1871 onward among the lodges sampled, a reflection of the diversification of local economies. The latter trend is suggested by the data from Vroomanton and Udora and it is most clearly indicated at Leslieville. Restructuring of the economy of Leslieville in the latter part of the nineteenth century transformed the rural lodge into an industrial-urban organization. The village's traditional community and farm service functions had been submerged by the creation of a major railway yard serving nearby Toronto. By 1890 the Leslieville lodge included fourteen men from the Grand Trunk Railway (GTR). Switchmen, brakemen, yardmen, and carmen had become a major component of both the local population and the local lodge and ten years later thirty of the sixty-two members worked for the GTR.

Professionals and clerical workers were found within the lodges in

TABLE 6
Occupational characteristics of Orangemen in rural and small town Ontario, 1850–1913

Lodge	Location	Date	Professionals	Merchants	Farmers	Tradesmen	Clerks	Labourers	Retired	Identified	Total membership
215	Leslieville	1850	–	2	2	–	–	6	–	10	20
		1871	–	2	6	–	–	2	–	10	29
		1890	3	1	2	4	–	9	–	19	32
		1900	2	6	13	14	–	26	1	62	64
570	Vroomanton	1854	2	2	26	1	1	1	–	33	33
		1871	–	1	14	4	–	13	–	32	51
		1913	1	3	20	0	0	0	1	25	41
571	Udora	1860	–	1	5	–	–	5	–	11	26
		1871	1	2	10	2	–	3	–	18	31
		1911	–	2	24	8	–	9	4	47	47
228	Unionville	1861	–	–	2	4	–	3	–	9	32
		1899	–	3	15	2	–	3	4	27	28
428	Dunnville	1862	–	2	–	11	2	1	–	16	38
706	Marvelville	1860	–	–	15	1	–	6	–	21	38
1139	Kinlough	1875	–	1	12	–	–	–	–	13	22
2296	Holstein (Grey Co.)	1913	6	7	16	4	2	6	1	42	42
2677	Apple Hill	1917–23	4	3	40	6	5	3	1	62	62

SOURCES: Manuscript records of lodges and censuses.

small numbers as would be expected given the composition of rural and small town Ontario. Two teachers were among the first members of the Vroomanton lodge where there was also a teacher in 1913. A local teacher was present in the Udora lodge in 1871. In Leslieville the three professionals in 1890 were two medical doctors and a teacher. By 1900 the doctors and teacher had left the lodge and an editor and a minister had joined. The range of professionals evident in the case of Leslieville was repeated in other communities. In the small town of Holstein, a lodge was organized in 1911 by a local clergyman who at the first meeting initiated seven new Orangemen – an undertaker, a veterinary surgeon, a miller, a salesman, a blacksmith, an agent, and a farmer. Within the next two years, despite the loss of four of the founding group, the membership had grown to forty-two men drawn from all classes in the community. Among the professionals were the community's moral and educational leaders – three ministers and two teachers – as well as the veterinary surgeon. It may even be inferred that the local professional and merchant elite played a leading role in the creation and maintenance of this local lodge but the inference could not be extended through Ontario. In the Scottish lodge at Apple Hill the professional and merchant groups were also prominent but in 1917 that lodge had been created by five local farmers 'out on certificate.' They were joined in subsequent months by a vet, a medical doctor, and two clergymen in addition to the merchants and large contingent of farmers. In this case leadership was definitely not provided by the local merchants and professionals. As Orangeism was able to transcend denominational and ethnic divisions so did it manage to bring together men of varied economic and occupational backgrounds.

The leadership of lodges in rural areas was drawn from the full range of the membership and was not confined to an elite group. Masters of the Leslieville lodge for the years listed in table 4 were respectively an innkeeper, the innkeeper's son, a doctor, and a farmer, and at other lodges comparable patterns existed. Vroomanton's first master was Nathaniel Bolster, the local merchant who had obtained the warrant, but in 1860 he was no longer a member and the master's chair was occupied by a farmer. In 1870 the master was also a farmer. The master of Apple Hill in 1922 was a blacksmith and the professionals were all ordinary members. The local lodges were fundamentally democratic and egalitarian clubs whose rules and operations prevented one group from controlling affairs for the wider membership. Masters and other officers were elected annually and consequently the potential for turnover in executive positions was great. To be sure, effective leadership was prized and men of ability would have returned again and again to the executive, providing they acted according to the wishes of the majority of members. The master's chair may have been commonly the preserve of an individual but rarely of a social elite. The democratic nature of the institution and the commitment of all to a common goal obviated against internal social divisions.

Lodge records for the other hearth of Canadian Orangeism, New Brunswick, indicate a variety of social and personal characteristics of Orangemen comparable to that shown for Ontario. The ethnic to native transition was made early. From mid-nineteenth century few immigrants settled in the province as the Maritimes were by then a backwater in the Canadian immigration route. The economy of New Brunswick, characterized by a seasonal swing between farming and winter lumbering, had given rise to a predominantly rural society. The lodges at Long's Creek and Prince William, neighbouring localities in the middle Saint John River Valley had as their members in 1848 a preponderance of farmers, rural tradesmen, and labourers and a relatively young age profile. These characteristics, summarized in table 7, highlight well the local community's makeup. Such communities of farmers and part-time lumbermen dominated much of New Brunswick Orangeism, well into the twentieth century. In 1904 the provincial grand lodge recorded: 'This province is largely a lumbering community and lumbermen must be in the woods before the snow comes; hence the lodge is closed, the members are scattered ...'[48]

In addition to the lumbering emphasis, other variations in local economies were reflected in Orange membership. That was clearly evident for the example of Campbellton, a town dominated by its role as a railway service centre. Campbellton sprang up in 1875 as an island of English speakers in the midst of the Acadian county of Restigouche. A lodge was formed there to serve the railwaymen. In 1923 that role remained paramount: the lodge had a total membership of eighty-five, forty-two of whom it is known worked for the Canadian National Railway and another twenty-four of whom, classified in the lodge records as labourers, probably also were attached to the railway. That case is reminiscent of conditions in the 1890s at Leslieville in Ontario. Urban centres such as Fredericton, Moncton, and Saint John were also important places of the order. Again, Orangemen came from many walks of life. During the nineteenth century LOL 1 Saint John, included 'a large number of prominent men both in political and mercantile life.'[49]

The religious composition of New Brunswick, marked by a large Baptist fraction was akin to that of New England from which many Loyalists had come. Unfortunately, data which would demonstrate the position of Baptists in the order are not available for early lodges. There were, however, a good number of lodges in Baptist localities which

TABLE 7
Occupational and age characteristics of LOL 71 and LOL 83,
New Brunswick, 1848

Occupation and age	LOL 71 Long's Creek	LOL 83 Prince William
Occupational group		
Professionals	–	–
Merchants	–	1
Farmers	31	20
Tradesmen	4	3
Clerks	–	1
Labourers	1	3
Age group		
18–19	8	2
20–9	17	13
30–9	2	9
40–9	4	3
50–9	3	1
Unknown	2	–
Total	36	28

SOURCES: Manuscript records of lodges.

necessarily would have drawn from that denomination. In Nashwaak Bridge, a farm settlement of Scottish descent, two Baptists, ten Presbyterians, ten Methodists, and one Anglican joined LOL 93 between 1905 and 1910. At a much later date (1948), a record of LOL 28, Bear Island, shows that of the twenty-eight founding members, only one was Anglican, five were United churchmen, and the remainder were Baptists. These records suggest that New Brunswick lodges, like lodges elsewhere in Canada, represented local denominational characteristics, and there is nothing to indicate that Baptists deliberately absented themselves from the movement. The nature of rural and small town lodge membership reflected the simple agricultural and resource bases of Canadian society. As might be expected, the order was more complex in the metropolitan centre of Toronto.

Toronto Orangemen

The membership of lodges in rural and small town Ontario was clearly representative of the nature of the communities which sustained them. In Toronto, a bustling and growing urban centre, the order proved able to attract a wide sample of the social spectrum. This correlation was established early in the city's development and continued through to the twentieth century. The only extant records of early Orangeism in Toronto are those of LOL 137, founded by Gowan in 1835. Its first initiates were an innkeeper, land agent, shopman, carter, and yeoman.[50] Gowan, while an MP during the 1850s, served as master of this lodge which by then may have become a more elitist club since it was popularly known as 'The Toronto Dandies.'[51] Among masters of Toronto lodges in 1857 were at least two members of the city's old tory families, W.H. Boulton, mayor of the city, and William Strachan, an alderman.[52] The mass of the city's Orangemen were of much less prestigious background.

Certainly, the records of the 1870s and 1880s indicate that Toronto's Orangemen were of diverse occupational backgrounds. From an analysis of four lodges for these two decades, Kealey developed the thesis that 'the Orange Order in Toronto was overwhelmingly working class in composition.'[53] In arguing this he is only partially correct; as his own data show, one-sixth to one-half of the membership of the selected lodges were composed of non-working and essentially middle-class elements. In Toronto as a whole a similar distribution of groups obtained, and the working-class element in the lodges was no greater than might be expected given the city's occupational makeup. Although each of the lodges studied had a sizeable non-working-class component, there was no indication that this group played an inordinate role in the running of lodge affairs. Kealey's examination of the background of lodge masters and other executive officers revealed that working-class men were just as likely to fill the positions of leadership as were their non-working-class brethren. The occupational mix among the rank and file was replicated in the executive. The patterns found in these four lodges undoubtedly would have been applicable to the full complement of the city's Orangemen. Comparable patterns can be demonstrated also for the mid 1890s.

The most complete information on the size and nature of Orange membership in Toronto is provided in an 1894 register of city Orangemen.[54] From this source the names and addresses of the members of forty-five of the fifty-five lodges operating in the city may be obtained. The known active membership was 3,250 and a projected total membership of 4,000 is reasonable. A random 10 per cent sample of the members in the 1894 list was cross referenced with information from directories and city assessment records to obtain the attributes of Toronto Orangemen. Of the 325 men in the sample, 272 were identified on at least one characteristic, and 117 on all. In terms of age, occupation, and religious characteristics the Orangemen of Toronto were to a large degree representative of the city's protestant population. Unfortunately it is impossible with the sources available to determine nationality or marital

TABLE 8
Age structure of Orangemen, 1894, and Toronto
males aged 20+, 1891, in per cent

Age	Orangemen 1894	Toronto males 1891
20–4	3.3	20.1
25–9	14.1	18.5
30–4	21.0	14.5
35–9	14.6	11.3
40–4	14.6	9.6
45–9	13.4	7.5
50–4	7.0	6.4
55–9	5.7	3.9
60–4	2.8	3.5
65–9	2.1	1.9
70+	1.4	2.8
Median age	38.9	34.0

NOTE: Sample size = 138.

status, but the data afford a reasonable description of the Orange membership.

Men were eligible for membership at age 18, although none that young was found in the sample (table 8). The very low proportion of Orangemen in the age group 20–4 years is striking but may well be an effect of the underrepresentation of young adult males in the city's directories and assessment records – sources which principally enumerate heads of household and homeowners. Even if the underrepresentation of those under 25 years is controlled for, the age structure of Orangemen remains biased in favour of those in the 30–9 age groups. This age distribution implies a stable and probably married group, an inference reinforced by home ownership characteristics. About 35 per cent of the Orangemen owned their houses, a proportion which could not have been much different from that of the city as a whole. Given the wide age distribution and the high proportion of home ownership it is clear that the order in Toronto was not merely a receiving institution for recently arrived immigrants or rural migrants, nor was it dependent upon them for its energy. In any event the immigration of protestant Irish to Toronto had for more than a decade been insignificant and could not possibly have sustained the numerical strength or demographic characteristics of the lodges in the city. The data do not permit analysis of birthplace of Toronto Orangemen but much later information for one lodge, LOL 275, in Toronto in 1912 demonstrates that immigrants were not an important component of new

ORANGEMEN

Orangemen. By C.W. Jefferys. (Public Archives of Canada)

members. Of the nine initiates in that year, one was born in England, one in Toronto, and the remaining seven in rural Ontario. Of the three who joined by certificate, one was born in Nova Scotia and two in rural Ontario. The non-immigrant character of the organization is further indicated by an analysis of those long service members in Ontario West (including Toronto) alive in 1962 and who had joined the order before 1912. Sixty-five of the seventy long service members had been initiated in Ontario, one in Newfoundland, one in Saskatchewan, and only three in Ireland.

In their denominational affiliations (table 9) Toronto Orangemen were drawn from all the major Protestant sects although Methodists and Anglicans were overrepresented in the order while Presbyterians were surprisingly underrepresented. Baptists, Congregationalists, and Lutherans were not important components. The ranking of religious denominations in the order did conform to that of the city: Anglicans were dominant with Methodists and Presbyterians in second and third places respectively. Those three comprised the vast bulk of protestants within the city and within the order.

There did not exist in Toronto towards the end of the century a recognizable association between religion and socio-economic strata. Orangemen, drawn from the three major sects, were also representative of all the major occupational groupings, and included drovers, porters, carpenters, steamfitters, clerks, teachers, lawyers, doctors, clergymen,

TABLE 9
Denominational characteristics of Orangemen, 1894,
and principal protestant sects, 1891, Toronto, in per cent

Denomination	Orangemen	Principal protestant sects
Anglican	45.4	37.8
Methodist	33.2	28.2
Presbyterian	19.7	24.0
Baptist	1.7	7.0
Congregational	–	2.4
Lutheran	–	0.6

NOTE: Sample size = 152.

TABLE 10
Occupational structure of Toronto
Orangemen, 1894

Occupational group*	Percentage
Unskilled	25.1
Semiskilled	27.1
Skilled	14.6
Clerical	12.5
Business	15.3
Professional	4.7
Private means	0.7

NOTE: Sample size = 246.
*Occupational structure according to
classification used by Goheen, *Victorian
Toronto, 1850–1900*, 229–30.

and businessmen. Table 10 indicates that two-thirds of the Orangemen belonged to the labouring and artisan classes, a finding similar to that presented in the work of Kealey. One-fifth of the Orangemen in 1894 were business and professional men and much of the emphasis on the cult of respectability, discipline, and literacy within the order may have emanated from this middle-class group. Leadership in the local lodges, however, was not their preserve. Executive offices rotated frequently and, as throughout rural Ontario, professionals and businessmen were no more prominent among the leadership than among the rank and file.

Three lodges, LOL 4, 342, and 506, were selected to demonstrate some dimensions of the social mix within the membership and executive (table 11). The executive of LOL 4, the oldest lodge in the city, was composed mainly of lower middle-class elements. The majority of members, however, were manual workers although three professionals, a barrister, an editor, and a student, also belonged. LOL 342 had a similar occupational mix in its membership but its executive, drawn overwhelmingly from semi-skilled workers, was markedly different from that of LOL 4. The third lodge, LOL 506, was the most socially homogeneous. The middle-class component, represented only by a doctor and barrister, was very weak. Subtle differences are evident between the three lodges, their executive, and ordinary members, and they suggest that there may have been some social differentiation among the lodges in Toronto. On one level this could have been a function of recruitment from a common work place. For example, the two tinners in LOL 506 worked in the same factory; LOL 342 had two workers from the same brewery and two policemen. However, the identification of lodges with places of work was extremely weak. There was not in Toronto any of the exclusiveness of membership found often among the lodges in Belfast where shipyard workers or policemen or others had their own separate lodges. In Toronto, the overall social pattern was one of a mix of a wide range of occupational groups within and between lodges.

The financiers and large industrial capitalists were the only group not represented among the Orangemen. Many of Toronto's entrepreneurial elite, such as William McMaster, founder of the Bank of Commerce, James Austin, who established the Dominion Bank, and the Methodist merchant, Timothy Eaton, were protestant Irish. Orange lodge rooms were not their forums.

The residential distribution of Orangemen in the city (figure 16) further illustrates the absence of that elite while at the same time emphasizing the pervasiveness of Orangeism otherwise. The density of Orangemen was lowest in the elite residential areas of Jarvis Street and Rosedale and on the expanding northern and western fringes of the city where subdivision was just underway. With these exceptions Orangemen were present throughout the city from the older central parts to the recently annexed villages of Yorkville, Seaton, and Parkdale, but they were found in their greatest density in the heavily populated and older residential eastern sector of the city known as Cabbagetown. It has been demonstrated that the Orangemen were not drawn from any single economic group and consequently they were able to transcend the residential segregation of economic classes which has been noted in studies of the city.[55] Orangemen were not a segregated minority confined to either economic or ethnic ghettos.

Individual lodges drew their recruits from many parts of the city and were not confined in their recruitment of members to demarcated and exclusive territories. Residential propinquity was not a determinant of

TABLE 11
Occupations of officers and occupational structure of members, three selected
lodges, Toronto, 1894

Occupations of officers and members	LOL 4	LOL 342	LOL 506
Officers			
Master	Engineer	Lather	Driver
Deputy master	Jeweller (owner)	Mover	Tinner
Chaplain	Salesman	Driver	Coachman
Recording secretary	Confectionist (owner)	n.a.	Tinner
Financial secretary	n.a.	Machinist	Cigarmaker (owner)
Treasurer	Foreman	Plumber	Carpenter
Director of ceremonies	Livery operator (owner)	Teamster	Carpenter
Lecturer	Cutter	Plumber	Carpenter
	Number of members		
Occupational group			
Unskilled	6	8	4
Semi-skilled	5	12	4
Skilled	3	4	3
Clerical	3	9	–
Business	4	4	1
Professional	3	5	2
Private means	1	–	–
Unknown	9	10	4
Total membership (including executive)	42	60	26

local lodge membership. Social links through work, worship, and recreation and residential mobility were important selectors mitigating against localization of lodge membership. Only in the cases of the three recently annexed villages was localization of lodge hall and membership apparent. Elsewhere in the city twelve meeting places were shared by the remaining fifty-three lodges. Twenty-five lodges met in the main hall on Queen Street East in the downtown core. The Western District Orange Hall, situated on Euclid Avenue, a residential side street, was the meeting place of eleven lodges. These two halls were accessible to all the developed parts of the city and the Orangemen meeting in them were drawn from wide and overlapping hinterlands. The majority of the 650 men who attended lodge at the Western District Hall resided within a radius of one and one-quarter miles, an area which included approximately one-third of

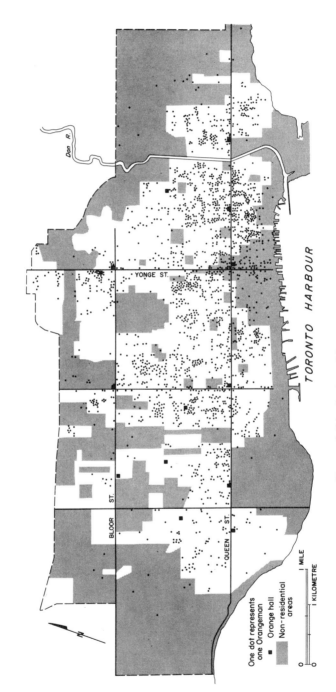

Figure 16. Distribution of Orangemen, Toronto, 1894

Toronto's population. Fifty-three Orangemen lived on Euclid Avenue itself. Twenty-eight of them were affiliated with nine different lodges meeting at the local hall and the remaining twenty-five men belonged to fourteen lodges which met elsewhere in the city. A one-quarter square mile tract centring on the Western District Hall (figure 17) has been chosen to illustrate the location of Orangemen in the residential pattern of their neighbourhood.

The district (figure 17) was predominantly protestant but there were a few Jewish families and a sizable catholic minority whose church was located outside the area two blocks south of the intersection of Queen and Bathurst streets. An analysis of householders in the area depicted in figure 17 clearly indicates the intermixing of Orangemen, catholics, and others. Orangemen were neither confined to the immediate vicinity of the hall nor were they segregated from the larger group of protestants and catholics. The greatest concentration of Orangemen was found along Euclid and Manning avenues and the catholics tended to be more evident in the south and west. However, the residential distinction of the two groups was subtle and obscured within the wider distribution of non-Orange protestants. No street, nor even a block face was held exclusively by any one of the three groups. Catholics lived side by side with protestants and nowhere did they form contiguous units of more than four houses. There was apparently no residential segregation on the basis of religion and in fact nowhere in the 'Belfast of Canada' was there an equivalent of the Shankhill-Falls divide.[56] Unlike Belfast, where residential segregation grew out of the nature of industrial entrepreneurialism and the attendant creation of large-scale terraced house developments, Toronto was not an industrial city dominated by a few industries and its housing stock was historically the product of piecemeal development by small speculators. Given the nature of the housing market the chances of large scale ghettos forming in Toronto were limited.

Conclusions on territoriality reached by S.E. Baker and F.W. Boal for Belfast are ill-suited to Toronto.[57] The ghettos of the type found in Irish and British cities are not identifiable in the Canadian city. Nevertheless, from the 1820s there had been protestant and catholic clashes, most of which were occasioned by marches on 12 July and 17 March. These sectarian riots have been described by Kealey in terms of ritualized violence and territoriality,[58] but the Orangemen did not see themselves as a mere minority group guarding and defending a specific neighbourhood. Their marches focused on the principal streets and major arteries of the city – clearly not a localized sense of territory. Orange parades were the expression of the power and control of a self-convinced charter group whose perceived duty it was to preserve and defend the very foundations

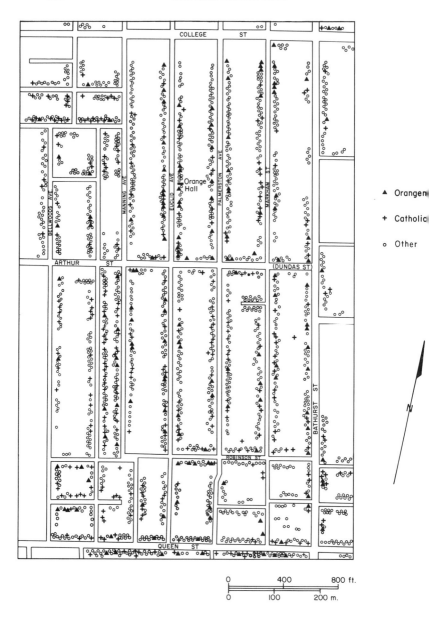

Figure 17. Household characteristics, Euclid Avenue district, Toronto, 1894

of the state. The Orange community was largely indistinguishable from the rest of the protestant city.

Canada's Orange lodges were not restricted in class and creed, and by their geography, their numerical strength, and social composition they reflected the integral part that Orangeism played in the country's protestant communities. By enlistment in the order all had indicated their commitment to a common cause. Settlements isolated by geography, history, ethnicity, and denominationalism were united within the order by their protestant and British identity. Regional variation in the character of the organization was expressed in its membership not in its tenets and aims. Even among the leading personalities of the order, a tremendous variety of background, outlook, vocation, and social status could be found. Canadian Orangemen who attained national prominence included such diverse figures as Gowan, the immigrant son of an Irish landlord; John Hillyard Cameron, a Scot and the leading barrister of his day; Mackenzie Bowell, English-born printer and later prime minister of Canada; Oronhyatekha, a Mohawk, Oxford-educated doctor and chief organizer of the Independent Order of Foresters; Sam Hughes, army general and flamboyant Canadian hero of World War I. It is impossible to create an Orange stereotype, except in terms of protestantism and loyalism.

The elite of the order derived a large measure of political support and power from association with the fraternity and many of them undoubtedly joined for that reason. The rank and file, because of its unifying ideology, community bonds, and place in a formal organizational structure, could on occasion be marshalled to support ambitious men. That potential was dependent upon the order's success as a functioning fraternity and social organization.

The Social Dimension

I'll sing and dance with any man ...
Now you look after me old boy
And I'll look after you

The Irish protestant coming to Canada in the early nineteenth century was faced by a bewildering social and physical environment. His land – probably a hundred-acre lot – was imprisoned by trees and nothing in his background had prepared him for the task of clearance. The alien quality of his new homeland was furthered by its seasonally extreme continental climate and compounding the immigrant's sense of alienation was the reality of isolated agricultural settlement. Population densities of more than four hundred persons per square mile in Ireland were replaced by densities of less than twenty. Familiar institutions were recreated as a defence against this new environment and the Orange lodge became as important to the Irish protestant immigrant as the church was to his catholic countryman. The early lodges provided a recognizable form through which social networks could be created and consolidated. Their meetings were social occasions.

For immigrant and native, the Newfoundland fisherman, the Nova Scotia miner, the New Brunswick lumberman, and the prairie settler, as well as a wide range of Ontarians, the lodges provided mythology, conviviality, and a sense of identity. Canadian Orangeism was a complex phenomenon and within its complexity a wide variety of personal desires could be accommodated.

Conviviality

The lodge meeting provided a regularized form of socializing. Gossip, tales of mutual friends, and, more usefully, information on job opportunities and techniques for day-to-day chores were all exchanged in the forum provided before and after the formal lodge business. In the male preserve, meeting under the auspices of a semi-secret body, the more ordinary community links would be reinforced and revitalized. The lodge also served to introduce newcomers into the community and to provide them with a useful set of contacts. No other formal infrastructure for social intercourse existed[1] except for churches which by their very multiplicity emphasized the denominational divisions in protestant society. The lodge recognized no such divisions and would be home for all.

The lodges served as men's clubs and early records indicate clearly that in terms of conviviality they were similar to contemporary local societies in England. As summarized by a prominent Orangeman: 'The item for refreshments was a regular monthly one, the expenditure often exceeded the receipts, and our brethern seem to have done little else in those days other than make Orangemen and then entertain them royally at the refreshment board.'[2] LOL 215 at Leslieville, Ontario, spent almost all of its 1839 budget of £3.16.5½ on refreshments viz.

	s.d.
April 3rd 1½ gal. whiskey, 2 lbs of brown sugar	5.8
May 1st " " " " " " "	4.11
May 1st 3 quarts of beer at 5d per quart	1.3
July 3rd 1½ gals. whiskey, 2 lbs of brown sugar	4.11
July 3rd paid Bro. Moffat for July 12th refreshments	4.9½
Aug. 7th Refreshments	5.6
Oct. 1st. 1 lb of candles, 1 qt of spirit, 1 gal. whiskey	4.9½
Nov. 6th 2 gal. whiskey, 2 lbs brown sugar, ½ lb candles	6.4½
	———
	£2.9.5½

Items were not specified for the expenditures in other months but, most likely, they were refreshments.[3]

The Leslieville lodge was by no means unique. During the twelve-month period August 1837 to August 1838, Peel County LOL 5 spent a total of £16.17.2½ on its fifty-one members. Of this sum £7.8.0 was spent on 12 July refreshments, a further £4.11.0 was spent on sashes for the parade, and thirteen shillings was spent on attending the funeral of a member. The remainder was spent on whiskey and candles.[4] The expenditure on drink was often encouraged by the fact that during the early period of Canadian Orangeism lodges commonly met in taverns. Such was the case for LOL 215 where Brother Moffat, the master, hosted the monthly meetings in his own tavern. John Craft's tavern in eastern Ontàrio and Montgomery's Inn on Dundas Street, west of Toronto, were also known as popular Orange meeting places.[5]

As the century progressed the place of alcohol at the lodge meetings yielded to a growing social emphasis on temperance. As early as 1847 Toronto's Loyal Orange Temperance Lodge no. 301 enacted in its by-laws

that this Lodge, having constantly before their eyes the pernicious dringing [sic] of spirituous liquors at the conclusion of their business, and deprecating the admission of such custom into this body, do hereby enact, that any brother proposing any part of the funds to be expended for such purposes, shall be suspended for a period not exceeding six months or receive his certificate, as a majority of the Lodge may determine.[6]

In keeping with its respectable image the business of this lodge was to be completed before 10:00 P.M. and should the meeting extend beyond that time the master would be fined one shilling and three pence for the first fifteen minutes and two and six for each successive fifteen minutes. In 1848 Cornwall had a lodge of thirty members also operating on temperance principles.[7] Strictures on drinking were publicized in 1854 by Gowan in an attempt to enhance the image of the order. He sanctimoniously urged that local lodges set up savings banks, libraries, and music lessons for their members who 'would soon learn to prefer the practice-room to the bar-room.'[8]

Such a radical change in the social atmosphere within which lodge business was conducted did not obtain unanimous support from the rank and file. LOL 215, for example, became a temperance lodge in April 1856 and as a compensation for the loss of liquor sales its innkeeper master was voted '3\9 each night as a remuneration for his room.' In December of the same year it was 'proposed and carried by a majority of the lodge that it be no longer a temperate lodge.'[9] The grand master of Quebec in 1858 was particularly disturbed by reports that 'some of the Lodges spend the funds, which should be transmitted to this Grand Lodge, in drinking and carousing at the conclusion of their Lodge Meetings, which, if true, is deeply to be regretted, as it will justify the assertion of our enemies, who denounce us as drunken and blood thirsty.'[10]

It became increasingly difficult for the grand lodge to tolerate such local behaviour. In 1857 Orange soirées, common on 5 November, Guy Fawkes' day, and 12 July, were forbidden except if held by the permission of district lodges and even then the presence of alcohol was discouraged.[11] After 1859 the grand lodge opposed any appearance of drunkenness, particularly at July parades, and local lodges were henceforth forbidden to meet in hotels or saloons.[12] A subsequent move to attach a vow of temperance to the Orange initiation oath was defeated,[13]

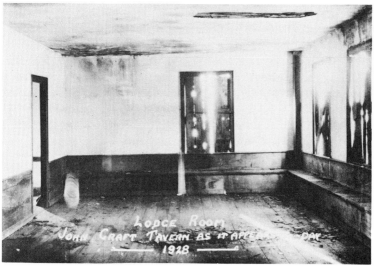

John Craft's tavern where, according to the lore of Brockville in 1928, the first Orange lodge in Canada was formed. (Courtesy of Mr Norman Ritchie)

but by the end of the century admission to the order was closed to those who made their living from the sale of 'spirituous liquor.' The regulations forbidding lodge meetings in public taverns were rigorously enforced and, for example, in 1883 LOL 1274 felt it had to petition the grand lodge for permission to meet in a hall adjoining a hotel. The grand lodge granted the petition on the grounds that 'the hall is only adjoining a hotel, and has an outside and independent entrance.'[14]

Much of the impetus for temperance came from the strong Methodist component within the order. In places such as Toronto where Orangemen were important in municipal government they joined with others in imposing a tone of temperance and strict sabbatarianism on the city. Similarly grand lodge reports from other provinces indicate a preoccupation with the issues of temperance and prohibition. In Newfoundland Orangemen were prominent in the successful 1915 campaign for prohibition.[15] The control which the order could exert over the personal use of alcohol by its members was however limited. Outside of actual lodge meetings and parades there was little the order could do except rely upon peer pressure and the personal responsibility of the members. Drinking persisted, especially after Twelfth festivities were officially closed. It was perhaps too much to expect that men, having marched for two hours in the hot sun, would not demand refreshment.

The record of the order's position on drinking merely reflected the social attitudes and mood of protestant Canadians. It had ignored heavy drinking during the pioneering phase of the first half of the nineteenth century, a period when British North America was notorious for its heavy consumption of alcohol. In subsequently rejecting that tradition, the order was neither a leader nor a laggard; it was in step with general sentiments. Changes in its official attitude had no effect on recruitment of members. Conviviality was simply provided in a changed format.

Ritual and colour

The aura of mystery and self-importance acquired through membership in a secret society with initiation rites, secret signs, symbols, and elaborate ritual added to the attraction of being an Orangeman. Particularly true in the early period of Canadian Orangeism, this appeal remains valid even today as is evident in the continuing popularity of the Freemasons, Shriners, and other ritual-bound groups. Much of the Orange ritual was borrowed from the Freemasons as were symbols such as the all-seeing eye, Jacob's ladder, and the sun, moon, and stars, the only major Orange additions being the figure of King William mounted on a white horse and the open protestant Bible. The Orange ritual and passwords were con-

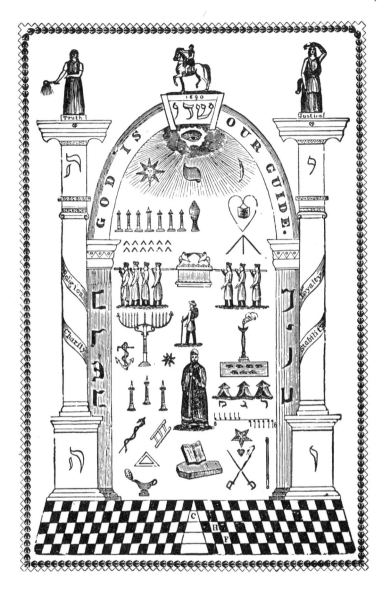

Orange symbols. From *Protestant Landmarks* (Toronto: G.M. Rose and Sons 1897).

tained in readings from the Old Testament and all lodge activities from initiations to the installation of officers were accompanied by prayers for the individuals concerned, the institution itself, and the reigning British monarch.

Lodge meetings were held regularly, usually once a month on a fixed day, never the Sabbath. In some local jurisdictions, however, meetings were held every two weeks. They were run by an executive consisting of a master, deputy master, past master, chaplain, secretary, and treasurer. Tylers, guarding the door, restricted admission to the lodge room to only those repeating the proper password. The meeting was held with the principal members of the executive seated at the cardinal points (figure 18), the ordinary members along the sides, and in the middle of the room was placed an altar draped with a Union Jack and topped by an opened Bible. According to the directions laid down in the constitution the form of business was as follows: 'Lodge to be opened with prayer. Lecture to be repeated. Minutes of former meeting read. Members to be proposed. Candidates to be initiated. Public business concerned with principles, honour and prosperity of the Association discussed. Roll called and dues collected. Lecture repeated. Lodge closed with prayers.'[16]

Within the formality of lodge business most of the colour and interest was generated and maintained by the ritualistic initiations of new members and the promotion of existing Orangemen. Internal ranking in the form of degrees provided a mechanism whereby a member entering the order would be initiated at the rank of the Orange degree. Subsequently he could pass successively through the purple, blue, arch purple, and scarlet degrees, each of those steps representing a greater commitment to the order, a fuller understanding of its principles, and a higher standard of social responsibility. The system of degrees represented a hierarchy within the order for the cumulative effect of new responsibilities at each stage reduced the numbers of men willing and able to ascend further. Only a minority reached the scarlet degree. Despite the apparent obstacles some men proceeded through all the ranks within a few years of their joining the order.

Initiations involved the candidate's submission to and acceptance of the principles and obligations of his degree. Each degree built upon the ones below and all had a clause demanding that the secrets be revealed to no man other than a holder of that degree. Thus it was possible to maintain a continuing sense of mystery and the lure of advancement into a progressively more committed and exclusive body. Cohesion at all levels was maintained by the candidate's agreement to give care and guidance to his brethren in times of difficulty and also admonish their misbehaviour.

The essential obligation upon which all else was based was that taken

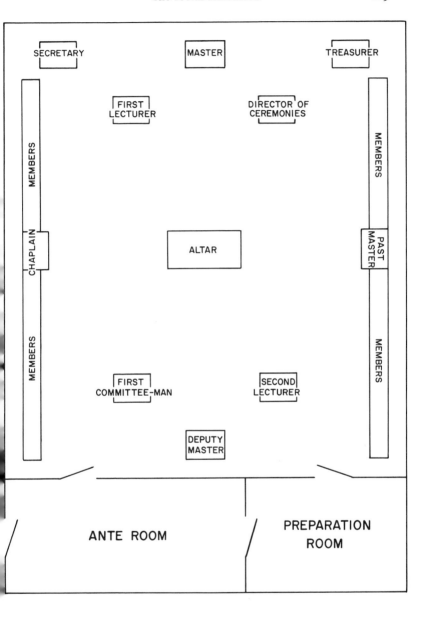

Figure 18. Plan of Orange lodge room arranged for an initiation ceremony

by an Orange initiate. The candidate, while kneeling, recited the following:

I, A.B., do solemnly and voluntarily swear, that I will be faithful, and bear true
allegiance to Her Majesty Queen Victoria, and to her lawful heirs and successors,
in the Sovereignty of Great Britain and Ireland, and of these Provinces dependant
on, and belonging to, the said Kingdom, so long as she or they shall maintain the
Protestant Religion and the laws of the country: that I will, to the utmost of my
power, defend them against all traitorous conspiracies and attempts, which I shall
know to be against her or any of them; that *I will steadily maintain the connection
between the Colonies of British America and the Mother Country, and be ever
ready to resist all attempts to weaken British influence, or dismember the British
Empire; that I will be true and faithful to every brother Orangeman in all just
actions, neither wronging him nor knowing him to be wronged or injured, without
giving him due notice thereof, and preventing it, if in my power.* I swear that I will
ever hold sacred the name of our Glorious Deliverer, King William the Third,
Prince of Orange; in grateful remembrance of whom, I solemnly promise (if in my
power) to celebrate his victory over James at the Boyne, in Ireland, by assembling
with my brethren, in their Lodge Room, on the 12th day of July, in every year; I
swear that I am not, nor ever will be, a Roman Catholic or Papist; *nor will I marry
a Roman Catholic or Papist, nor educate my children, nor suffer them to be
educated in the Roman Catholic Faith; nor am I now, or ever will be, a member of
any society or body of men that are enemies to Her Majesty and our Glorious
Constitution*; that I never was, to my knowledge or belief, rejected in, or expelled
from, any Orange lodge; I further declare, that I will do my utmost to support and
maintain the Loyal Orange Institution: obey all regular summonses, and pay all
just dues, (if in my power,) and observe and obey the Constitution and Laws of the
same; and lastly, I swear that I will always conceal, and never in any way
whatsoever, disclose or reveal, the whole or any part of the signs, words, or
tokens, that are now about to be privately communicated to me, unless I shall be
duly authorized so to do by the proper authorities of the Orange Institution, of
which I am now about to become a member. So help me God, and keep me
steadfast in this my Orangeman's Obligation.[17]

The above version of the obligation, current in 1869, differed from the
original 1830 Canadian version[18] by the inclusion of those parts itali-
cized. The added material reflected more inclusive strictures on fraternization with Catholics, an acknowledged intent to maintain the integrity
of the empire and, a clear denial of radical or subversive organizations, as
a reaction to the rebellion of 1837 and the Fenian invasion of 1866. A
further consequence of Canadian conditions was that those Orangemen

'on certificate' coming from Ireland and Britain were required to affirm that part of the obligation concerning the maintenance of the connection between the colonies of British America and the mother country.[19] Further elaboration and definition of the basic tenets were made as conditions demanded. By 1923 the obligation reflected a softening of the Orangemen's attitude to Catholics toward whom they were to 'abstain from all unkind words and actions.'[20] Strictures on fraternization with Catholics remained but with the pragmatic exception that children of Orangemen could attend a Catholic school 'where no Protestant or public schools exist.'[21] The revised obligation also included a promise, formerly part of the royal arch purple degree, that 'I will not unlawfully have any carnal knowledge of a brother's wife, sister, daughter or mother, and that I will also honour and respect the chastity of womanhood.'[22] From this obligation the Orangeman could proceed to the purple degree.

The obligations of the purple and blue degrees merely required an oath to keep their secrets but in the royal arch purple the initiate was required also to promise 'that I will not know a Royal Arch Purple Marksman to be in Want, Hardship or Distress (which has not been brought upon him by his own misconduct,) without rendering him such reasonable relief and assistance as may be in my power, without injury to myself or family.'[23] The fraternal assistance promised in the arch purple degree was more concisely defined in the highest degree, the royal scarlet, in which candidates pledged to pay a 'monthly offering, (if in my power,) to such person as the Sovereign [master] may appoint to receive the same.'[24]

Initiates to all degrees professed their obligations in rituals, heavily religious in tone, and all the secrets and codes imparted to them were based on biblical allegories. An emphasis upon kneeling and the imposition of hands is more reminiscent of an Episcopal than a Presbyterian tradition and probably emanated from the early dominance of the order in Ireland by Anglicans. Within a setting of biblical readings, prayers, hushed tones, and flickering candlelight men were solemnly given fundamental secrets of their order and it is easy to understand how the drama of the situation could provide an escape from the monotony of everyday life. Impromptu and unofficial rites were often incorporated into the formal ceremony. Riding the goat (being blindfolded, thrown into a blanket, and tossed repeatedly) and even, in a few isolated cases, branding on the chest by a heated lodge seal[25] added to the excitement of the occasion.

Candidates for the purple degree were invited to sprinkle warm ashes from the stove, a representation of Moses invoking a curse on the pharaoh. The action served to remind them that just as the Jews had once been oppressed by the Egyptians so also were their 'Protestant Fathers persecuted by Popery.'[26] Advancement to the blue degree involved in part the following ceremony.

The preparation of the candidate is to take place in the ante-room, as follows – He is to be stripped of his coat and vest, and his left arm bared to the shoulder, and a Blue Ribbon tied round that arm above the elbow. All being ready, the Candidate shall be led to the Lodge-room door, when a sudden alarm shall be made by the Sponsors, and they shall knock.

The door is then opened, and the Candidate (having the Bible in his hand) shall be introduced between his two Sponsors, each bearing an Orange Rod, decorated with Blue Ribbon, and one carrying, also, the Blue Book of the Lodge, with the Obligation thereon and open, and the other an Inkstand; he shall then be conducted to the side of the room, and then East, towards the Deputy-Master, before whom shall be burning one *bright* light; and before the Master there shall be placed eleven candles, in a semi-circle, and also one candle placed in the centre of the circle. The eleven candles are not to be lighted until the Candidate has reached the Deputy-Master; the one in the centre is not to be lighted.[27]

After a series of readings from the Old Testament and several prayers recited by the kneeling members, the candidate was initiated into the blue degree and charged to live a life of virtue and faith so that he might 'arrive at as near a state of perfection as sinful man can expect to attain.'[28]

In addition to the private ritual of the lodge meeting the order, in common with most other secret societies, had a specific ritual which was exhibited publicly in the annual walks or parades. Guy Fawkes day (5 November) and especially 12 July were celebrated by Orangemen in public demonstration, marches, and picnics. Upon initiation all Orangemen had to promise to celebrate the Boyne victory 'by assembling with my brethren, in their Lodge Room, on the 12th day of July in every year.'[29] From there, after a formal meeting had been called to order, the members would proceed to the parade in open session. Consequently every lodge carried an open Bible, the symbol of an Orange meeting in progress. Not until after the parade when the marchers returned to their hall was the meeting formally closed. The parade, therefore, was a public spectacle introduced into the regular conduct of lodge business and during it members were subject to the discipline of the master. By the same token, the participation of women and children was not permitted until the formal closing, whereupon games, picnics, or supper would be enjoyed by all.

Generally, a number of local lodges would gather in some convenient town. The venue of the walk would be altered from year to year and only

The Church of England's St James' Cathedral and the solid commercial front of
King Street provide a fitting backdrop to Toronto's 1874 Orange parade.
(*Canadian Illustrated News*, 1 August 1874. Photo courtesy of Metropolitan
Toronto Library Board.)

Toronto by virtue of its large number of lodges merited an annual parade.
In 1890, the bicentennial of the Boyne, Toronto's *Globe* reported:

The hour fixed for the starting of the procession was 11:30. Long before that time
Queen, Bond, Church and Jarvis streets were glorious with banners and musical
with the rub a dub dub of the drum and the pipers strains of Lilleballero, or the
Boyne Water as it has been called since that battle day. Lodges were marching and
counter-marching, crossing and recrossing each other, searching for the places
assigned in the order of the processions, but which all the heroic efforts of the
besworded marshalls could not find for them.[30]

Invariably a man in the role of King Billy on a white horse, the symbol of
the royal house of Hanover (to whom the English protestant succession

had been entrusted),[31] led the procession. Behind him came the lodges in order of seniority, the lowest numbered lodges coming first. Each lodge would carry its own silk banner with a hand-painted depiction of King William on one side and perhaps a scene from the Old Testament on the other. The marching members would be regaled with sashes and orange rosettes and past masters wore medals indicative of their status. Where possible, a lodge would try to obtain a band or at least a drummer and fife player. Preparations for the display involved the outlay of considerable capital, not only for the refreshments but also for regalia and instruments. In 1841, LOL 215 spent £2.10.0 for a drum and £5 for a banner.[32] Some lodges laid down strict regulations regarding dress appropriate for the occasion. Toronto LOL 301 stated in its by-laws of 1847 that 'in summer, the members shall dress in black coat and hat, white trousers, and white or fancy vest. In winter and at funerals the clothing to be as dark as possible.'[33] For all, 12 July was the greatest day in the year and they willingly dressed up for it.

In Newfoundland, because of the demands of the summer fishing industry, Orangemen were unable to march on 12 July. Instead, their celebrations usually occurred on either St Stephen's or Candlemas days in the dead of winter. On the Change Islands of Notre Dame Bay, 'around Candlemas the Fishermen and Orange societies would have their annual 'times' – a parade through the village, a church service, and in the evening a big supper and dance in their respective halls. The men's colourful regalia made a brave display as they wended their way up hill and down dale or across a frozen harbour, and we boys looked forward to the time when we too could join and be part of all that ritual and splendour.'[34]

It was a day of community festivities, a midsummer break, and an occasion for meeting and gossiping with old friends. The route of the parade and other residential streets would be decked with Orange bunting and Union Jacks. At traditional locations arches emblazoned with Orange symbols and slogans would be erected and under them marchers and spectators would be required to pass. After the parade men in their regalia would mill about in the lingering crowds and frequently drummers and fifers would give spontaneous performances of Orange tunes. Platforms specially arranged for the event were used by clergymen, politicians, and high ranking Orangemen to propagate their views and elicit support from the masses attracted by the spectacle. For protestants, it was a day of triumph. For catholics, it was a symbol of the dominance of protestantism, a reminder of their own insecurity within the society and frequently the occasion for much bitterness.

Discipline

Through the obligations imposed upon candidates at initiation and extended by a series of by-laws the lodges maintained a code of discipline
that, on the surface at any rate, appeared comprehensive. Members could
be punished for betraying the secrets, speaking ill of the order, marrying a
catholic, or succumbing to any other immorality or social misdemeanour.
Civil or criminal convictions were punishable within the Orange lodges as
well as within the courts. Orange discipline was maintained and enforced
by a standing committee in each lodge, and its verdict was usually final,
although appeals could be made to higher jurisdictions. Particularly
serious infringements of the code, if denied by the accused, might be
brought before a special tribunal of local members and higher officials
within the order. Punishment could take one of three forms; fines,
suspension for a specified time – usually three to twelve months – or
expulsion. The latter penalty was particularly severe, not only because it
permanently placed an individual beyond the Orange fold, but also
because the accused could be placed under censure by the community at
large in areas where the majority of adult males were in the order. Tales of
expelled Orangemen being forced to leave a district are not unusual. The
local importance of lodge censure is indicated by an incident in Udora in
the mid 1850s. An Orangeman had stolen an item from a local shop. The
shopkeeper, not a member of the lodge, reported the matter to the local
master in the hope that the culprit would be disciplined by his brethren
and that the affair would not have to be taken to the civil authorities.

   The annual reports of the provincial grand lodges contained a summary
of expulsions, suspensions, and fines meted out by local lodges and also
in many instances gave the names of the offenders. The number who
came under the disciplinary proceedings increased as the nineteenth
century progressed, a consequence of the growing size of the order and its
increasing emphasis on respectability. In 1884, sixty-seven men were
expelled in Ontario.[35] In 1898 the number was ninety-two. In any given
year, suspensions for non-payment of dues, the bulk of the punishments,
would number several hundred. Records reveal these and a host of more
serious infringements. For example, LOL 5 in Peel County in 1839 fined a
member ten shillings for being drunk on the Twelfth and using abusive
language towards a fellow Orangeman. A few weeks later another member of LOL 5 received a three-month suspension for 'bad conduct on the
Sabbath day at a camp meeting.'[36] In 1880 Ontario East recorded the
suspension of three members for defrauding a brother. In addition two
members were expelled for drunkenness and a similar penalty was im-

posed on a member who had been 'convicted of felony,' on another who was accused of 'deserting wife and eloping with prostitute' and on a fifth who was guilty of 'seducing a brother's daughter.'[37] Two other men were expelled for marrying Roman Catholics.

Marrying a catholic guaranteed expulsion from the order and even if the woman became a protestant the offending member had to furnish written proof of his wife's conversion. Thus in 1853 the minute books of LOL 215 record that: 'The members of 215 have come to a decision that Thomas Truman shall be suspended for the space of six months providing he gets satisfactory proof by getting a satisfactory sertificate [sic] from a Minister's hand of the Church of England that his wife has renounced the Roman Catholic faith to the satisfactory [sic] of this lodge.'[38] Twenty years later Robert Glockling, a prominent trade unionist and master of LOL 657 in Toronto, was expelled from his lodge for marrying a catholic. He appealed the decision to the district lodge which subsequently appointed a review committee of five local masters. The committee's report found in favour of Glockling, noting that a certificate of recantation had been obtained from an Anglican minister before the marriage and that the 'wife was a Protestant at the time [of the wedding] and for some days previous.'[39] The report was adopted by the district lodge by a vote of twenty-four to twenty-three. Glockling returned to his lodge where he served as secretary from 1877 to 1880.

An issue which had a much more controversial disciplinary dimension was that of voting behaviour. The Orangeman's oath, while pledging loyalty to the monarchy, laws, and constitution of the country, did not involve any obligation to vote for a specific political party or candidate. Nevertheless, it was generally assumed that the defence of the public good required the support of solidly protestant candidates. Some lodges attempted to direct and control voting behaviour. For example, LOL 137, Toronto, passed a resolution in 1858 'that it is the opinion of this meeting that any brother voting against Brother Cameron at the coming election is not worthy the name of an Orangeman, and should be expelled from the institution.'[40] LOL 140, Toronto, even went so far as to expel Samuel Parker for voting for J. O'Donohoe, a catholic, in the East Toronto election of 1874.[41] Such action within the order was not justified by the constitution. At the grand lodge meeting of 1856 it had been proposed that members should, if at all possible, support only Orangemen and in those instances where Orangemen ran against each other the preferred candidate should be determined by the grand master.[42] Although a committee was appointed to study the matter, the necessary changes in the constitution required to sustain the proposal were never made.

In the quest for an act of incorporation during the 1870s the grand lodge did resolve that it was the duty of Orangemen to support only those candidates willing to vote for an Orange incorporation bill, but the duty of members was specified in terms of supporting individuals, not a specific party.[43] The grand lodge could comment on voting behaviour but according to the constitution it could take no disciplinary action against those voting contrary to its wishes. It was restricted to passing such motions as: 'We greatly regret to find that Orangemen should so far forget the duty they owe themselves and the Association, as to prefer in anywise a Papist to a Brother.'[44] Had they managed to enforce political solidarity the order would have become a powerful voting bloc. However, it proved impossible to realize that potential. The informal entente that existed between the order and the Conservatives was maintained not by organizational edict but by their complementary ideologies and by subtle social and peer pressure.

The emphasis upon discipline was directed at maintaining coherence in the organization (hence the stress on payment of dues) and ensuring respectability. The order was aware of criticisms that it was a riotous and drunken lower-class assembly bent upon introducing and continuing Old World conflicts in the New. Its insistence upon a high standard of private morality, reminiscent of the cult of respectability emphasized by contemporary British self-help societies, was a reflection of the middle-class values of Orange leaders. The code of discipline introduced, formally and effectively, a set of principles which could be used for ordering personal and social life. As such Orangeism acted as a conservative force in the moral sphere and, in conjunction with protestantism which it supported, it contributed to much of the dourness, sabbatarianism, and sanctimonious tone of nineteenth- and early twentieth-century Canada.

Self-help and mutual aid

Drawn together by a common ideology, friendship, and an aura of conviviality and glamour attendant upon a secret society, Orangemen formed a community within themselves. They were obliged to be aware of the needs and interests of their brethren and were expected, where possible, to offer support. Such support could take the form of financial aid in times of sickness or unemployment and even the provision of business and employment patronage. In rural protestant communities aid to a brother whose barn had burnt down or whose crops had failed was both spontaneous and non-monetary. On the other hand, self-interest and antipathy towards catholics would have been sufficient guarantees of patronage. In a mixed community an Orange employer, faced with the choice of hiring a fellow Orangeman, another protestant, or a catholic, required no written by-laws to guide him in his decision. Written records and by-laws were, however, necessary to regulate financial aid, and it is from those sources that much information on the self-help and mutual aid functions of the order can be gleaned.

The third virtue, charity, featured prominently in the Orange creed.[45] The general regulations drawn up by the grand lodge alluded to the necessity of offering 'assistance to distressed members of the Order,'[46] and the ritual for the initiation of members contained further reminders of their fraternal responsibilities. The grand lodge guidelines for aid and benevolence were necessarily vague, and it was left to individual lodges to devise and regulate specific schemes better attuned to the needs and financial ability of the local membership. Although by-laws including those concerning benevolence were submitted to the grand lodge for ratification, aid was administered solely by the local lodge. Only on occasions of major disasters did the grand lodge intervene in the collection and distribution of emergency funds.

One of the earliest sets of by-laws containing provisions for benevolence was that of LOL 301, Toronto, printed in 1847. Article XXI decreed:

As soon as the funds in the hands of the Treasurer shall amount to the sum of twenty pounds, they will be devoted to benevolent purposes, in the relief of sick brethern and the burial of deceased members. Any brother who may be taken sick, and unable to attend to his employment, shall receive the sum of 7\6d weekly until he recovers, provided such sickness is not brought on by his own misconduct; and should a member die the sum of four pounds shall be paid towards the expenses of his funeral.[47]

Only those who had been members of the lodge for more than six months and who were fully paid up in their dues were entitled to these benefits. Moreover, the actual payment of benefits, since it was conditional upon the lodge having a minimum of £20, was not automatic insurance against personal misfortune. Another Toronto lodge, LOL 328, known as Virgin Lodge and founded 'for the purpose of giving unmarried young men, students or mercantile men, etc., a Lodge where they could assemble together,'[48] provided another unstructured benevolence scheme in its revised by-laws of 1852. Officials of the lodge were 'authorized to examine into all applications for Charity during vacation, and advance any amount in their discretion, not exceeding one pound from the funds of the Lodge.'[49] Five years later, however, the same lodge had moved into a much more organized program and had retained a physician, Dr W.C. Buchanan, as the lodge doctor.

During the last quarter of the nineteenth century most lodge by-laws

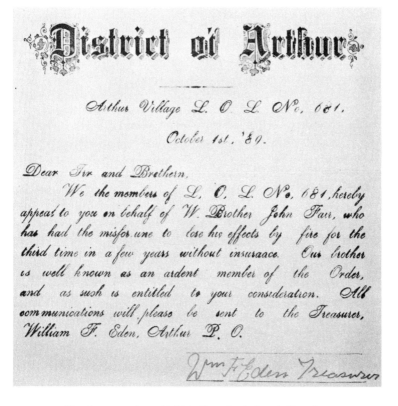

District of Arthur

Arthur Village L. O. L. Nᵒ. 681.

October 1st, '89.

Dear Sir and Brethern,

We the members of L. O. L. Nᵒ, 681, hereby appeal to you on behalf of W. Brother John Fair, who has had the misfortune to lose his effects by fire for the third time in a few years without insurance. Our brother is well known as an ardent member of the Order, and as such is entitled to your consideration. All communications will please be sent to the Treasurer, William F. Eden, Arthur P. O.

Wm F Eden Treasurer

Circular requesting relief distributed to lodges in Ontario

contained a fixed scale of benevolence payments. Urban lodges, in particular, usually retained a physician. As early as 1858 LOL 216 in Weston, Ontario, had its own doctor,[50] and in 1877 an Ottawa lodge, LOL 126, enacted that any member in good standing who was unable 'to attend his usual employment through sickness or accident shall receive the sum of: Orange $2, Purple and Blue $2.50; Royal Arch $3, weekly until his recovery.' Because of its unqualified guarantee of sick benefits the lodge required all new members to pass a medical examination before admission and in furtherance of the self-help function the lodge provided a physician, free of charge, in times of sickness.

The Physician shall be a legally qualified physician and surgeon ... he shall visit (or cause a competent medical gentleman to visit) every sick member as often as the case may require, but not less than three times a week, or, if he considers him able, may require the sick member to visit him ... for the faithful performance of such duties he shall receive from the Lodge the sum of fifty cents per member, per annum; he shall be required to give three months notice of his desire to resign his office, and shall receive the same from the Lodge if they may wish to dispense with his services.[51]

Some lodges provided a pharmacist's service as well as those of a doctor and it was usual to select both through an evaluation of competitive bids. For example, in 1886 Dr Parry of Toronto underbid two other physicians to obtain a contract from LOL 342[52] and eight years later he was recorded as serving two lodges in the city.[53] Of the fifty-five lodges operating in Toronto in 1894, thirty-five had their own physicians and medical insurance, and it is probable that the remaining lodges also provided some less formal assistance.[54] Having a lodge doctor and sickness payments anticipated the state-run scheme of the twentieth century. It worked in the interests of both the lodge members whom it served and the doctor to whom it guaranteed a regular clientele and income in an era when medical practitioners had to seek out their clients.

In times of widespread unemployment or prolonged sickness lodge funds were often exhausted and the formal self-help mechanism would break down. Some lodges provided for such an eventuality by assessing an additional amount from the healthy and employed members,[55] but others simply cancelled the benefit scheme. Financial disaster was an inherent risk for the lodge benefit schemes founded, as they were, on weak actuarial principles and, paradoxically, the lodge was thus least effective in times of extreme crisis. During periods of severe economic depression many unemployed members were unable to pay their dues and so ceased to be members, although attempts were made to carry them on the books for as long as possible. In more normal times and in transient crises the lodges did offer a degree of financial insurance.

The order also provided non-material comfort; 'members with the 'Blue' degree were required to sit up with sick brethren.'[56] Each lodge had its sick committee whose duty it was to visit members who were ill and confined to their homes. Ottawa LOL 126, appointed a visiting committee of six members who served six-month periods and in the course of their duties they were required to 'visit brethren who are reported sick, and render them such assistance as circumstances may require, and if requisite they shall notify the members two by two, as they stand on the list, to attend on the sick brothers during the night, or find a substitute.'[57] Only in a case of contagious disease or where illness was due to immoral conduct was the sick committee relieved of its responsibilities.[58] As well as providing company, and in many cases a death watch, the sick committee also acted as a monitor and could cancel sick benefits if it found a member to be feigning illness.

Further aid was given by lodges at the time of a member's death, or occasionally the death of his wife. Peel County LOL 5 expended thirteen shillings attending a brother's funeral in 1835,[59] and throughout the century most lodge minute books recorded the purchase of black crepe for funeral purposes. By-laws commonly stipulated a fixed sum to be paid towards a funeral but the amount varied from lodge to lodge through time. LOL 301 in 1847 stipulated a payment of £4; LOL 126 in 1877 offered the handsome sum of $50 – each lodge member paying an assessment of $1. Lodge 711 in Toronto enacted in 1898 'that upon the death of a brother in good standing a sum of thirty dollars be appropriated in aid of defraying the funeral expenses; and that on the death of a brother's wife the sum of ten dollars be appropriated for the same.'[60] The lump sum payment ensured that burial would take place with some dignity and that perhaps some of the financial burden of the family might be relieved. A pauper's funeral would be avoided. Additional respect, and indeed some pomp and ritual, was provided with the attendance of the lodge at the funeral, a duty which was recognized by the grand lodge in that it published the form of the ceremonies to be performed at the burial of an Orangeman. Orange funerals would be held only with the consent of the deceased's relatives. Preparations for the funeral would be undertaken at an emergency meeting on the morning of the burial. Members, having been furnished with an orange rosette to be worn on the left breast and crepe with an orange ribbon for their left arm, formed a procession and marched to the dead man's home and thence accompanied the coffin to the graveyard. Following the normal church service at the graveside the Orangemen would proceed with their own ceremony. 'Here in solemn silence the Master shall drop his Rosette or Orange Ribbon into the grave, upon the coffin. The Brothers shall then move from East to West round the grave in single fyle, each stopping at the foot of the grave and depositing his Rosette or Ribbon in the grave; until the whole have performed this duty.'[61] The by-laws of LOL 375 stipulated in addition that 'it shall be the duty of the visiting committee to cause the notice of the funeral to be inserted in the daily papers.'[62]

The system of benefits designed to relieve the stress of working and lower middle-class life in nineteenth-century Canada was reminiscent of the contemporary Friendly Societies and providential associations which had developed in Britain in the post-1760 period.[63] The British model contained provisions for sickness, unemployment, and death benefits paid out of regular dues. In the design of by-laws, the scale of payments, and pattern of secret ritual-bound meetings there are clear parallels with the subsequent development of benevolence within Canadian Orange-ism.[64] Given the size of the British movements and their public images it is reasonable to assume that the Orangemen of Canada would have been well aware of them. During the nineteenth century the British societies developed along two distinct lines – the local societies and the more national associations such as the Oddfellows and the Foresters. The Orange Order in Canada contained similarities to both. In terms of its hierarchical administration and its geographical extent the Canadian order resembled the national associations. However, until the formation of the Orange Mutual Benefit Fund in 1881 and its legal incorporation in 1890, the Orange Order did not function as a national self-help and benevolence association. Aid was arranged and supported by each local lodge and consequently there were limits in the scale of self-help functions. Only through a national organization could actuarial principles be applied effectively to ensure smooth operation of a benevolent fund.

Orange Mutual Benefit Fund

In 1877 the Provincial Grand Lodge of Ontario West ambitiously announced the beginning of a campaign to raise within a year $10,000 to aid the widows and orphans of deceased Orangemen. Some four years later, with the approval of the national grand lodge, the Orange Mutual Insurance Society of Ontario West was formed. This new benevolence wing of Orangeism provided a structure similar to that of the affiliated Friendly Societies for collecting dues and administering funeral, sick, and medical benefits together with life insurance on a national scale. The scheme was designed to rationalize the diverse benefits offered by the local lodges but it was prompted also by the recent appearance of the Oddfellows and Foresters. The grand master of Ontario West argued in 1882 that 'we are obliged to have recourse to this in order to place our Order on an equal footing with numerous other societies which have come into existence in our province and who were bidding and offering better terms for candidates to join their respective societies.'[65] One of the principal organizers behind the fund was the Mohawk, Oronhyatekha. He drew on his experience with the Independent Order of Foresters (IOF) to help the Orange scheme on its way. With his advice and supervision the order was made aware of actuarial science and through him avoided many of the major problems which led to the financial ruin of other benefit funds.

Despite Oronhyatekha's competence and advice the benefit fund grew slowly. By 1890, when it was transferred from Ontario West to the jurisdiction of the Grand Orange Lodge of British America, death benefits to the amount of only $54,000 had been dispensed. The diligence of the medical referee in vetting candidates had kept the mortality rate at a lower level than those of other fraternal societies and thus had enabled the scheme to remain solvent.[66] However, a few years later an anticipated rise in membership had not materialized and heavy demands on the insurance fund threatened insolvency. In 1897 it was suggested that the scheme be terminated but in 1899, having been given a temporary reprieve, the fund reported the first increase in membership for four years.[67]

Despite the traditions of self-help within the order only a small minority of Orangemen joined the insurance scheme. In 1900 there were only 2,029 members enrolled, although there were probably 60,000 active Orangemen in the country at the time. A large proportion of them would have been eligible for insurance. The number of men insured increased slowly during the early 1900s and reached a peak of 6,436 in 1913, declining to 3,424 by 1920.[68] Compared to the numbers of policies given out by the IOF, the major fraternal insurance company, those registered with the Orange fund were few. The IOF had 35,657 policies in effect in 1900 and 77,125 by 1920.[69] The discrepancy in the size of the two funds reflected a number of factors. The sole object of the Foresters' organization was insurance and their fraternalism was employed merely as a sales device. On the other hand, the Orange Order had a much wider set of objectives and insurance was only an ancillary function. Furthermore, the crises which beset the Orange fund during the 1890s may have deterred many potential investors. A great many Orangemen did, in fact, hold policies in the IOF, whose leader and many administrators were Orangemen.[70]

The Orange life insurance scheme was operated by the national grand lodge but other Orange bodies, the Ladies Orange Benevolent Association, and the provincial grand lodges, offered sickness, medical, and funeral benefit schemes. The Provincial Grand Lodge of Ontario West operated the largest fund, but compared to the primary organization in this field, the Oddfellows, its scale was limited. Total net assets of the Ontario West Orange scheme in 1900 were $1,800 whereas those of the Oddfellows amounted to $900,000. By 1920 the Oddfellows' assets were $3 million and those of the Orange less than $50,000.[71] As with the life insurance schemes this Orange fund suffered competition from other bodies whose primary function was insurance and which included many Orangemen in their ranks. Toronto's policemen, firemen, and printers, for example, all operated their own funds and reduced the potential subscription lists of the Orange. If organized benevolence had been its sole raison d'être, the Orange Order quickly would have expired in bankruptcy.

The Orange landscape

The order's role had a much wider social significance, a significance clearly manifest in the Canadian landscape. From St John's, Newfoundland, to British Columbia, Loyal Orange Lodge halls proclaimed the presence of the order and the importance of King Billy within the surrounding neighbourhood. They became an important feature in the settled landscape of Ontario and New Brunswick from the mid-nineteenth century and their importance was duly recognized by Ogle R. Gowan. The first grand master saw them as a natural appurtenance to his organization's growing respectability and an indicator of its solidity and permanence in the protestant community. The lodge hall was often the first institutional structure erected in pioneering settlements and sometimes served temporarily as a schoolhouse or church. Its basic function however was to serve as a private place where Orangemen could initiate their candidates and conduct their ritual meetings. Although formal meetings usually occurred once a month the buildings were utilized on many other occasions by formal and informal community gatherings. In fact, the Orange hall through its functions, form, and location reflected the centrality of the fraternity within much of protestant Canadian society. It also augmented the plain simpleness of that society's landscape.

Most of the halls were built through the cooperative efforts and shared labour of the members. The decision to build was the culmination of a lodge's commitment to fraternal principles. It demanded some but not excessive financial cost, rarely a mortgage, but it required that the burdens of planning and construction be shared. The lodge would decide what size of building was needed given the number of members and alternative uses to which the building might be put. Floor dimensions were rectangular as required by the form of the ritual space (figure 18) and ranged from as little as twelve feet by twenty feet to extremes of thirty-five feet by one hundred feet.[72] The most common dimension was twenty by thirty-five feet, a size that easily accommodated thirty to sixty members. Often a second storey was decided upon – upstairs reserved as a room for the lodge and downstairs for community affairs. Two-storey halls constituted about half the total. Once building size had been determined a site was sought. Land may have been obtained from the crossroads corner of a farmer's field or from subdivisions within village and town limits. Quite often a member donated the building lot or sold it at nominal cost. Generally, the parcel of land was little larger than the floor area of the building. The lodge's functions took place solely within the hall.

Most of the halls were constructed of timber or lumber frame, clad with horizontal board siding. In the early period, and even occasionally in the later nineteenth century, log buildings were usual. Generally the wood was cut, squared, and cured by the members themselves, sawn in a local mill, and carted to the hall site where, perhaps under the direction of a hired carpenter, the building was erected. As late as 1944 such a communal operation took place at Wareham, Newfoundland. Logs were cut and floated in the autumn from an offshore island to a mainland sawmill. From there the lumber was sledded across foreshore ice to the site about three miles down the coast.[73] In this case and most others there was little outlay of cash except for nails, glass and hardware, and perhaps payment of sawyers and a supervising carpenter. Materials were cheap and labour communal. Even when communal labour was not used expenses were minimal. At the August 1893 meeting of LOL 1516 in the mixed German and Irish-Canadian settlement of Ladysmith, Quebec, it was 'proposed by Bro. F. Bretzlaff that [Bro.] W. Kennedy get the job of building our lodgeroom, plan and size of main building 18 × 26 × 12 ft. ceiling. Anti-room 6× 8 × 7 ft. to be boarded rough on outside with 4 windows and double floor and finished inside with chimney stand and arch to be completed for the sum of $55 for Nov. 1st.'[74] Only brick buildings entailed much expense, but few halls were built in this material and as might be expected, given the rural and small town architectural patterns of Canada, they were confined largely to Ontario.

Rarely were the halls of architectural excellence or distinction. Their form was basic; a simple pent roof, a gable end doorway, and two or three windows arranged symmetrically along each side. The identifying plaque over the front door and the adjacent flagpole, sometimes painted in bands of British red, white, and blue, were the only adornments on an otherwise austere and anonymous structure. The anonymity of the building was heightened by shutters and heavy curtains on the windows. The Orange halls lacked pretension and reflected the anonymity of vernacular architecture. They did not approach the level of ostentation achieved by Masonic temples, in large part because Freemasonry represented a narrower and more urban middle-class constituency. Neither could LOL halls approach the monumentality of the Oddfellows halls, except in Newfoundland where settlement conditions different from those on the mainland prevailed. In mainland Canada Orange halls were generally unlike

LOL 1313
Danford Lake
Quebec

LOL 856
Cargill, Ontario

LOL 324
Dungannon, Ontario

LOL 2111
Woody Point
Newfoundland

LOL 1459
Cupids
Newfoundland

LOL 1126
Brookfield
Prince Edward
Island

LOL 109
Richmond Corners
New Brunswick

LOL 1133
Hazzard's Corners
Ontario

ORANGE HALLS

those of other fraternal societies: they were architecturally akin to community halls. They reflected a broad social spectrum and the generally humble condition of rural and small town Canada.

There were exceptions to the inconspicuous vernacular hall. In the downtown core of Toronto near the city hall, Orangemen in 1886 erected a brick edifice that through its central location, size, and ostentation emphasized the order's position in the city and the nation. Victoria Hall served more than a local function for it housed not only some two dozen local lodges and the Toronto County lodge but also the national headquarters of the movement. In a neighbouring building the *Sentinel* was published. Around the First World War another elaborate hall with classical lines was built on College Street in Toronto at a cost of $70,000. The only other Orange buildings which approached the scale of the Toronto halls were the Scott Memorial Hall, built in Winnipeg in 1905 at

Although eroded badly, the engravure of a mounted King William is still recognizable on this marker on the grave of George Reid, an Orangeman of Churchville, Peel County, Ontario.

a cost of $30,000,[75] the main Orange hall in Vancouver built around the same time, and another in Bonavista, Newfoundland. The Bonavista hall was undoubtedly the most remarkable in the Orange world. It rivalled Toronto's Victoria Hall in size, and in aspect completely outclassed it and all others, including those of Belfast. It is a two-storey frame building with an excessively large cupola. Situated on an extensive lot beside the courthouse and on a high point overlooking the harbour, the Bonavista hall has only one architectural rival in the town, the Anglican church. The Bonavista hall is an Orange fortress. It and other large halls such as at Grand Bank and Woody Point illustrate the grip that protestantism, loyalty, and fraternity had on outport Newfoundland. They are also among the few symbols shared by the outports and mainland Canada.

Orange halls bespoke the lodge's role in the community. In farming areas they were sometimes found along bleak roads seemingly isolated but actually central to the local neighbourhood. More likely they were found at a major intersection or junction, reflecting their function as a central place, and often in juxtaposition with the church and school – a summary of the complete social milieu. Pierce's Corners near Ottawa is an excellent example of this settlement type. In the extant core of this village are two former secondary schools, an Anglican church, the township hall, and a now abandoned Orange hall. Life in such a community revolved around these institutions and services, each fulfilling an essential local function. In towns, the hall was found mainly in residential areas at locations comparable to those occupied by churches or schools. A few lodges were found in the centre of commercial blocks, renting out the ground floor to a merchant and using the upstairs for lodge functions.

But for the exception of Newfoundland, protestant Canada's Orange landscape was typified by strategically located but rather plain vernacular halls. The Orangemen's meeting place blended well with the rest of a rather simple, even mundane setting. In Newfoundland the situation was different. In practically all of the two hundred or so outport settlements where it was found the Orange hall shared a place with only the church of the main protestant denomination. It and a church standing on a high point in a simple institutional compound dominated the outport landscape. They had few rivals. Schools, split into denominational roles, were small. The fraternal halls of the Society of United Fishermen were fewer and with one or two notable exceptions also smaller. In only a few ports were Freemasons or Oddfellows buildings significant and in even fewer did they surpass the Orange. Blatantly displayed symbolism, unparalleled in British North America, also contributed to the Orange predominance on the secular landscape. Newfoundland Orangemen built into, cut into, or painted onto their halls elaborate arches and symbols

PRINCIPAL ORANGE HALLS

LEFT Victoria Hall, Queen St East, Toronto. Designed by Orangeman E.J.
Lennox, it was erected in 1886, and demolished in 1971. (Courtesy of City of
Toronto Archives)
RIGHT Orange hall, Bonavista, Newfoundland
BELOW Vancouver Orange hall (Photograph by D. Holdsworth)

such as the 2½, five-cornered stars, half moons, and ladders. Above entrance doors they presented large boldly drawn names, in contrast to the rather obscure, barely recognizable nameplates stuck to halls in the rest of Canada. In the protestant graveyards of Newfoundland Orange symbolism is more readily apparent than anywhere else in the country. The unique features of the island's Orange landscape did not arise from Orangeism but from the island's society.[76]

Through lodge halls and headstones and the many place-names of Orange significance such as Derry, Aughrim, Enniskillen, Boyne, Orange Corners, Purple Valley, and Prince William, the meaning of Orangeism was stamped upon the Canadian land.

Conclusions

At the local level the social dimensions of Orangeism were a primary attraction and many of the earliest lodge meetings appear to have revolved around the consumption of whiskey, beer, and tobacco amid an atmosphere of boisterous good cheer. Despite official censure of intemperance in the second half of the nineteenth century, camaraderie and a sense of local importance continued to draw many into the order. This appeal was strengthened, particularly in large urban centres such as Toronto, by the hope of obtaining some form of patronage through association with the fraternity. Orangemen did not join their order for pecuniary benefits alone. Like the other fraternal organizations, it crystallized 'an ethos of mutuality'[77] but unlike the others its ideology embraced a whole set of political and religious ideals which appealed to a wide range of protestants, regardless of class. In the political sphere it exuded a sense of power which was perhaps more mythical than real but nevertheless proved effective as an agent for recruitment. Total Orange membership increased despite the fluctuating fortunes of its benevolence functions. Within the lodges conviviality and the glamour of ritual acted together to reinforce the feeling of brotherhood among the Orange community. Benevolence was an offshoot of the whole social meaning of Orangeism.

The Ideological and Political Dimension

And we'll keep the old flag flying
The old red, white and blue

Nineteenth-century English Canada embodied the triumph of ideology and politics over geography. It was separated from the United States not by any physical barrier but by a set of beliefs in which the link with Britain was central. Canada was North America minus a revolution. Its tory tradition was at once conservative, loyal, and protestant, and within such a tradition the tenets of Orangeism were supportive, not anachronistic. At the outset the order was not welcomed: its social composition, immigrant character, and the blatancy of its anti-catholicism clashed with an entrenched elite. However, as the century progressed, the order moved closer to the centre of the political stage. It is almost impossible to distinguish the Orangemen's unique contribution in an era when the Bible and church affiliation were an accepted part of the political life of the nation at large.

Religion and politics were inseparable in nineteenth-century Canada.[1] In French Canadian culture, catholicism and the rural ideal were jointly upheld as the defence of the integrity of a community faced with the onslaught of modernization and the antagonism of English-speaking protestants. In English-speaking Canada politico-religious controversies were also paramount and were most clearly represented in the community divisiveness engendered by the issue of religious instruction in elementary schools. At a higher level of education, the University of Toronto's college system evolved on the basis of religion not ethnicity, class, or academic interest. Religion was not simply a matter of 'private salvation' or theological debate. In the words of the historian W.L.

Morton, 'religion – not wealth, and not politics – was the chief concern, the main ideal occupation of Canadians, both British and French. The Age is indeed to be comprehended only in terms of the idea of Providence, that God and His Church were very present actors in the World ... Religion was thus the chief guide of life for most Canadians; it touched all matters from personal conduct to state policy. All politics were indeed sectarian.'[2] The order took its place, albeit an important one, in the ranks of a society which drew a shadowy line between the realm of politics and religion, public good and Christian values. For example, in Toronto during the 1850s contempt of catholics and French Canadians was elevated into a patriotic duty.[3] George Brown, the founder and editor of the widely influential but anti-order *Globe*, published some of the most venomous anti-catholic propaganda of the century. As historian Carl Berger has noted, 'Religion was the mortar of the social order,'[4] and Orangeism was clearly a part of it. The Orangemen voiced their enmity and distrust of catholics perhaps more directly and loudly than other elements of protestant Canadian society, but their views differed only in degree, not in kind, from the norm of anti-catholicism.

Spurred on by a desire to keep Canada protestant and British the order was one of the foremost advocates of a united country stretching *a mari usque ad mare*. Extension of the order into Muskoka and to Manitoulin Island in the 1870s was heartily applauded, and in 1893 further progress was announced at the grand lodge meeting:

In these northern districts of Ontario is the great growth of the Order especially gratifying. North of the line of the French River, where a decade ago were but a few white settlements, there are now forty Orange Lodges in full working order. The lumbering, mining, farming and fishing industries in these parts have, as in Manitoba and the north-west, called the last and bravest of the young men from the older provinces. These young pioneers are losing no time in implanting in their new homes the principles of our noble Order, which today form the keystone of all responsible government and true religion.[5]

Through migration Orangeism could extend its defences and consecrate new territories in the name of Britishness and protestantism. With its network of lodges stretching from St John's to Vancouver Island the order was in a position not only to enunciate dreams of national unity but to use its political power to influence the realization of those ideals. During the preparations for Canadian confederation in 1867 the order, although not vocal, lent its tacit support to the venture.[6] In the rest of the century, and indeed until 1949, the order played a more active role in seeking inclusion of Newfoundland within Canada. Its attitude towards the offshore colony

was best expressed by Grand Master Clarke Wallace in 1892: 'Newfoundland has long formed a federated Province in Orange British America. May the day not be far distant when it shall be added, a rugged
Province, the sentinel on the wild Atlantic, to the Dominion of Canada.'[7]

Imperialism and Orangeism

In their view of a Canada united and part of the British Empire, Orangemen differed little from Canadian imperialists in general, except that they
added, in their minds at least, the qualification that the protestant religion
should be a further hallmark of the British connection. Historian Allan
Smith has argued that by 1860 there had definitely emerged in Ontario a
frame of mind which 'supposed a Canadian future within the imperial
system.'[8] As the settlement of the Canadian west unfolded, Ontario's
sense of nation was extrapolated to embrace that of the country at large.
Perhaps the process of 'Ontarianization' was most evident in Manitoba,
but it also embraced Saskatchewan, Alberta, and British Columbia. In the
view of Canadian imperialists there was no conflict between the desire for
a close link with Britain and the dream of a strong Canadian nation. In the
words of Berger, 'for Imperialists the sense of nationality and the ideal of
imperial unity were interlocked and identical.'[9] Only by first attaining a
strong internal unity could Canada hope to be accepted as a respectable
member of the British Empire – an institution which the imperialists
hoped might even be transformed by the new country. The commitment
to the empire did not arise merely from a sense of colonial inferiority or a
quest for economic security. 'Long before the surge of imperialism in the
late nineteenth century, British North Americans had looked upon the
Empire as the vehicle and embodiment of a progressive civilization which
was designated by Providence to spread its culture, religion, and political
institutions across the face of the earth.'[10] Canada, like the empire,
should be united by a common set of laws, schools, language, and
symbols. Orangemen subscribed wholeheartedly to these sentiments and
proclaimed their slogan 'One flag, one language, and one school, equal
rights for all, special privileges for none.' Orangemen were not the sole
proponents of imperialism but few could exceed their ardour.

As early as 1833 Ogle R. Gowan had suggested for the Orange lodges
scattered around the world some form of imperial union, but it was not
until 1867 that his dream was realized. In that year the pervasiveness of
Orangeism in the empire received concrete expression when the inaugural meeting of the Imperial Grand Orange Council of the World was
convened in Belfast. The council which became a triennial affair met next
in Toronto. It was hoped that just as the British North American Orange

organization served as a model for national unity so might its international council provide an example and stimulant for federation of the British
Empire. Clarke Wallace, in his grand master's address of 1892, expressed the hope 'that the plan of Orange federation throughout the
British Empire in every part of the world, so long in successful operation,
may form a precedent for the Motherland and her rising dominions, to
establish at an early date a federation of the great British Empire.'[11] It was
the aspiration of the order that the thin red line of empire be inset by an
Orange stripe. As a garrison of fundamental British and protestant values
the order sought to unite and defend the legacy of those values extended
overseas.

Imperialism was inherent in Orangeism and received its clearest arti-
culation in the Boer and First World wars. Patriotic duty was the driving
force behind Orange war efforts and lodge halls were frequently used as
recruiting stations. To Orangemen it was incomprehensible, yet hardly
unexpected, that French Canadians expressed little sympathy for the
imperial wars. The frenzied reaction to Quebec at the time of these crises
is to be seen in the context of the French Canadians' fulfilling the Orange
prophecy that catholics were disloyal by virtue of their religion.

At the 1900 grand lodge meeting Clarke Wallace, feeling the moment
had arrived for Canada to receive its baptism in an imperial war, uttered
this proclamation: 'In a moment, the Army of England became the Army
of an Empire. From every Colony and Dependency, from India, Australia, the Cape, the West Indies, and Canada, contributions of men and
means poured into the Motherland. The people beamed with a patriotic
zeal marvellous to witness, and in no part of the Queen's domains did the
spirit of loyalty glow more brightly than in this our Dominion.'[12] The
grand lodge proudly published a list of members and sons of members
who had enlisted and it was announced with pride that LOL 1527 at Fort
McLeod had closed down because so many of its members had gone to
war.[13]

The outbreak of the First World War provided Canadians with another
opportunity to demonstrate their imperial devotion and out of it there
would emerge a sense of nationhood. Led by their fellow Orangeman
General Sam Hughes, the minister of militia, members of the order turned
their attentions to the war effort. They claimed to be the backbone of the
expeditionary force, but it is impossible to assess accurately the size of
their contribution. In 1916 they argued that 'fifty thousand of our members from this jurisdiction [Canada] are on active military service.'[14]
Tremendous peer pressure was put on young Orangemen to enlist and in
turn this deprived the order, temporarily at least, of its more active
members and the functioning of the association was disrupted. In 1916 it

was claimed by the York County master of the Orange Young Britons that 'the Orange Young Briton Association are playing their part in this great war, over sixty per cent, of the membership of this County are either in France, or in training camps preparing themselves to do their part, which has resulted in two lodges going dormant, while others are working with a bare quorum.'[15] In 1917, the Grand Orange Lodge of British America was unable to meet for the first time since 1830. The presence of Orangemen in the army meant an extension of Canadian Orangeism overseas in the form of military lodges. Such lodges were active in recruiting new members among the soldiers – members who were highly prized as they were believed to be 'thoroughly imbued with the Imperial spirit and ideals.'[16] Many lodge meetings and 12 July parades testified to the presence of 'the Orange in Khaki.'

The First World War offered to the order the opportunity to carry its psychological and moral garrison into a military reality. Duty to the empire was expressed with religious fervour and those who opposed the war, or appeared less than enthusiastic, were denounced. On 12 July 1917, resolutions were passed by a Toronto lodge.

Resolved that McKinley LOL 275 petition the Government at Ottawa to put the Conscription bill in force immediately on its receiving the signature of the Governor General, as the lads at the front need help and need it at once.

And be it further resolved that we urge the Government to take proceedings against those who are putting forth treasonable utterances, whether they be in Quebec Province, or in any other Province of this fair Dominion and this Lodge recommends that the parties, when found guilty, be taken out and shot at sunrise.[17]

In the aftermath of the war the lodges enshrined their dead in the folk memory of Orangeism. The order had been tried and not found wanting. With the passing of years the dimension of its role was embellished until it appeared that the order and the army had been virtually synonymous.

National party politics

From the formation of the grand lodge in 1830 Gowan marshalled the order as a political force. Throughout its history Canadian Orangeism would serve as a defender of the status quo. In the early 1830s Gowan and other Orangemen worked to create an immigrant party voice in Upper Canadian affairs.[18] Personal ambition and the expressed resentment from the older established and privileged families were motivating forces but so too was the perceived republican threat to the colony posed by the reformer, William Lyon Mackenzie. In 1837 when Mackenzie led an abortive rebellion Orangemen actively defended the tory government,[19] and Gowan raised at his own expense a company of militia. But even in their loyalty Orangemen were distrusted. Sir George Arthur, the last lieutenant governor of Upper Canada, wrote to Lord Durham in July 1839 that 'there is a numerous and very troublesomely disposed class of persons in this Province – Orangemen – who consider lenity of any kind [to the 1837 rebels] under such circumstances to be an insult to their Order.'[20]

In the aftermath of the rebellion the order was unable to establish a comfortable rapport with either of the two major political groupings in the country. Despite the inclusion of officers and gentry in the grand lodges of the 1830s, Orangeism was not a tory institution, although it had been so described by Lord Durham.[21] Orangeism and toryism were philosophically complementary but socially incompatible. Nevertheless, the order provided for tory candidates a measure of voting power and public obstructionism at the polls. Others in the Reform party were similarly averse to the order and its tactics, and a Reform government introduced two bills aimed directly at curtailing Orange power. Only the Party Processions Bill of 1843 became law, and until it was repealed eight years later Orange demonstrations and parades were banned. The proscriptive intent of the bills was more than most Orangemen would endure and their fortunes became even more clearly associated with anti-Reform and tory interests.

Gowan sided with John A. Macdonald, an Orangeman from 1841, in his efforts to create a Conservative party incorporating Catholics from French Canada and in so doing clashed with many in the order. Grand Master Benjamin saw Gowan's activities as a deviation from basic principles and judged that 'a few members have openly repudiated religion as our primary function and contended that our association is a mere political organization.'[22] The tensions engendered by the attempts at balance between religion and politics were fully exposed. Gowan, faced with the need to enhance his own position within Macdonald's circle and seeing the order's organizational apparatus resting idle in the hands of a tory, determined once again to be grand master. At the grand lodge meeting in 1853 he orchestrated his own election, but as a result the order was split. Fifty-four lodges sided with Benjamin and all but three were located in the eastern and older half of Ontario.[23] Benjamin's constituency reflected a higher degree of toryism and vested privilege than did the much larger group of lodges which held with Gowan. In class terms the split represented a division between an established genteel tory leadership within the grand lodge and the more recently arrived and politically aspiring Irish. It also mirrored the division between Macdonald's Conservatives and the tory elite. Two grand lodges operated until 1856 when a compromise board of officers, reflecting Gowan's views, was installed.

Relations between the order and Macdonald's Conservatives were not easy and the order did not provide bloc support. In Macdonald's attempts at compromise, a purely protestant stance had to be forfeited; in any case the order lacked the power to marshal its own vote. One of the most successful attempts to detach part of the Orange vote from its developing allegiance to the Conservatives was made by the Clear Grits in Toronto during the election of 1857. The Clear Grit platform insisted on policies of 'rep by pop,' the separation of church and state, and efficient government, issues that appealed to Orangemen wishing to see further reduction of the power of vested tory interests. A critical factor in attracting Orange support was the Clear Grits leader, George Brown. There was no one in the Orange leadership whose anti-catholicism surpassed that of the *Globe*'s protestant owner. In the election of 1857 he successfully carried Toronto, supposedly with the aid of six hundred Orange votes.[24] Those six hundred, had they been cast by men in active connection with the order, would have represented half the total Orange vote. Certainly Orange power in the city was no myth for as Harcourt Gowan pointed out, their 'influence, properly wielded, is sufficiently strong to hold the balance of power, if not to elect, the Member of the Legislative Council or "Upper House of Parliament," – there being ... 1217 members in actual connection.'[25] Brown had been nominated by John Holland,[26] master of LOL 551[27] and Orange grand secretary of British America. Much of the credit in securing Orange votes may be given to him and his allies in the Toronto lodges, the masters of LOL 328 and LOL 621. Together, they were censured by both the Toronto district and York County lodges[28] and Holland was consequently replaced as grand secretary, but their activity as Grits continued. In 1858 Holland was again instrumental in a move which saw four of twenty lodges in Toronto refuse to agree to a district resolution that Orangemen vote for John Hillyard Cameron in the local elections that year.[29] Cameron's opponent was none other than George Brown. Cameron lost. The order would continue to have difficulty bringing out the vote in favour of its chosen party, the Conservative.

Although a close contact had been established between the order and Macdonald's Conservatives, no formal political alliance was ever made. Only an exceptionally strong-willed and single-minded hierarchy of leaders, from the grand master down through the county and district organizations to the masters of the local lodges, could have enforced party discipline. That sort of unity did not exist. In 1863 while he was grand master and member of the assembly Cameron supported an act giving increased power to catholic separate schools despite opposition from several lodges. Cameron challenged them and argued that if they persisted in their condemnation 'I would feel it my duty not merely to vacate this chair [the grand master's], but to withdraw from the Order altogether, as I should be in my judgement ... debarred from that freedom of action and opinion which I have a right to exercise in all matters that come before me as a member of the legislature.'[30] Cameron managed to convince the grand lodge of the correctness of his views. Subsequently he also managed to ward off the effects of criticism of his acting as lawyer for the assassin of D'Arcy McGee in 1868.[31] Party compromise, variable leadership, actual disagreement with many of the policies of the Conservatives, and local political interests made the order an ineffectual party machine.

Nevertheless there can be no doubt that the Orangemen were a power in the land and in succeeding decades the association with the national Conservatives was firmly cemented. Conservative cabinets usually included two Orangemen[32] who provided the link with a critical vote. Sir Richard Cartwright, a Liberal who served in parliament during the period, estimated that 'from 1870 to 1891, the fate of the several governments of the Dominion depended to a most unusual degree, as far as Ontario was concerned, on the action of the Orange Order.'[33] When that support was temporarily divided in the elections of 1872[34] and hopelessly at odds with government policies in 1896 the Conservatives' fortunes suffered. The events which led to the temporary fracturing of relations between the order and the Conservatives in the latter year provide a measure of the extent to which Orangemen constituted a wing of that party.

An act of the Quebec government in 1888 to compensate the Roman Catholic church for properties confiscated from the Jesuits in the aftermath of 1759 marked the first stage of the eventual split between Orangemen and the Conservative party. Many protestants were incensed by what appeared to be concessions to catholicism and parliament was called on to nullify the provincial act. Only thirteen 'noble' supporters for the motion could be found, among them the Orange grand master, Clarke Wallace. The Orangemen in parliament however were not unanimous on the issue since Mackenzie Bowell, a former grand master and cabinet minister, stood with his party and voted against the motion. Macdonald managed to stem further loss of Orange support by softening the impact of the Jesuits' Estates Act. As a concession to Orange interests a bill for the incorporation of the Orange Order was pushed successfully through parliament by the Conservative party.[35] In the subsequent election the Conservatives focused on the issue of trade reciprocity with the United States and were able to appeal successfully to economic and nationalist above protestant and Orange sentiments.

With the death of Macdonald soon after the 1891 election, the Conservatives, deprived of effective leadership and beset by growing protestant unrest, found it increasingly difficult to govern and retain Orange allegiance. Senator J.J.C. Abbott, former Orange deputy master of Quebec[36] and mayor of Montreal, acted as prime minister during the remainder of 1891 and part of 1892 until bad health forced his retirement. He was replaced by John Thompson, a Methodist convert to catholicism, whose appointment required some adjustment of Orange positions within the government. Clarke Wallace was admitted to the cabinet and added to the Orange weight already provided by Mackenzie Bowell. However, during the next few years the issue of French language instruction in the separate schools of Manitoba emerged as a national crisis with the potential to rupture the harmony of Orange-Conservative relations. Bowell who had become prime minister on the death of Thompson in 1893 favoured federal legislation which supported French catholic rights in Manitoba. There were serious objections to such interference. The cry of 'hands off Manitoba' was raised by protestants throughout the dominion, and under pressure from his lodges, Grand Master Wallace resigned from the cabinet and with him went the order's Conservative vote.

By the early 1900s the entente had been reestablished with a new set of participants. Clarke Wallace had died in 1901 and Mackenzie Bowell had been elevated to the Senate. Colonel Sam Hughes, T.S. Sproule, and millionaire A.E. Kemp provided able Orange replacements.[37] Following the Conservative victory in the elections of 1911 Hughes became minister of defence and militia, and Sproule resigned as Orange grand master to assume the role of speaker in the house. Kemp entered the cabinet without a portfolio but in 1915 was appointed chairman of the War Purchasing Commission and in the following year took on responsibility for military affairs when Hughes was forced to resign. There were others who followed in the steps of Kemp, Hughes, and Sproule but the role of Orangemen among the federal Conservatives declined as Orangeism itself declined after the First World War. Orange power was further weakened by the fact that the Conservatives were to form a government for only a few years during the next half century. During the First World War, with its expressions of patriotic ardour and distrust of 'foreign' Canadians, the party alliance that had been forged by Gowan and Macdonald during the middle decades of the nineteenth century was at its height.

Toronto, Aug. 7, 1911

Dear Sir and Worshipful Brother,

The following Protestant Platform was adopted by M.W. Grand Orange Lodge of British America at the Annual Meeting held in the City of Winnipeg June 28th and 29th, 1911, and a copy of it ordered to be forwarded to every Primary Lodge in the jurisdiction.

Yours fraternally,

JAMES H. SCOTT, Grand Master.
WILLIAM LEE, Grand Secretary.

PROTESTANT PLATFORM

I. The entire separation of Church and State.

II. Opposition to any interference of the Dominion Government with the different provinces in educational affairs.

III. The resistance of any further special privileges to any section of the population either on account of race or religion; and the elimination of any special privileges which they now possess except those included in the Confederation compact.

IV. Opposition to any extension of lingual privileges beyond those conferred by the British North America Act.

V. The maintenance of British Connection and the support of any movement which tends to make closer and more binding the relation between Canada, Newfoundland and the Mother Country.

VI. A close supervision of all new settlers and the encouragement of suitable white immigration from the British Isles, the United States and Northern Europe.

VII. A Federal marriage law recognizing the validity of marriages performed by the qualified clergyman of every religious denomination or other person vested by the law with that power; and the enactment of criminal penalties against persons using their influence to separate legally married couples by questioning the validity of marriages performed in accordance with provisions of this law.

VIII. Government inspection of all religious, educational and charitable institutions and the inspection of the books of all institutions receiving aid from the public treasury.

Circular sent from the grand lodge to local lodges throughout Canada on the eve of the 1911 national election. (Courtesy Mr A. Murray, Clyde River, P.E.I.).

Provincial party politics

The federal constitutional arrangement, which gave to Ottawa control
over external relations and national goals, restricted at the provincial
level the range of concerns in which the Orange Order could have a vital
interest. Separate schools and language were the only issues on which
Orangemen could effectively present a united voice to the public and on
those issues they were only one section, albeit a strident one, of a greater
protestant and English-speaking constituency. From the beginnings of
public education the rights of separate schools were scrutinized assid-
uously and any move which was thought might increase their role hotly
decried. In most provinces accommodation was reached which allowed
for some minority language and religious instruction at the primary level,
while maintaining a semblance of a public school system agreeable to
most protestants. For example, in New Brunswick during the early 1870s
a vigorous and often violent schools controversy with full Orange involvement had led to a political compromise. Similar compromises were
arrived at in Nova Scotia and Prince Edward Island, and Laurier's
national government achieved a comparable result in Manitoba at the end
of the century. Laurier's acceptance of one hour of minority language
instruction would become an often used model.

In most provinces, because of the catholic French-speaking minorities,
it was difficult for protestants to separate the religious and language issues
and it was for Orangemen simply impossible. For Orangemen, the
non-British were suspect and, since they were also generally not protestant, their attempts to acquire fuller religious or language services in the
schools were doubly protested. In New Brunswick in the 1890s the
provincial grand master, loyalist, and Conservative H.H. Pitts doggedly
attempted to inflame protestant opposition to catholic and French
instruction.[38] His efforts eventually came to nought, but in the controversies that he promoted, the alignments of loyalist protestants and
Conservatives were more clearly evident. In the federal election of 1900,
when Pitts was particularly active, the Conservatives lost four and won
only five of New Brunswick's fourteen seats and 'most of the five ridings
held by the Conservatives were strongholds of the Orange Lodge.'[39]
Without the backdrop of other popular concerns, provincial schools
issues were generally insufficient to sustain the vote occasionally
enlivened by Orange rhetoric. Besides, astute non-Conservative politicians, such as Mowat in Ontario, Greenway in Manitoba, Blair in New
Brunswick, and Gardiner in Saskatchewan, generally managed to divert
potential Orange Conservative votes by their handling of the transient
crises. Nowhere was that more apparent than in the Orange heartland,
Ontario.

Ironically, despite many elected Orangemen in Ontario, a Conservative provincial administration was not formed until 1905. The Liberals had dominated Ontarian politics from confederation and much of their success was derived from the tremendous personal ability of Oliver Mowat (premier, 1872–96). He was able to appeal to a broad section of the electorate and balanced both protestant and catholic interests. In his first electoral campaign he had employed the slogan 'Mowat and the Queen, or Morrison and the Pope'[40] but subsequently his anti-catholicism was much subdued. In fact, 'he built so much confidence amongst Catholics all over Canada that Laurier made him Minister of Justice so that he could deal with the aggrieved Catholic minority in Manitoba. In this capacity he was able to facilitate the betrayal of that minority.'[41] Despite his anti-catholic sentiments and background, the Orange Order could not find in him a ready ally. In 1873 a bill to incorporate the Orange Order passed through Ontario's Legislative Assembly with Mowat's support but was disallowed by the lieutenant governor. Mowat failed to press the issue and on the occasion of another Orange incorporation bill being presented six years later he suggested that the Orangemen should incorporate themselves under an extant general act of incorporation.[42] Not until the federal government passed its act in 1890 did the order receive the legal right as an association to hold valuables and property in Ontario.

Within a year of the Ontario Conservatives' securing their first election victory in 1905 the peculiar concerns of the Orange wing of the party were revealed on the issue of language instruction in the schools. Since 1885 Ontario had maintained a school curriculum that required the compulsory study of English, a policy redefined during the early 1890s to make English the language of instruction wherever possible. Some separate schools in French-speaking areas did not fulfil the intent of the regulations and starting in 1906 the public was made aware of this.[43] The issue was publicized first by the actions of Ottawa English-speaking separate school supporters and subsequently by the Orange Sentinel and the Grand Lodge of Ontario East. The movement of French Canadians into both eastern and northern Ontario in the previous two decades had doubled the French proportion of the population to almost 10 per cent of the province's total. That fact and the growing demands for French schools provoked the reaction. The debate was intensified by the internal struggle within the catholic hierarchy between French and Irish clerics, the latter wishing to avoid the issue of French instruction being confused with the wider issue of separate schools.[44] In 1910, G. Howard Ferguson, Orange leader of the ultra-protestant group in the Conservative party, brought the school language issue to the floor of the assembly. The issue proved important in the 1911 Conservative election victories, both in Ontario and federally.

In the aftermath of the electoral victories the Ontario government created a new school language policy, popularly known as Regulation 17. It reduced considerably the position of French, and besides isolating the French-speaking communities from the rest of Ontario, Regulation 17 served also to promote the political interests of Orangemen and none more so than Howard Ferguson.

Ferguson, 'a small town Ontario Protestant, to many an Orange bigot, narrow, fanatical and anti-French,'[45] led the Orange faction in the provincial Conservative party. In 1915, probably one-third of the Legislative Assembly was Orange, few of whom were not Conservatives.[46] That position was weakened by the election victory of Labour and the United Farmers of Ontario in 1919. Despite Ferguson's role as Conservative organizer during the campaign, many Orange votes had been lost. By 1923, Ferguson, now leader of the Conservatives, managed to rally the Orange vote and carried the election, primarily because of his position on Regulation 17. Of the 110 seats in the legislature, the Conservatives won 72, and of those, 38 were held by Orangemen.[47] While they remained in power Ferguson's government epitomized the Orange tone of Ontarian affairs.

Newfoundland was also an area wherein the Orange vote played a decisive role. There, a tradition of Orange involvement in administration had been evident since the 1890s. J.S. Winter, prime minister and attorney general from 1897 to 1900, was one of the colony's first prominent Orange politicians.[48] He was followed by Richard A. Squires, who was 'Prime Minister of Newfoundland on three occasions, and occupied the highest chair in the Orange Order, not only in his own Provincial Grand Lodge, but also in the Grand Black Chapter and the Grand Lodge of British America.'[49] The order in Newfoundland acted as a strong confederationist force and in this no one was more dedicated than Brother Joseph Smallwood, Orangeman and eventual provincial premier, who on the eve of the 1948 confederation referendum personally visited the lodges along Conception Bay to marshal the pro-confederation vote. Newfoundland's joining Canada was the realization of a long-cherished Orange dream.

Other ultra-protestant movements

The tradition of ultra-protestantism in Canada was maintained not solely by the Orange Order; on notable occasions it was outdistanced by blatantly sectarian but emphemeral political movements. Late in 1891 the Protestant Protective Association (PPA) appeared in Ontario to supplant temporarily the extremist sentiments in the established order. It set as a policy the boycotting of catholic businesses and the exclusion of catholics from public office and drew support from disaffected Orangemen and remnants of D'Alton McCarthy's Equal Rights Association. The first council of the PPA was established by Orangemen in Windsor, principally through the instigation of W.J. Traynor, deputy master of the Grand Lodge of the United States and the editor of Detroit's *Patriotic American*.[50] Traynor, a native of Brantford, Ontario, had moved to the United States but retained connections with his home province. He was elected vice-president of the Triennial Orange Council of the World when it met in Toronto in 1892.[51] Meetings of the PPA were held in Orange halls across Ontario,[52] but although it received support from local Orangemen it was generally snubbed by the grand lodge.

The PPA represented a threat to the organization's solidarity especially after the Catholic Thompson became Canadian prime minister, but it was also perceived as republican in tone, missing that essential element of professed Britishness and loyalism.[53] Orange officers initially pursued a policy of ignoring the new group, but when it became apparent that the PPA also posed a threat to the Conservative party the order confronted it directly.[54] Clarke Wallace was given authority to suspend lodges but that extraordinary power represented no more than a vote of confidence in the grand master and could not be applied. Wallace's weapon was not only ineffective, it was unnecessary. The PPA, without adequate leadership[55] and a base no wider than extreme protestantism, could not sustain popular interest in its political platform. It did not have the social and cultural depth nor heritage of the Orange Order and it faded as quickly as it had arrived.

The United States was the origin of another ultra-protestant movement which came to Canada in the 1920s and built upon endemic protestant sentiments there. The Ku Klux Klan subscribed to 'Protestantism, racial purity, Gentile economic freedom, just laws and liberty, separation of Church and state, pure patriotism, restrictive and selective immigration, freedom of speech and press, law and order, higher moral standards, freedom from mob violence and one public school.'[56] Considerable curiosity was shown when Klan organizers came into a Canadian community to speak in the Orange lodge room, Masonic temple, or other hall, and there were local citizens familiar enough with American lore to wear hoods at the inaugural meetings in many places.[57] Only in Saskatchewan in the years 1927 and 1928 did a common brand of bigotry give full but fleeting support to the Klan. In Saskatchewan the Klan managed to forge cordial links with the Orange Order. The *Sentinel* provided sympathetic accounts of its presence, Orangemen were prominent in its ranks,[58] and in many ways the two were interdependent. They were also to a large extent geographically coterminous.[59] The Klan drew support from communities of the same British and Ontarian character which supported the Orange Order.

The Protestant Protective Association and the Ku Klux Klan represented a much more narrowly defined extreme of protestant sentiment than did the Orange Order and as a consequence were unable to conjoin with the established pattern of political compromise found within Canada's parties. The order's great strength rested in its ability to provide an ideological and social focus at the community level while at the same time projecting its aspirations into party politics. Its success and longevity were determined by needs for a social ordering greater than that provided by churches and more direct than that provided by parties. The order, while apparently adapting to changing conditions, was at the same time constant, an essential bulwark to encircled protestants and a natural vehicle for their political influence.

Local politics: Toronto

The vigilance with which the order guarded against the advances of catholic power was as evident at the local level as it was in the provincial and federal areas. Throughout Canada, but especially in Ontario, New Brunswick, and Newfoundland, local councils had their complement of Orange mayors, reeves, aldermen, councillors, wardens, and trustees. Their position as office holders did not necessarily represent a polarization of catholic and protestant electoral support but merely implied the symbiotic relationship of Orange tenets and local community sentiments. Temperance and prohibition, sabbatarianism and a public good defined in terms of protestant morality, and an undercurrent of anti-catholicism characterized the tone of local affairs. That tone was steadfastly maintained by Orange administrators who otherwise conducted municipal business by accepted economic and administrative practices. There was no conflict between good administration and the nature of Orangeism. The Orangemen's contribution cannot be measured in terms of efficiency but in their injection of a particular tone and creation of an easily recognizable identity.

The image of Toronto was that of overriding Britishness and protestantism, qualities frequently commented upon by visitors. As historian D.C. Masters has written: 'All Torontonians, of course were not strict Protestant moralists, but there were enough of the type to fix the tone of the city. The constant insistence of a strict observance of Sunday was one indication of their attitude.'[60] For many citizens to be on the streets on the Sabbath, for reasons other than church-going, placed their souls or their social position in jeopardy, and whether or not streetcars would run on Sundays was a hot subject of public debate during the 1890s.[61] In this respect Toronto was a mirror image of Belfast blueness. The common epithets of 'Toronto the Good' and 'British Town on American Soil' were extended by most to include the 'Belfast of Canada'[62] and 'the bush metropolis of the Orange lodges.'[63] The conservative and ultra-protestant Orange society was an integral component of the city's flavour, or flavourlessness as many would say.

The Orange presence in the city had been noted as early as 1818 and within a few years the town council received its first Orange member. In 1844 six of Toronto's ten aldermen were members of the fraternity[64] and the first Orange mayor, W.H. Boulton, took office in the following year. During the rest of the nineteenth century twenty of Toronto's twenty-three mayors were Orange. The order was pervasive in the city and an examination of its various political and civic links around 1894 demonstrates its solidly entrenched position. An analysis of the city's elected representatives in that year reveals that the mayor and nine of twenty-four aldermen were members of the order. The nine identified Orange aldermen had acquired almost seventeen thousand votes,[65] obviously a lot more than the number of paid-up Orangemen in the city (about four thousand). The city's six wards had all returned at least one Orangeman to council and the Orange mayor, Warring Kennedy, who was elected on a city-wide constituency, polled 13,830 votes, 60 per cent of the total cast.[66] In his nomination speech Kennedy expressed the principles common to both his fraternity and the protestant city. 'We hold that the high moral tone of this city gives strength to our finances, it gives strength to our real estate properties, it gives strength to our government, it gives strength to our institutions, a high moral tone pervading all the city of Toronto. It is the finishing of our success, and it be that which will sustain her Majesty on Her Royal throne.'[67] Similarly, in the week before the election, Alderman Bailey at the annual general meeting of LOL 469 'spoke somewhat at length on the necessity of Protestants standing by one another to resist the encroachments of the Church of Rome in municipal matters, giving some instances where gross injustices in favour of Romanists had been discovered by him in civic management and promptly checked by his vigorous action. He urged on the Brethren the need to elect only Protestants as aldermen and to the Mayor's chair.'[68] As might be expected, the election was not fought on an Orange platform but on the common issue of tax reduction, and in council the Orange aldermen did not consistently operate as a voting block. Nevertheless, the lodges did provide a nucleus of candidates, basic electoral support, and a forum from which campaigns could be launched. As historian G.P. de T.

Glazebrook has noted 'no doubt exists that the Orange Order was a very powerful force.'[69]

The Orange aldermen were representative of a wide range of economic interests. Only their fraternity and its concomitant protestant and loyalist ideology were common to all. Edward Hewitt of ward 2 was a builder. John Shaw, a lawyer from ward 3, sat for a total of seventeen years on city council, acting as mayor from 1897 to 1899 and as a city controller in 1904–5. Later in 1908 he was elected MPP for North Toronto. Thomas Crawford of ward 5 was a cattle dealer and aldermanic partner of John Bailey, deputy master of the Toronto County lodge. Bailey, Hewitt, and Shaw, nicknamed 'the gang' by John Ross Robertson's *Evening Telegram*, formed a triumvirate that controlled the council. The mayor, Warring Kennedy, was a member of Temperance LOL 301 and former president of the Irish Protestant Benevolent Society. Born in Ulster he had emigrated to Canada in 1857 where, ten years later, he and two partners formed a wholesale dry goods firm which by 1879 had an annual turnover of one million dollars.[70] Kennedy was a Methodist lay preacher and at various times a director of such diverse interests as the Upper Canada Bible Society, the Necropolis, the House of Industry, the Saskatchewan Land and Homestead Company, and the Real Estate Loan and Debenture Company.

The political strength of the order was also reflected in the civic administration where many departments were directed by Orangemen. The city solicitor, the treasurer, deputy treasurer, and the commissioner, the most powerful officers in the civic administration, were all members of the order. Consolidation of this power had been progressing through the previous half century and had not gone unnoticed by the public press and other non-Orange figures. The Liberal *Globe*, commented in 1893: 'The most important service accomplished by Mayor Fleming during his tenure of office, however, is in the breaking of secret society influence at City Hall. This has long been recognised as a prolific source of bad government and too many of the chief executive offices have been filled with the nominees of the lodges, who in their turn nominated as their subordinates, at the request of the aldermen, members of some secret order.'[71] The claim of breaking the Orange control of patronage was premature. Mayor Fleming's tenure was only an interlude and Orange power continued to be manifested in the city until after the Second World War.

From this position of power, patronage was distributed among the Orange rank and file. In the 1894 Orange register, twelve men gave the city hall as their address, but the Orange component at all levels in city hall was much greater. The Toronto *Evening Telegram* on the occasion of the 1893 July parade reported in rhyme

> Like the temple of old Egypt
> Empty as a noxious mine
> Stood the City Hall deserted
> For 'the byes' were all in line.[72]

Many in the police force were Orangemen and such was also the case for the fire department. In the 1894 register, four members of LOL 207 gave their address as the Parkdale fire station and in LOL 781 eleven members were firemen. Patronage probably also extended into the school system where five of the twelve trustees elected in 1894 came from the ranks of the order as did the superintendent and then Orange grand master of Ontario West, James L. Hughes. In such critical administrations under Orange guidance there was ample scope for preferred treatment towards members of the fraternity.

The Orange strength in the municipal administration had been engineered over many years and in turn provided federal and provincial Conservative parties with experienced members. Emerson Coatsworth, Conservative MP for Toronto East in 1894, was a member of LOL 781 as were his brother and his father, the Toronto city commissioner. Coatsworth served as MP from 1891 to 1896 when, because of his support of the Conservatives' remedial legislation for Manitoba's school policy, he was defeated by a fellow Conservative and Orangeman, John Ross Robertson. However, in 1906 Coatsworth was elected mayor of the city. He ended his career as a Conservative political appointee on Ontario's Board of Licensing Commissioners which at the time was bent on reducing the number of licensed taverns in Toronto. E.F. Clarke, former mayor of Toronto, completed his term as Conservative MPP in 1894. In that year he was also the deputy Orange grand master and the editor of the *Sentinel*. In the Conservative electoral debacle of 1896 he was elected to the federal parliament from Toronto West. During the 1894 provincial elections Orangeman and Toronto alderman Thomas Crawford successfully carried the tory banner in Toronto West and another Orangeman, George Ryerson, MD and professor at Trinity College, was successful in Toronto East. Ryerson, however, had run for the extreme Protestant Protective Association not the Conservatives, and although not supported by the Orange hierarchy he did receive considerable sympathy from the rank and file. The mid 1890s were not exceptional in the history of Orange Toronto and for another half century the order would continue to hold sway in the municipal administration.

8

The Collapse

Since the Second World War the bang of the Lambeg drum and lines of marching men draped in Orange sashes have been much less evident. The annual parades still occur but they tend to be smaller and cover a shorter route out of respect for both traffic regulations and an aging membership. The 1977 parade in Toronto received no prior publicity in the newspapers and attracted little interest. Only a few hundred people watched it depart from the grounds of the parliament building, even fewer awaited its arrival in Bellwoods Park. The *Toronto Star* in an article the following Monday referred to the event as a relic from the past.[1] Compared with other annual parades in the city, for example, the million-dollar Santa Claus extravaganza sponsored by Eaton's department store and the Caribana festival staged by West Indian immigrants, the Orange is an unpolished and feeble spectacle. Unlike its earlier days it stimulates few passions, incites no riots, no buildings along the parade route are bedecked with Orange bunting, and the Union Jack is rarely seen. The parade is largely ignored. The demise of this annual event has been rapid; even as late as the 1950s it was an important occasion in the city's social calendar. Today Orangeism, not only in Toronto but in most places in Canada, is a peripheral movement restricted to a minority of aging participants and incomprehensible to most observers. Few under twenty years of age are even aware of the symbolic meaning of the Twelfth or know of the battle of the Boyne. To the thousands of new Canadians the term 'Orange parade' is more likely to conjure up images of a citrus fruit festival, not the triumph of British protestantism over catholicism. Falling membership, a diminishing number of lodges, and weakened representation in municipal and parliamentary politics illustrate the reality of decline.

Attrition

The order reached its peak about 1920 and since then there has been a steady reduction in the number of lodges. There were over two thousand active lodges in Canada and Newfoundland at the end of the First World War but by 1970 that figure had fallen to less than one-half (figure 19). The precipitous decline of the order during the twentieth century mirrored its rapid rise in the nineteenth. Ontario, always the major Orange province, had reached a plateau in its own development by 1870 and a subsequent increase in its complement of lodges around the time of the First World War was stimulated by developments in Toronto and in the northern resource centres. The rapid acceleration in the Canadian total after confederation had been a product of territorial inclusion and demographic expansion. Since 1920 decline has been gradual. The virtual disappearance of lodges in the western provinces since 1930 has exaggerated the rapidity of the national collapse. In Ontario the loss in numbers of lodges has been steady and somewhat more gradual than the national trend. Of all the provinces only Newfoundland has avoided the twentieth-century forces of attrition. There, the position attained by 1920 remains relatively unchanged. Overall, the patterns of diminishing strength imply the inevitable extinction of the order in Canada.

The number of Orangemen has been declining at a time when the Canadian population has been rising rapidly. The national population has more than doubled during the past half century and the contemporary numerical decline of Orangemen has relegated them to a very insignificant component. Heavy immigration has contributed to the high rate of population growth, but the fact that immigrants have been drawn increasingly from non-protestant areas outside of the British Isles has reduced the recruitment potential of the order. In 1901 almost 60 per cent of Canadians claimed the British Isles as their origin and by 1921 the percentage was 55. Every census since 1931 has recorded a relative decline in the number of persons of British background. In 1971 this group constituted only 45 per cent of the total population. A high birth rate in Quebec (at least until 1960), growing immigration from southern and eastern Europe, and more recently from Asia and the Caribbean have been responsible for the altered British position. In 1970, out of a total of 147,713 immigrants to Canada, only 26,497 were from Britain, and of those a mere 1,620 from Ulster.[2] The ongoing process of cultural change in Canada reflected in the changing demographic character of the country has weakened the base of the order, and without the infusion of sympathetic immigrants it has been unable to renew itself. One of the few positive benefits which the order gained from the new wave of immi-

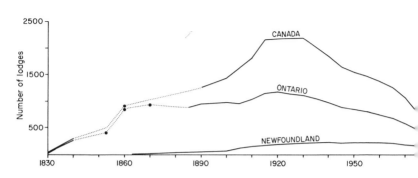

Figure 19. Number of lodges in Canada (including Newfoundland), Ontario, and Newfoundland, 1830–1975

grants was the creation in 1930 of the Giuseppe Garibaldi lodge in Toronto. It was formed by, and catered to, members of the small protestant Italian community and among that group it still functions today.

The relationship between the order's development and population growth is well illustrated by the example of Toronto (figure 20). The general association between population and number of lodges during the nineteenth century, apparent in the graph, reflects the coincidental growth of the city and Orangeism. Until 1860 the pattern was extremely close but in the last forty years of the century a growing deviation between the two variables is evident. However, this dichotomy cannot be interpreted as a weakening relationship. Although the number of lodges did not keep pace with population growth, increases in average lodge size were such that the number of Orangemen in the city relative to the total protestant population was the same at the end of the century as it had been in the middle. In 1857, some 1,165 members were distributed among twenty-two lodges and in 1894 the fifty-six lodges had a registered membership of some 4,000 men.[3] The average membership had increased from fifty-three to seventy-two and the ratio of Orangemen to protestants in the city had barely changed. During the twentieth century the growth of the city was not matched by comparable Orange vitality. As the century progressed the stagnation and eventual post-1940 fall of the order contrasts markedly with development of the metropolitan centre. As Toronto became a more cosmopolitan place the position of the order became untenable and its power base in the city was undercut.

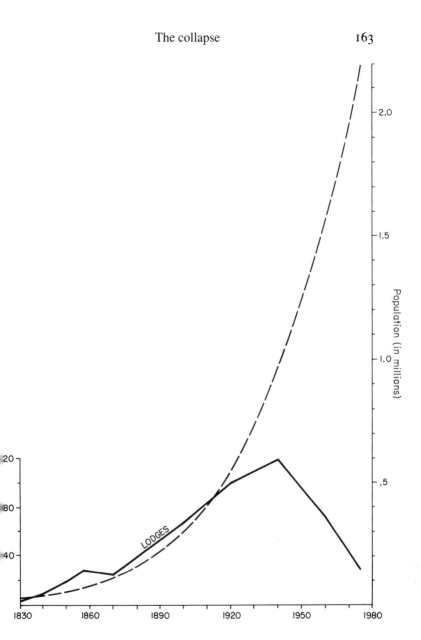

Figure 20. Orange lodges and population, Toronto, 1830–1976 (territory of Metropolitan Toronto in 1976)

Geographical retraction

Just as growth of the order had been marked by territorial spread so has its decline been reflected in geographical contraction. Throughout the history of Canadian Orangeism, Ontario, the heartland, has retained at least half of all the lodges. New Brunswick can rival the central province in terms of the longevity and strength of its Orange traditions, but Ontario's population size gave it a much larger number of lodges. At the peak of the order's strength in the 1920s Ontario had 54 per cent of the lodges (table 12), Saskatchewan followed with almost 10, and Newfoundland was third with almost 9. New Brunswick had less than 7 per cent of the lodges in the country. By 1970 the pattern had altered dramatically. Ontario retained its share of a diminishing number of lodges but Newfoundland with almost 20 per cent of the national total ranked second. New Brunswick was in third place but Saskatchewan had dropped almost to the bottom. Although British Columbia was unchanged in its percentage, there and in the other provinces the order was virtually obliterated. The few lodges still operating in the west were confined primarily to the larger urban centres where there remained enough local supporters to maintain a lodge. In those regions Orangeism is today a total irrelevancy in cultural and political affairs. Nova Scotia's Orange lodges also have almost disappeared. In that province the order's bases in the industrial and mining regions of Springhill, Pictou County, and northeast Cape Breton have been undermined by economic stagnation and out-migration. In Prince Edward Island the order is insignificant and its lodges are relic features in the cultural landscape.

The present strength of Orangeism rests essentially in three provinces. Ontario and New Brunswick had been the original centres of the British North American order and in their case the order has apparently folded in on itself and retracted to its original cores. In Newfoundland, on the other hand, Orangeism is little more than a century old and within that socially conservative society modernization has been retarded and diminution of Orange strength consequently restricted. Religious divisions are still significant in the Atlantic province and in its isolated outports there are few forms of social recreation capable of competing with the order. The lodge hall still functions as a local community centre and the Monday closest to 12 July remains a provincial holiday (Orangemen's Day). Newfoundland is certainly the most vibrant Orange province. The number of lodges operating on the island in 1970 was actually four more than in 1920, a period when declines of 50 per cent or more were registered in all other provinces. Newfoundland may within a decade or so become the largest Orange jurisdiction in the country. However, the current rapid rate

TABLE 12
Percentage distribution of Orange lodges,
1920 and 1970

Province	1920	1970
Newfoundland	8.7	18.8
Prince Edward Island	1.9	1.7
Nova Scotia	3.6	2.7
New Brunswick	6.5	8.2
Quebec	3.0	4.0
Ontario	54.0	55.0
Manitoba	6.2	3.7
Saskatchewan	9.6	1.9
Alberta	3.9	1.4
British Columbia	2.6	2.6

SOURCES: Provincial grand lodge reports,
1920 and 1970.

of modernization on the island contains within it for the order a promise of impending disaster.

The national pattern of geographical retreat is expressed similarly within the province of Ontario. Retention has been highest in those areas which had the greatest density of lodges in the nineteenth century. Toronto's twenty-nine lodges still form the greatest concentration outside of Ulster but the real expression of Orangeism in Ontario today lies in three distinctive residual rural cores (figure 21). South of Ottawa, in Leeds, Lanark, and Carleton counties, an initial heartland of the order in eastern Ontario, there is a pronounced cluster of lodges from which a thin line extends eastwards towards Quebec in an interpenetration of local French districts. The other strong concentration of lodges in eastern Ontario is in Hastings and Peterborough counties where among the small decaying villages the lodge still performs an important role for older residents. Kingston, once an important Orange stronghold and formerly titled 'the Derry of Canada,' now has only one lodge. On the other hand western Ontario still retains a belt of lodges stretching northwest from Toronto towards the Bruce Peninsula and embracing Grey, Dufferin, and Simcoe counties in particular. Elsewhere in the province lodges are sporadic. The strength of Ontarian Orangeism rests on farming communities and in particular upon people born between the two world wars. In many instances the hall is maintained by no more than half a dozen members, and although it may be rented to a wider public for euchre parties and bingo the ultimate function of the building is understood by few under twenty years of age. Perhaps no more significant index of the cultural and social transformation of the province can be found than this

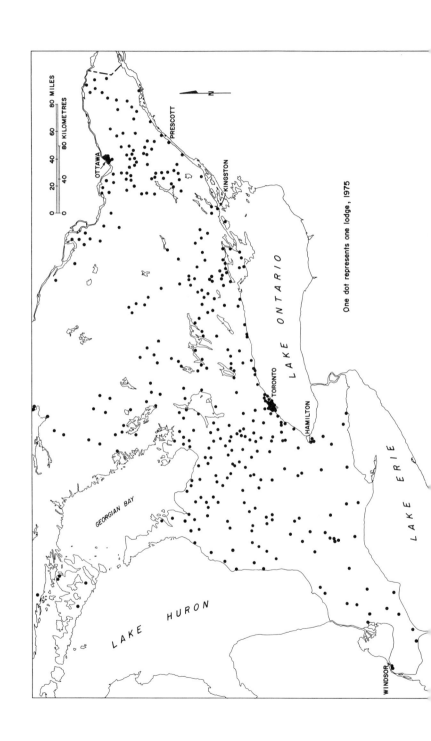

One dot represents one lodge, 1975

age-related ignorance of the role which the Orange lodge and its members formerly played in the community.

Orangeism had established its initial strength in Ontario and New Brunswick, and it is perhaps indicative of some fundamental qualities in those provinces that they, along with Newfoundland, remain as core areas. However the order cannot hope to sustain strength for much longer in Ontario. The forces of change are strong in that province, even in rural areas, and the aging membership, infrequent attendance at lodge meetings, and the deteriorating structures of the halls themselves clearly articulate the process of decay. With the general attrition of the order Orangemen have become a minuscule and aging minority within Canadian society.

There are now fewer than twenty thousand active members in the country and their average age cannot be less than fifty years. Proof of that is to be found in the faces of those who attend lodge meetings and march in the Twelfth, as well as in growing lists of death notices published in the *Sentinel* and grand lodge proceedings. This membership is a clear testimony to the order's failure to attract young recruits in the past twenty years. Deprived of much significant sustenance from the young the order must rely on men, the bulk of whom joined no later than the late 1940s. It is a decaying institution. The process of decay has been protracted because of the consistent efforts and support of the older group, but it has reached the stage where the decline in membership is exponential. The growth of cities and out-migration from rural areas have undermined the demographic basis of the order by contributing to the aging of rural communities. Many small hamlets have virtually disappeared, others have become ex-urbanite and commuter centres – communities which are usually young, educated, ethnically mixed, and without attachment to the local rural traditions. It might be argued, therefore, that just as the order's growth provides a surrogate for the spread of settlement in nineteenth century protestant Canada so also does its decline reflect the changed components of the twentieth century rural community.

The decline of the order is evident in the landscape. Former Orange halls now provide premises for antique stores, summer cottages, and local museums in many small towns. Others are simply abandoned, their rotting structures standing at now remote intersections testifying to the former existence of a rural community. Rural churches and schools likewise have suffered as a result of depopulation and the more general pattern of rural decay. In some of the declining areas the local Orange lodge has taken over the relic schoolhouse or church, the structure of these buildings being usually superior to that of the old Orange hall. Orange relics can also be found by the careful observer in graveyards.

Former Orange hall, Rockport, New Brunswick (Photograph by D. Holdsworth)

Twelfth of July parade, Bayfield, Ontario, 1977

Derelict rural halls and poorly attended parades testify to the changed fortunes of Orangeism in Canada.

Lodge symbols or the figure of King William riding a horse may be found engraved on some tombstones. In death as in life, the symbol of the defeat of James II was important. King William representing the defence of the British crown and protestant Bible was the inspiration of an institution whose landscape legacy affirms the former Orange identity of many localities.

Causes of decline

Orangeism grew in Canada because of two factors. It provided in an adequate manner a social and, to some extent, religious focus for community development. Secondly, it developed as part of widely held colonial sentiments of protestantism and Britishness and their corollaries, anti-catholicism and distrust of republicanism. Orangeism was a garrison of unswerving principles, a defender of the foundations of the state, and as such became more British and more protestant than the state itself. The twentieth century unfolded in Canada with the order riding the crest of the waves of imperial fervour sweeping the country. For Canada the First World War was a catalyst; for the order it was confirmation of its role as a garrison. The country not the order had begun to change and in that drift lay the roots of the eventual decline of the order. The holocaust of war and the growing sense of useless sacrifice had by 1918 instilled in many Canadians a resentment towards the nature of their imperial duties.[4] In addition, their ability to meet the challenge of war and acquit themselves on foreign battlefields had stimulated a new sense of Canadian nationalism. The paradox of imperialist sentiment that desired both a strong Canada and close imperial ties was being rejected in favour of a new arrangement of less pronounced colonial dependence. Within the growing sense of national assurance and weakening colonialism the order was anachronistic. It could not adjust because that would have required rejection of its basic principles and it would be unable to survive as a garrison in a community that no longer had a place for its vigilance.

The order did not acquiesce easily in the changing national condition and its reactions were voiced frequently and forcefully. The loss of British character was deplored and blame attributed to catholics, foreign immigrants, and a new enemy, communists. The provincial grand lodge of Ontario East in 1931 praised 'Premier Bennett and his cabinet in regard to having no truck or trade with Bolshevik Russia,' but they demanded that the national government do more.

Search out the agitators of Bolshevism. If they are foreigners or even naturalized citizens, cancel their Canadian citizenship and send them home. To the Governors of our Universities and leaders of our Canadian Churches, we might suggest that you search out professors and clergymen from our own Canadian-born College graduates, examine their records carefully, and especially examine the Faith and records of men from other lands, and not run so great a risk as that of having the minds of our youth warped and twisted by churches poisoned with modernism and colleges polluted with Atheism and un-belief.[5]

Much of their fear of communism grew out of the resentment of the increasingly non-British character of immigration. 'Canada needs more British,' argued the *Sentinel*, and active encouragement of immigration from Britain was a policy of the order. 'We backed our belief by voting $8,000 from our meagre finances and have done more than any other organization of like numbers in encouraging the placement of British youths in Canada and in educating our governments and transportation systems as to the practicability of our plan and our ability to utilize the machinery of our Association in a practical and effective manner.'[6] The order responded to the Canadianization of the national symbols in a similar vein. It denounced attempts to replace the Union Jack with a distinctive Canadian flag and similarly opposed the changing of the national anthem from God Save the Queen, to 'O Canada' which some considered to be a 'Roman Catholic Religious Hymn.'[7] In 1960 the grand master of Ontario East exhorted,

Brethren, we must stand fast for these great symbols of freedom and justice, and let us in whatever capacity that may be ours, see to it that these ties are not broken or destroyed, but rather strengthened and maintained. We note also, at this time, that the appointment of a new Governor General, within the last year, was made not from Britain but for the second time from Canada and for the first time in the long history of our Country, a member of the Roman Catholic faith. This by a Government from which we did not expect such action, and under protest from our Orange Association. These things show how alert and vigilant we must be at all times if we would maintain a true democracy and preserve our way of life.[8]

The weakening of the imperial links as Canada moved 'from colony to nation'[9] was a blow to one of the order's basic tenets.

Growing secularization and a decline in church going struck at the other keystone. A secular organization dedicated to observing and obstructing Catholic advances had little appeal for the young men of the post Second World War period. Disinterest in the order was for some an expression of their general lack of interest in religion; for others, a growing mood of ecumenism had pushed Orangeism out of the field of religious debate. By the second half of the twentieth century the union of

Former Western District Orange hall, Euclid Avenue and College Street, Toronto. This hall, built during the peak of Orangeism in the early twentieth century, is now an Italian Dance Club in the middle of Little Italy. (Photograph 1977)

religion and politics had clearly been broken, and within the new social and political reality there was little scope for the operation of a die-hard politico-religious fraternity. Decolonization and secularization of Canadian society were but two manifestations of a greater process of cultural change. Northrop Frye has argued that it was only from the late 1920s that Ontario began to develop an identity in art and literature.[10] He described nineteenth-century southern Ontario as 'one of the most brutally inarticulate societies the world has ever known,'[11] characterized by emotionalism and rhetoric. The processes of change which led to the creation of excitingly new Canadian art were reflections of a new certainty in public affairs. Frye's assessment of the timing and nature of cultural change might do much to explain the demise of the Orange Order's emotional appeal.

The convivial possibilities which lodge membership provided became increasingly anachronistic during the twentieth century. Fundamental changes in attitudes to alcohol, camaraderie, and institutionalized occasions drew young people away from the set formality of the lodge. Recreational patterns in the nineteenth century offered little variety; lodge meetings were one of few alternatives for social enjoyment beyond the home and church. As the twentieth century progressed new media had profound effects. Commercial replacements for community and family forms of recreation allowed alternatives to the local and narrowly confined forms of socializing. The dance halls, bars, movies, and professional spectator sports deflected interest from fraternalism. Domestic entertainment provided by phonographs, radios, and later televisions offered a passive form of recreation obviating against lodge attendance. Their effects were felt not just by the Orange Order but by Freemasonry and Oddfellowship. For Canadians, the convergence of secularism, a mood of national confidence, and a vastly increased range of recreational activities undermined the raison d'être for Orange membership.

Its decline was hastened by the obsolescence of the self-help function and economic crisis. The depression of the 1930s dealt a severe blow to the order and nowhere were the detrimental effects more evident than in Saskatchewan where from 1930 to 1940 the number of lodges declined by 30 per cent. Nationally, the number of lodges fell by 15 per cent in the same period. In the prairie province the fabric of society was rent by the severity of the agricultural depression and many small centres disappeared in the consequent outflow of migrants. The process of resettlement continued into the early 1950s by which time the number of lodges was only one-quarter of the 1930 total. The patterns evident in Saskatchewan were only an exaggeration of those found throughout rural Canada. During the depression local lodges were called upon increasingly to make benevolence payments at a time when members, finding it difficult to pay the monthly dues, were withdrawing. Many lodges carried the unemployed on their books free of charge for months, but as the crisis deepened and the lodge coffers were emptied, some lodges were forced to close. Most lodges lost considerable proportions of their members in this period of difficulty. Even when the depression ended, however, the lodges did not recover. One of the national consequences of the 1930s was the growing degree of state intervention and assistance in most crises of life, for example sickness, unemployment, and death, and as a result all fraternal societies lost important elements in their social functions.

Metropolitanization and suburbanization also contributed to deterioration of the order. In a city such as Toronto the order had depended upon local in-migrants and the sons of Torontonians, but those sources of recruitment were progressively cut off. After the Second World War international migration fuelled the growth of Toronto, and few of the insignificant numbers of local in-migrants were interested in Orangeism. The sons of Toronto Orangemen also failed to join. Their neglect of the order was precipitated by the suburban extension of Toronto society. Many Toronto Orangemen left the order during the 1950s and 1960s upon moving from the city to the suburbs, and the order, already weakened, was unable to accommodate the movement by creating suburban lodges. Only east Toronto, least affected by the process, retained a large number of Orangemen into the 1970s. It may also be argued that inherent in the suburban movement was a weakening of community bonds. Suburban neighbours had no need for local community organizations such as the Orange lodge which presupposed a particular social, religious, and political conformity. A comparable fracturing of traditional social networks has had an adverse effect on lodge membership in rural areas. On practical and ideological grounds the Orange Order now appears redundant to Canadians, including sons of previously Orange families.

The Orange Order in the 1970s

Today the order has few members among elected politicians. A few members of the order do hold seats in the Ontario, Newfoundland, and federal parliaments but they have little weight. Of those parliamentary figures the most colourful is certainly the irascible Leonard Jones, MP for Moncton, New Brunswick. William Dennison, the last Orange mayor of Toronto, retired in 1972 and there is currently only one Orangeman on the Toronto city council.[12] Generally, Orange votes are still cast for the Conservative party but an unofficial entente with the order no longer exists. Many other Orangemen in large cities cast their vote for the socialist New Democratic party. Only at the level of local politics in a few scattered places does the order retain political power of any significance.

Recently, through the monthly *Sentinel*, grand lodge addresses, and occasionally letters to the press, the order has been making known its position on such issues as immigration, bilingualism, and the ever present criticism of the monarchy. The order was one of the public groups from whom the minister of manpower and immigration solicited a statement for the preparation of the government's Green Paper on Immigration in 1974. The grand master, the Reverend C.K.S. Moffatt, submitted a brief in which he argued that an immigrant quota system should not be established, but 'the preferred countries of origins, we believe, should be the United Kingdom, the Commonwealth, the United States, the northern European nations, and other countries whose way of life is essentially similar to ours and who have proven to be the source of smooth, successful immigration.'[13] It was argued that it would be wrong to implement an immigration program which would 'change the composition and characteristics of the nation as it now exists' and it was particularly emphasized that Canada should not become a haven for immigrants from Third World countries or 'international criminals, drug traffickers, revolutionaries and other undesirables' – the latter categories referring to the earlier influx of American draft evaders.[14]

More recently, a *Sentinel* editorial by Norman Ritchie, the grand secretary of British America, reiterated the fear that the Anglo-Saxon stock in Canada was being relegated to the status of just another ethnic minority. 'We believe the time is right for all like-minded persons and organizations which are patriotic, law-abiding, loyalist in sentiment, and supporting such institutions as the Monarchy, to come together as an united people ... [to] speak as one voice in the defence of our Canadian-British Heritage and Culture.'[15] Although the order has shown considerable intransigence towards non-Anglo-Saxon immigrants it has recently demonstrated a slightly more flexible attitude on the issue of the French language. In 1974 Grand Master Moffatt rejected the national policy of bilingualism arguing that 'Canada is not only English speaking theoretically and legally, but it is so in practice as well.'[16] However, in the 1977 address to the grand lodge by Grand Master Reside it was acknowledged that although the order disagreed with the official policy of bilingualism, some concessions should be made to French language speakers outside Quebec. Objections to bilingualism were phrased in terms of the program's impracticality; no opposition was offered on ideological grounds. In a set of counter proposals the order suggested government services be made available in both languages where required and that the provinces undertake a concerted effort 'to improve the teaching of the second language in all school systems.'[17] Neither proposal offered any real challenge to government policy and it might be suggested that the order's willingness to compromise on this issue was a pragmatic reaction to the fear that Quebec would separate from Canada. This latest statement on national unity represents the only major ideological concession made by the order during its century and a half in Canada.

The concession acknowledges the order's realization of its own weakness in modern Canada. To improve its position, a campaign to attract new members to the lodges was carried out through protestant church newspapers in 1977. Advertisements parodying a familiar slogan of Canadian Pacific Airlines announced that 'Orange is more than beautiful.' Interestingly, in those advertisements the Christian, fraternal, and insurance functions of the order were stressed heavily and little space was given to the Orangemen's political role. An article in the Toronto *Globe and Mail* referred to the Orange advertisement under a headline 'Once-mighty Orange Order advertises for new recruits'[18] and summarized thereby the present state of the organization.

Among many older Orangemen willingness to compromise the basic tenets of the order is less evident. Bigotry is still expressed by this legion of the rearguard. Nowhere was this more clearly illustrated than in Cavan Township, Ontario, during the summer of 1977. National headlines recorded the refusal of the local municipal council to grant a land rezoning application by Cistercian monks from Oka, Quebec, wishing to establish a monastery in the township. One of the councillors was quoted as saying 'Cavan is a Protestant township and it shall stay like this.'[19] The area had been settled originally around 1820 by protestant Irish and among its present population of thirty-seven hundred, there are fewer than fifty catholics. The township never had a Roman Catholic church in its history and no catholic has ever sat on the local council.[20] In many ways the township represents a unique relic of a society in which Orange-ism had been able to flourish for more than a century.

The present irrelevance of Orangeism may be inferred from a recent retirement notice which appeared in the *Globe and Mail* for the order's last important Toronto politician, Leslie H. Saunders, former grand master of British America.

In earlier years, his career as a municipal politician was marked by headlines prompted by his strong views about the Catholic Church, the French language and liquor. He says that if these headlines have become less frequent it is not because he has changed his Protestant, pro-British, pro-temperance views but because the newspapers have become less vicious and some of the issues are 'dead as dodos.'[21]

Conclusions

For one hundred and fifty years the Orange Order was part of Canada. It contributed to a sense of loyalism, sustained a particularly protestant viewpoint, and coloured political life in the country. The order is no longer acceptable, however, and its collapse, although protracted, has been inevitable. A group, which was once known by almost all Canadians, now elicits a response from only a handful of the older generation. It is remarkable that the Ulster-born secret society took root, spread so far, and persisted for so long in the new country. Canada was home to an organization which, by definition, was the embodiment of outmoded tradition, and the success of the order there raises questions not only about Orangeism itself but also about the communities and nation into which it was inserted.

It is difficult to find another secular organization as successfully implanted in the New World as was the Orange Order. The Masons and Oddfellows are the only comparable examples, but the success of these organizations in Canada postdated that of the Orange. Also, the ideals of those fraternities stressed self-help and mutual aid, universal values whose appeal was not couched in ethnic terms. There were, however, numerous voluntary associations and societies clearly identified by ethnic group interests. Through affiliation with them, members maintained a semblance of a familiar Old World atmosphere and occasionally, in times of distress, financial aid. They were created to solve New World problems, and not simply to maintain intact the full compendium of Old World values. Ultimately they were creations of the American side, not transfers from Europe. In this important respect most ethnic societies in America differ from the Orange. The order differs further from them in that, although initially a creation and transfer of protestant Irish immigrants, it rapidly transcended its ethnic base. It was not a mere social refuge for nostalgic emigrants. The success of the order arose from the wide appeal of its principles. The ideals of protestantism and loyalism were not peculiar in a country whose existence was underwritten by those same values.

Although Orangeism's arrival in the country was inauspicious, from 1815 its advance was sure. In the first years of the 1800s, in a few army garrisons, Orange militiamen held cordial gatherings whose intent was no more than to remember the Irish events of 1798 or rekindle the memories of an Irish townland or village. Its success was ensured by the subsequent immigrant droves from Ireland, whose mentality and views were imbued with those of Orangeism. They carried the Orange principles to the lumber camps of the Saint John River valley. They carried them up the St Lawrence to the ports of Montreal and Brockville and into the territories behind, and they carried them up the Ottawa River to the Pontiac. The garrison mentality of protestant Ireland was transferred to Canada where it flourished in colonies perceived to be threatened by French Canadian catholicism and American republicanism. It was the Orangeman's self-imposed duty to ensure that the destiny of the new colony would develop along lines unmistakably protestant and British. The order would present itself as a sentinel on a protestant frontier watching over and directing the ideological foundations and colonial inheritance of the country.

Development of the organization proceeded from two hearths, New Brunswick and Ontario, separated by the intervening space of Catholic Quecbec. Ontario was unquestionably the more important for it was there that the order was given a constituted form and it was from there that the organization was directed. That Ontario should have been the greater core of the fraternity is easily understood – its population was much larger, its Irishness greater, and its protestantism more complete. The maritime province was nevertheless important, for the New Brunswick wing of the order, in its functions, its social importance, and in its rise and fall, mirrored its Ontario counterpart. The fact of two hearths is a consequence of geography and not the reflection of ideological differences. In the order's march across the country, the mode of observance of the tradition may have been altered slightly from place to place in response to local conditions, but the principles were unchanged.

The order's development was spontaneous, a fact reflected well by the simultaneous advance of the fraternity and the settlement frontier. Lodges, established in the Irish immigrant districts along the St Lawrence and north shore of Lake Ontario during the 1820s, were among the first in the country, and when a centralized administration was formed at Brock-ville in 1830, they were among the first incorporated within the new organization. The first steps of the order were into the known Irish districts in the bush and in the larger towns. In subsequent decades the order continued to spread into the new farm settlement regions of Ontario, into the lumbering and mining centres of the Canadian Shield and across the Great Lakes to the Ontarian cores of the prairie lands. Similarly, expansion of the order had proceeded from New Brunswick eastward into Nova Scotia and Prince Edward Island. Later, the addition of Newfoundland completed the order's Atlantic realm. The pace and scale of the advance, its completeness, and its coincidence with new settlement could not have been orchestrated other than through a spontaneous and mass movement of committed supporters. There had been no more than a handful of Orange missionaries seeking out communities which might accept the tenets, but there had been tens of thousands of ordinary Orangemen, of whom some three thousand had taken the requisite steps to obtain a warrant and establish a lodge.

By the end of the First World War the land frontier of the nation had been achieved and strung along it a line of Orange garrisons – 'protestant fortresses from which have been fired the red hot Gospel truth.'[1] From the exposed outports of Newfoundland, through the mining and farming communities of maritime and central Canada, the railway hamlets of the prairies, and the isolated mining towns of British Columbia, Orangemen were known. Together, they constituted a representative sample of the English-speaking population of Canada. Irishness defined the core of the group nationally, but the importance of that identity had waned within the organization from the 1850s. Irish immigration by then had declined significantly and, besides, native-born Canadians of Irish, English, Scottish, and mixed ethnic descent, as well as Indians, were taking their place in the organization. Later in the century, the addition of a group of German descent from Lunenburg and a few other localities practically completed within the order the full range of Canadian protestantism. The order by no means incorporated all protestant adult males within its fold but it had appealed to at least one-third of them.

The ethnic variety within the order from the mid-nineteenth century onwards was clear proof that the fraternity no longer functioned as an immigrant institution. Because of that, it becomes difficult to treat the order within the contex of ideas already developed on the nature and role of voluntary immigrant associations. Models of ethnic assimilation and acculturation are inappropriate to a group which quickly had assumed a place in the mainstream of Canadian society. Likewise, it is difficult to examine the order's social composition only in terms of class divisions. The range of social classes and occupational groups within the membership of any one region and also the range of regional economic identities exemplified within the order's realm, preclude any inference that Orangeism was a homogeneous movement. The only identification was provided by those two principles of protestantism and loyalism which each member swore to maintain.

The fraternity attracted men from many walks of life and was to a large extent socially egalitarian. In the rural lodges farmers mixed with the local merchants, clergy, teachers, and others from the community. Among the outport lodges of Newfoundland, fishermen mingled with the clergymen and teachers. Any adult male protestant able to provide the small membership dues was eligible. The destitute rung of protestant Canada was thus excluded and for other reasons the upper elite excluded itself. The rungs in between, which encompassed the working and middle classes of Canada, the mass of Canadians, were represented by the Orange Order. Recruits were selected with respect to neither class nor ethnicity. The degree of religious commitment and orthodoxy was small and recognized no denominational divisions. The order showed little concern for the form and fitness normally demanded by the churches. A belief in basic Christian principles, a standard of public respectability, was all that was required. Commitment to the British and monarchical link was expected, a distrust of catholicism assumed. In colonial Canada, the philosophy of Orangemen was the comfortable adjunct of a pervasive mood.

The order was unquestionably attractive. Canadians were drawn to it by its internal functions and its perceived external role. Internally, the order offered its members a form of social recreation, opportunities for conviviality, and fraternalism in an era when few alternatives to family and church-centred activities existed. Meeting at lodge and walking on the Twelfth were escapes from the mundane. The charitable functions of the order reinforced among its members their sense of neighbourliness and solidarity. It tended to weld them into a community which was at once local yet operated at the level of province, nation, and empire. The order was the institutional social focus for many who believed that protestantism and loyalty to the crown underlay the very destiny of the country. Those two values were fundamental, in essence beyond politics and partisan behaviour, but in practice, crises, both real and imagined, drew Orangeism into Canadian politics at all levels.

Orangeism's ideological interpretation of the politico-religious nature of society was reminiscent of the pre-Enlightenment eighteenth century. It would, however, be too simple to argue that its decline during the past fifty years was the inevitable outcome of the twentieth century catching up with Orangeism. Rather, it was a case of the twentieth century catching up with Canada, effecting changes which altered fundamentally the character of the country and destroying those colonial conditions which had given Orangeism a role in the New World. During the nineteenth century Orangeism had been an ideological constant in an era of unparalleled social and economic change; it faltered and eventually failed because it could not accommodate itself within the process of modernization in the twentieth.

Notes

AO   Archives of Ontario

GOLBA   Grand Orange Lodge of British America (Canadian grand lodge, 1868–)

GOLBNA Grand Orange Lodge of British North America (Canadian grand lodge 1830–67)

GOLCC   Provincial Grand Orange Lodge of Central Canada (Ontario, east of Durham County, 1860–8)

GOLOE   Provincial Grand Orange Lodge of Ontario East (Ontario, east of Durham County, 1869–)

GOLOW   Provincial Grand Orange Lodge of Ontario West (1882–)

GOLWC   Provincial Grand Orange Lodge of Western Canada (provincial grand lodge of western Ontario, 1860–7)

GOLWO   Provincial Grand Orange Lodge of Western Ontario (1868–81)

LOL   Loyal Orange Lodge

OA   Archives, Loyal Orange Association of British America

PAC   Public Archives of Canada

CHAPTER I

1 The basis for this assertion is presented in chapter 5.

2 Cited in Gowan, *Orangeism: its origin and history*, 191.

3 The qualifications essential for membership in the Canadian order, as given in the pamphlet *Orange: who needs it?* issued by the Grand Orange Lodge of British America in 1977, are:

(1) 'TOWARD GOD – An applicant for admission should have a sincere love and veneration for his Heavenly Father; a steadfast faith in Jesus Christ, as the only Mediator between God and man; and a firm reliance in the guiding,

witnessing, and sanctifying power of the Holy Spirit. He should be a diligent reader of God's Word, a sincere observer of the Lord's Day, and a regular attendant at His House; endeavouring to bring forth the practical fruits of righteousness and obedience to God's commands, as a humble and consistent servant of God and follower of his Saviour.'

(2) 'TOWARD QUEEN AND COUNTRY – He should be loyal in thought, word and act toward the Crown, being Protestant; seeking the prosperity and integrity of the Constitutional Monarchy; strengthening its concepts and supporting the principles which have been the foundation of the Dominion of Canada; ready to promote civil and religious liberty; to maintain the Protestant faith as the purest form of Christianity, and the basis of Constitutional Government of the people, by the people, for the people; and to foster unity and Godliness in Canada and throughout the Commonwealth.'

(3) 'TOWARD MANKIND – He should be of temperate and kindly habits, striving to be an example to others, as a true Christian citizen. He should abstain from swearing and profane language, from dishonesty and from intemperance of every kind. He should seek the welfare of others, be just, considerate and tolerant in his judgment, especially toward those who are opposed in faith and principles; ready to assist those who are needy or oppressed, and to promote the spirit of friendliness and brotherly love.' 'The Glory of God, the Welfare of Man, the Honour of his Sovereign, and the Good of his Country should be the motives of all his actions.'

4 With the exception of Kealey's 'The Orange Order in Toronto: religious riot and the working class' which in part examines the social composition of four Toronto lodges in the late nineteenth century, historians have confined their attention to the political activities of the Canadian order. Moir in *Church and state in Canada West*, 17, concluded that during the 1850s the order 're-mained basically a Tory political machine rather than a religious cult.' A somewhat similar assessment of pre-confederation Orangeism was suggested in Mood's pioneering thesis, 'The Orange Order in Canadian politics, 1841–1867.' The role of the order in one election campaign was examined by Livermore in 'The Orange Order and the election of 1861 in Kingston.' The political aspect of the fraternity has received most attention from Hereward Senior. In his book on the order in Ireland and his monograph and several articles on Canadian Orangeism, he has written from the perspective of a political historian, although he does indicate an awareness of the social dimension. See Senior, *Orangeism in Ireland and Britain, 1795–1836, Orangeism: the Canadian phase*, 'The genesis of Canadian Orangeism,' 'Ogle Gowan, Orangeism, and the immigrant question, 1830–1833,' 'Orangeism in Ontario politics, 1872–1896.'

5 Glazebrook, *Life in Ontario: a social history*, 65, noted that Orangemen 'have been more prominent in Canadian history for their political activities and battles rather than for their more peaceful and non-political activities.' In *The developing Canadian community*, S.D. Clark indicated that the early Orange lodges fulfilled an important social function in that 'they provided the one means of social intercourse familiar to the earlier settlers from overseas'

(p. 79). Similarly, A.R.M. Lower was conscious of a sense of community which typified Ulster areas in Ontario: 'Wherever the countryside is strongly Ulster and Orange, there will usually be an Anglican church in the community and a Tory member in Parliament' (*Colony to nation*, 195).

6 The Orange Order flourished in New Zealand and Australia. The United States also had their lodges and at one time or another lodges were established in India, Bermuda, Hong Kong, Bahama Islands, Cuba, Togo, and Ghana. An Orange parade of African lodges under the jurisdiction of the Ghana-Togo Grand Lodge took place in July 1979 (*Sentinel*, October 1979, 13).

7 Morton, 'Victorian Canada.'

8 Saunders, *The story of Orangeism*, 47.

9 This represents a new theme within the established field of cultural transfer and there is little in the North American literature to provide a model for such a study. Folklorists and cultural geographers who have dealt with themes of cultural transfer have produced a rich body of literature for groups in the United States. With the notable exceptions of the geographical works of A.H. Clark, R.C. Harris, and John Mannion little comparable work has been done on Canada (Clark, *Three centuries and the Island*, and 'Old World origins and religious adherence in Nova Scotia'; R.C. Harris, *The seigneurial system in early Canada*; and Mannion, *Irish settlements in eastern Canada: a study of cultural transfer and adaptation*). Even so, studies of cultural transfer have in general confined their attention to artifacts, not institutions and ideologies. They have concentrated upon elements that survive best in isolated and backward areas. In more accessible regions the transferred tools, field systems, house styles, and furniture quickly become anachronistic and yield to technological adjustments dictated by both economic realities and contact with other cultures. Yet much remains of a group's culture in the aftermath of technological conformity. Social ideals, values, and institutions persist long after the last Old World spade or plough has been abandoned.

10 In exasperation with the genre of Canadian cultural enquiry the historian Ramsay Cook exclaimed in 1967: 'Perhaps instead of constantly deploring our lack of identity, we should attempt to understand and explain the regional, ethnic and class identities that we do have. It might just be that it is in these limited identities that "Canadianism" is found' ('Canadian Centennial Celebrations,' *International Journal* 22 (1967):663). Paradoxically, Canadian writers faced with the model of a mosaic have paid less attention to cultural variety than have their American counterparts operating within the context of a melting pot.

CHAPTER 2

1 Beckett, *The Anglo-Irish tradition*, 64.

2 Crawford and Trainor, *Aspects of Irish social history*, xiv.

3 Beckett, *The Anglo-Irish tradition*, 45.

4 Cullen, *An economic history of Ireland since 1660*.

5 Quoted in Crawford and Trainor, *Aspects of Irish social history*, 74.

6 Senior, *Orangeism in Ireland and Britain*.
7 Gibbon, 'The origins of the Orange Order and the United Irishmen.'
8 Dewar, Brown, and Long, *Orangeism: a new historical appreciation*, 99.
9 Senior, *Orangeism in Ireland and Britain*, 58.
10 Ibid., 78.
11 Dewar, Brown, and Long, *Orangeism: a new historical appreciation*, 107.
12 Ibid.
13 Senior, *Orangeism in Ireland and Britain*, 93–4.
14 See membership lists of two County Down lodges, presented by Aiken McClelland, 'Composition of two Orange lodges, 1853,' in *Ulster Folklife* 14 (1968): 62–5.
15 Farrell, *Northern Ireland: the Orange state*, 16.
16 Senior, *Orangeism in Ireland and Britain*, 151.
17 Ibid., 152.
18 Ibid., 265.
19 Ibid., 167.
20 Suggested in Senior, *Orangeism: the Canadian phase*, 64.
21 Senior, 'The genesis of Canadian Orangeism,' 14.
22 Harris and Warkentin, *Canada before confederation: a study in historical geography*, 118.
23 Interview with Mr Lee Murphy, Orange grand master of Quebec, August 1977.
24 Senior, 'The genesis of Canadian Orangeism,' 15.
25 Ibid., 14.
26 Bull, *From the Boyne to Brampton*, 57.
27 Grand Orange Lodge, *Orangeism* (pamphlet, n.d. but issued in the 1970s, copy in OA).
28 Senior, 'The genesis of Canadian Orangeism,' 16.
29 Strachan letterbook, Strachan to A.M. Campbell, 6 October 1841.
30 Bull, *From the Boyne to Brampton*, 132.
31 Quoted in Senior, 'The genesis of Canadian Orangeism,' 26.
32 Quoted in ibid., 24.

CHAPTER 3

1 The best account of the early career of Gowan is to be found in Senior, 'Ogle Gowan, Orangeism, and the immigrant question, 1830–1833.'
2 John Richards, quoted in Cowan, *British emigration to British North America*, 64.
3 *Rules and regulations of the Orange institution of British North America, 1830* (Brockville 1833), 4. (OA)
4 Saunders, *The story of Orangeism*, 28.
5 The date of issue of warrants and localities to which they were issued are recorded in the Loyal Orange Association of British North America, 'Register of warrants, 1830–1963' (4 vols., manuscript, OA). The data in these sources have been cross-checked and verified through a directory of lodges in western

Ontario provided in Saunders, *The story of Orangeism*, and the annual proceedings of the national and provincial grand lodges. The New Brunswick data, unfortunately, are unsuitable for inclusion. The New Brunswick Grand Lodge, which had its own warrant issuing authority, did not keep an updated register of warrants, nor did it number its warrants according to date of issue. It kept to a habit of reissuing the warrant numbers of dormant lodges to new lodges.

6 Only four or five warrants were issued between 1974 and 1979 and at least three of them were to Newfoundland. Information from recent issues of the *Sentinel*.

7 GOLBNA, *Proceedings*, 1840, 10. (OA)

8 Hackett was killed following the 12 July march in Montreal. His death and the execution of Scott by Riel at Fort Garry in 1870, were used frequently in subsequent decades to stir anti-catholic and anti-French sentiments.

9 *Rules and regulations of the Orange institution of British North America, 1830*, 3–4.

10 Quoted in Pauline Roulston, 'The urbanization of nineteenth century Orangeville, Ontario: some historical and geographical aspects' (unpublished MA thesis, University of Toronto 1974).

11 Oral lore of Streetsville, Ont.

12 The Reverend John Kay, quoted in Jean R. Burnet, *Ethnic groups in Upper Canada* (Ontario Historical Society research publication 1, 1972), 105.

13 GOLBNA, *Proceedings*, 1840, 10.

14 AO, Misc. collection, 4, 1840, Letter of instruction to the Reverend George Montgomery West, signed by Ogle R. Gowan, 6 July 1840.

15 Senior, 'The genesis of Canadian Orangeism,' 22.

16 GOLBNA, *Proceedings*, 1840, 11.

17 GOLBNA, *Proceedings*, 1848, 15.

18 *Perth County historical atlas*, xx.

19 Saunders, *The story of Orangeism*, inset list of Orange warrants in York County; and Harcourt P. Gowan, *Annual return of the Loyal Orange Institution in the County of York, Upper Canada, December, 1857*. (OA)

20 John Barnett, 'John Button of Buttonville,' *Ontario History* 34 (194): 75–89.

21 In 1857, Alderman William Strachan was master of LOL 375 in Toronto and the Reverend Henry Bath Osler was master of LOL 736 in Lloydtown. Gowan, *Annual return of the Loyal Orange Institution in the County of York, Upper Canada, December, 1857*.

22 Senior, 'The genesis of Canadian Orangeism,' 14.

23 Robina and Kathleen Lizars, *In the days of the Canada Company* (Toronto 1896), 432.

24 Interestingly, a proposal to translate the Orange ritual into German was introduced at a grand lodge meeting in 1878 (GOLWO, *Proceedings*, 1878, 57–9). No action was taken. In 1905, the Grand Lodge agreed to print the ritual in German (GOLBA, *Proceedings*, 1905, 50), but no further reference to the subject appeared nor have any copies been located.

25 The estimates of protestant Irish were arrived at by subtracting the estimated

number of catholic Irish from the number of Irish in each township as given in the 1871 census. The catholics were determined as the Roman Catholic population less Canadians of French ancestry and others such as catholic Germans and Scots known to be significant in some townships. The methodology, given the cartographic objective, does provide good estimates.

26 The opinion of Mood, 'The Orange Order and Canadian politics, 1841– 1867,' and Cross from whom the quote is taken. Cross, 'Stony Monday, 1849: the rebellion losses riot in Bytown,' 179.

27 Following the estimation procedure outlined in note 25, it was estimated that there were 377,000 Ontarians of protestant Irish background in 1871 and 182,000 of catholic Irish extraction.

28 GOLWO, *Proceedings*, 1870, 8.

29 *Guide book and atlas of Muskoka and Parry Sound districts*, 37.

30 GOLOW, *Proceedings*, 1899, 18.

31 The geography of rural depopulation in nineteenth century Ontario is discussed in Spelt, *Urban development in south-central Ontario*, 101–50.

32 GOLOE, *Proceedings*, 1886.

33 Cartwright, 'Institutions on the frontier: French-Canadian settlement in eastern Ontario in the nineteenth century.'

34 R. Sellar, *The tragedy of Quebec*, 288.

35 Blanchard, *Le Canada français*, 78; Harris and Warkentin, *Canada before confederation*, 98.

36 Senior, *Orangeism: the Canadian phase*, 7.

37 Estimate made in same manner as outlined in note 25.

38 *Proceedings of the Grand Orange Lodge of the Province of Quebec*, 1886, 10. (OA)

39 GOLBNA, *Proceedings*, 1886, 24.

40 *Proceedings of the Grand Orange Lodge of Canada East*, 1858. (OA)

41 *Proceedings of the Grand Orange Lodge of the Province of Quebec*, 1886, 7, 10.

CHAPTER 4

1 Silver, 'French Canada and the prairie frontier, 1870–1890,' 12.

2 Morton, *Manitoba, a history*, 117.

3 Silver, 'French Canada and the prairie frontier.'

4 Senior, *Orangeism: the Canadian phase*, 73.

5 *Proceedings of the Provincial Grand Orange Lodge of Manitoba*, 1935, 84. (OA).

6 Ibid., 1930, 53.

7 Ibid., 53.

8 Ibid., 57.

9 Ibid., 53.

10 GOLBA, *Proceedings*, 1873, 30.

11 GOLOE, *Proceedings*, 1871, 15.

12 Talman, 'Migration from Ontario to Manitoba in 1871.'

13 Rea, 'The roots of prairie society,' 48.

14 Macdonald, *Canada, immigration and colonization, 1841–1903*, 190.
15 *The Carberry plains* (Carberry: Carberry Agricultural Society 1959).
16 Ida Clingan, *The Virden story* (Virden 1957).
17 Information provided by Professor Desmond Morton. See PAC, MG 27, ID3 (papers), vol. 118.
18 *Report of the Grand Orange Lodge of the North-West Territories*, 1895, 48. (OA)
19 Ibid.
20 Loyal Orange Association of British North America, *Register of warrants*.
21 Quoted in *Proceedings of the Grand Orange Lodge of Manitoba*, 1930, 51.
22 Quoted in ibid.
23 Ibid.
24 GOLBA, *Proceedings*, 1892, 15.
25 *Proceedings of the Grand Orange Lodge of British Columbia*, 1901. (OA)
26 Quoted in Keyes, *The Sentinel*, 18.
27 Robin, 'The social basis of party politics in British Columbia.'
28 GOLBA, *Proceedings*, 1889, 22.
29 J. Edward Steele, comp., *History and directory of the Provincial Grand Orange Lodge and primary lodges of New Brunswick, 1690–1934* (Saint John 1934), 11. (OA)
30 Ibid., 17.
31 Ibid., 11.
32 GOLBNA, *Proceedings*, 1849, 9.
33 Steele, *History and directory of the Provincial Grand Orange Lodge and primary lodges of New Brunswick*, 13.
34 *Proceedings of the Provincial Grand Orange Lodge of New Brunswick*, 1864, 16. (OA)
35 GOLBA, *Proceedings*, 1900, 22.
36 The founding of Marysville is discussed in Acheson, 'The National Policy and the industrialization of the Maritimes, 1880–1910.'
37 Senior, *Orangeism: the Canadian phase*, 63.
38 Stanley, 'The Caraquet riots of 1875.'
39 *Novascotian* (Halifax), 27 Sept. 1847, 307.
40 Census of Canada, 1871, *Nova Scotia*.
41 Public Archives of Nova Scotia, MG 20, vol. 507, no. 1 (List of incorporated Loyal Orange Lodges).
42 Erskine, 'The Atlantic region.'
43 Cameron, *Pictou County's history*, 170.
44 According to information in the census of 1871, 93 per cent of Nova Scotians were native born. The corresponding figure for Cape Breton was 83 per cent.
45 Cameron, *Pictou County's history*, 202.
46 Ibid., 198.
47 Ibid., 203.
48 GOLBA, *Register of warrants*.
49 Murphy, *A story of the settlement of the townships of Truro, Onslow, and Londonderry*.
50 Cameron, *Pictou County's history*, 202.

51 A good discussion of industrial decline in Nova Scotia is to be found in Acheson, 'The National Policy.'

52 One of the best descriptions of Prince Edward Island is that in Clark, *Three centuries and the Island.*

53 Ibid., 126.

54 Robertson, 'The Bible question in Prince Edward Island from 1856 to 1860.'

55 Ibid.

56 *Proceedings of the Grand Orange Lodge of Prince Edward Island,* 1900. (OA)

57 Ibid.

58 OA, LOL 2298 (Brackley Point, P.E.I.), Minute book, 1911–9.

59 Ibid.

60 Ibid.

61 E. Senior, 'The origin and political activities of the Orange Order in Newfoundland, 1863–1890,' 4.

62 Mannion, *Irish settlements in eastern Canada,* 23.

63 *Journal of the House of Assembly of Newfoundland, 1909,* App., 463–576. We are indebted to Dr Michael Staveley, Department of Geography, Memorial University of Newfoundland, St John's, for drawing this source to our attention.

64 Smallwood, *I chose Canada,* I, 300.

65 Noel, *Politics in Newfoundland,* 5.

66 GOLBA, *Proceedings,* 1884, 53.

67 Aly O'Brien, St John's, personal communication, November 1977.

68 GOLBA, *Proceedings,* 1899.

69 Noel, *Politics in Newfoundland,* 104.

70 E. Senior, 'The origin and political activities of the Orange Order in Newfoundland,' 148.

71 Ibid., 171.

72 GOLOW, *Proceedings,* 1891, 20.

73 Noel, *Politics in Newfoundland,* 91.

74 Sanger, 'The evolution of sealing and the spread of settlement in north-eastern Newfoundland.'

75 E. Senior, 'The origin and political activities of the Orange Order,' 121–2.

76 Noel, *Politics in Newfoundland,* 83.

77 Ibid., 89.

CHAPTER 5

1 *Rules and regulations of the Orange institution of British North America,* 1830, 15.

2 GOLBNA, *Proceedings,* 1835, duplicated in 'Report from the select committee appointed to enquire into the nature, character, extent and tendency of Orange lodges, associations or societies in Great Britain and the colonies,' 205.

3 J.H. Cameron cited by Mood, 'The Orange Order in Canadian politics, 1841–1867,' 77.

4 GOLBNA, *Proceedings,* 1861, 33.

5 GOLCC, *Proceedings*, 1864, 20.
6 GOLOW, *Proceedings*, 1886, 24.
7 *Report of proceedings of Grand Orange Lodge of New Zealand*, 1889, 22. (OA)
8 GOLBNA, *Proceedings*, 1861, 33.
9 Ibid., 34.
10 Derived from data in Gowan, *Annual return of the Loyal Orange Institution in the County of York, Upper Canada*, 1857.
11 OA, Toronto Loyal Orange District Lodge, Minute book, October 1869–January 1884.
12 Ibid.
13 Data from *Register and directory of the Loyal Orange Association of the City of Toronto*, 1894. (OA)
14 OA, Annual county returns of the Provincial Grand Lodge of Ontario East, 1884.
15 *Proceedings of Provincial Grand Orange Lodge of Prince Edward Island*, 1898. (OA)
16 *Proceedings of the Grand Lodge of Manitoba and the NWT*, 1890, 19. (OA)
17 *Proceedings of the Grand Lodge of the North-West Territories*, 1895, 12.
18 *Golden jubilee report of the Provincial Grand Lodge of Newfoundland*, 1914.
19 An approximate figure based on data in *Report of proceedings of the Imperial Grand Orange Council of the World*, 1900, 17–25 (OA); GOLOW, *Proceedings*, 1896, 35; GOLOE, *Proceedings*, 1901.
20 *Report of proceedings of the Imperial Grand Orange Council of the World*, 1900, 17–25.
21 Ibid.
22 Estimate based on Canada census, 1901.
23 GOLWO, *Proceedings*, 1872.
24 GOLOE, *Proceedings*, 1908.
25 Ibid., 1940.
26 Ibid., 1921.
27 Livermore, 'The Orange Order and the election of 1861 in Kingston.'
28 Kealey, 'The Orange Order in Toronto: religious riot and the working class,' 18.
29 GOLWO, *Proceedings*, 1880, 26.
30 GOLWO, *Proceedings*, 1881.
31 GOLWO, *Proceedings*, 1863, 1866, 1894, 1900; GOLOE, *Proceedings*, 1897; GOLBA, *Proceedings*, 1882, 10.
32 Kealey, 'The Orange Order in Toronto, 18.
33 OA, Toronto Loyal Orange District Lodge, Minute book, October 1869–January 1884.
34 Mayor Beaudry of Montreal infuriated the order in 1878 when he prevented Orangemen from marching on the Twelfth and commemorating the death of Hackett at the previous celebration. The militia were called out to support the civil authorities – an indication of the episode's seriousness.
35 Rarely would an Orangeman, after withdrawing from the fraternity, renege on

his oath. This has been impressed emphatically upon the authors in their field interviews with formerly active Orangemen in many parts of Canada.

36 Gagan, 'Geographical and social mobility in nineteenth century Ontario: a microstudy.'

37 Katz, *The people of Hamilton, Canada West, 1851–1861.*

38 GOLBA, *Proceedings*, 1897.

39 (259 net on certificate plus 1386 net suspensions plus 92 expulsions)

40 Summation of initiation records cited in GOLBA, *Proceedings*, 1891–1900.

41 GOLBA, *Proceedings*, 1904, 28; 1905, 28.

42 Orange claims of general membership ranging from 200,000 in the 1870s to 400,000 in the early 1900s are feasible given the turnover potential of the organization. The figure of 400,000 was offered in 1905 by T.S. Sproule, then grand secretary and later speaker of the Canadian House of Commons (GOLBA, *Proceedings*, 1905, 27). Those figures would represent about one-third of Canada's protestant adult male population at the time. Historian P.B. Waite has also indicated that one-third of all protestant adult males was a reasonable estimate of Orange strength in the late 1870s (*Arduous destiny: Canada, 1874–96*, 87).

43 GOLWO, *Proceedings*, 1869, 5–6.

44 Ibid., 1880, 27.

45 Data from *Report of Proceedings of the M.W. Grand Lodge of Orange Young Britons, 1902* (Russell, Ont., n.d.), 52–6. (OA)

46 GOLOW, *Proceedings*, 1892, 39.

47 GOLCC, *Proceedings*, 1866, 13.

48 *Report of proceedings of the Provincial Grand Orange Lodge of New Brunswick*, 1904, 26. (OA)

49 Steele, *History and directory of the Provincial Grand Orange Lodge and primary lodges of New Brunswick, 1690–1934*, 17.

50 Lovelock, 'Reminiscences of Toronto Orangeism,' 9.

51 Ibid., 10.

52 Gowan, *Annual return of the Loyal Orange Institution in the County of York, Upper Canada*, 1857.

53 Kealey, 'The Orange Order in Toronto.'

54 *Register and directory of the Loyal Orange Association of the City of Toronto*, 1894.

55 Glazebrook, *The story of Toronto*, and Goheen, *Victorian Toronto*.

56 This term has been applied by Boal, 'Territoriality on the Shankhill-Falls divide, Belfast.'

57 Baker, 'Orange and Green: Belfast, 1832–1912'; Boal, 'Territoriality on the Shankhill-Falls divide, Belfast.'

58 Kealey, 'The Orange Order in Toronto.'

CHAPTER 6

1 Although the Masonic Order and the Oddfellows both appeared in Ontario in the early nineteenth century, it was not until after 1870 that either became numerically strong.

2 Lovelock, 'Reminiscences of Toronto Orangeism,' 11, 15.
3 OA, LOL 215 (Leslieville, Ont.), Minute book, 1839.
4 Region of Peel Archives (Brampton, Ont.), Peel County LOL 5, Lodge minute book, 1838–1839.
5 Bull, *From the Boyne to Brampton*, 137.
6 *By-laws and regulations of the Loyal Orange Temperance Lodge no. 301*, (Toronto 1852), 5.
7 GOLBNA, *Proceedings*, 1848, 20.
8 Ibid., 1854, 30.
9 OA, LOL 215, Minute book, 5 Dec. 1856.
10 *Report of Proceedings of the Grand Orange Lodge of Canada East* [Quebec], 1858, 9–10.
11 Bull, *From the Boyne to Brampton*, 220.
12 Ibid., 138.
13 GOLBNA, *Proceedings*, 1863.
14 GOLBA, *Proceedings*, 1883, 47.
15 Noel, *Politics in Newfoundland*, 132.
16 *Forms to be observed in private lodges of the Loyal Orange Institution of British North America* (Toronto 1869), 5. (OA)
17 Ibid.
18 *Rules and regulations of the Orange Institution of British North America*, 1830.
19 OA, Toronto Loyal Orange District Lodge, Minute book, October 1869–January 1884.
20 *Forms to be used in all lodges of the Loyal Orange Association of British America* (Toronto 1923), 11–12. (OA)
21 Ibid., 12.
22 Ibid.
23 *Forms to be observed in the royal arch purple mark order, of private lodges, of the Loyal Orange Institution of British North America* (Belleville 1860), 13. (OA)
24 *Forms and ritual of the royal scarlet order to be observed in private chapters of the Orange Association of British North America* (Cobourg 1846), 9. (OA)
25 Information gained during field work in the Napanee district, Ontario, September 1977.
26 *Forms to be observed in the purple order of private lodges, of the Loyal Orange Institution of British North America* (Belleville 1860), 8. (OA)
27 *Forms to be observed in the royal blue order of private lodges, of the Loyal Orange Institution of British North America* (Belleville 1860), 7. (OA)
28 Ibid., 13.
29 *Rules and regulations of the Orange Institution of British North America*, 1830.
30 *Globe* (Toronto), 14 July 1890.
31 Dewar *et al.*, *Orangeism: a new historical appreciation*.
32 OA, LOL 215, Minute book, July 1841.
33 *By-laws and regulations of the Loyal Orange Temperance Lodge no. 301*, 12.

34 Arthur R. Scammell, 'Outport memories,' in J.R. Smallwood, *The New-foundland book*, vol. 4 (St John's 1967), 240.

35 GOLBA, *Proceedings*, 1885.

36 Bull, *From the Boyne to Brampton*, 139.

37 GOLOE, *Proceedings*, 1881, 52–4.

38 OA, LOL 215, Minute book, 16 Sept. 1853.

39 Toronto Loyal Orange District Lodge, Minute book, April 1876.

40 Lovelock, 'Reminiscences of Toronto Orangeism,' 11.

41 GOLOW, *Proceedings*, 1875.

42 GOLBNA, *Proceedings*, 1856, 86; 1857, 22.

43 GOLBA, *Proceedings*, 1874, 43.

44 Ibid., 1870, 18.

45 As well as supplying aid to fellow Orangemen in times of crises, the order was also instrumental in establishing protestant orphanages in most provinces. Toronto Orangemen spent more than four thousand dollars on charity in 1880.

46 *Rules and regulations of the Orange Institution of British North America*, 1830.

47 *By-laws and regulations of the Loyal Orange Temperance Lodge no. 301*, 9.

48 *By-laws of the Loyal Orange Virgin Lodge no. 328* (Toronto 1872). (OA)

49 Ibid. (1852), 7.

50 OA, Toronto Loyal Orange District Lodge, Minute book, 1858.

51 *Constitution and by-laws of Ottawa Loyal Orange Benevolent Lodge no. 126* (Ottawa 1877), 8. (OA)

52 Letters from Dr Parry included in OA, LOL 342 (Toronto), Roll book, 1874–88.

53 *Register and directory of the Loyal Orange Association of the City of Toronto*, 1894, 45.

54 Ibid.

55 *Constitution and by-laws of Ottawa Loyal Orange Benevolent Lodge no 126*, 10.

56 Saunders, *The story of Orangeism*, 31.

57 *Constitution and by-laws of Ottawa Loyal Orange Benevolent Lodge no. 126*, 10.

58 *By-laws of York LOL no. 375* (Toronto 1894), 16.

59 Region of Peel Archives, Peel County LOL 5, Lodge minute book, 1835.

60 *By-laws and regulations of the Loyal Orange Temperance Lodge no. 301*, 9; *Constitution and by-laws of Ottawa Loyal Orange Benevolent Lodge no. 126*, 12; *By-laws of LOL no. 711* (1898), 15.

61 *Forms to be observed in performing the ceremonies prescribed for the burial of an Orangeman; the dedication of an Orange hall; the opening of a new Orange lodge; and the laying of the corner stone of an Orange hall* (Belleville 1873), 6. (OA)

62 *By-laws of York LOL no. 375* (1894), 18.

63 The better writing on British Friendly Societies is that by Gosden, *The*

Friendly Societies in England, 1815–1875; Fuller, *West Country Friendly Societies*; and Supple, 'Legislation and virtue: an essay on working class self-help and the state in the early nineteenth century.'

64 As early as 1803 a total of 700,000 members in British Friendly Societies was recorded and by 1872 their strength was estimated at 4 million (Gosden, *The Friendly Societies in England*, 6).

65 GOLOW, *Proceedings*, 1883, 98.

66 Ibid., 1891, 28.

67 GOLBA, *Proceedings*, 1899.

68 Ontario, *Report of the inspector of insurance and registrar of Friendly Societies*, 1900–20.

69 Ibid.

70 Wayne Roberts, Department of History, McMaster University, Hamilton, Ont., commenting on IOF administrators at a symposium at University College, University of Toronto, November 1977.

71 Ontario, *Report of the inspector of insurance and registrar of Friendly Societies*, 1920.

72 Based on field observations of about five hundred Orange halls across Canada.

73 Information obtained during field enquiry, Wareham, Newfoundland, July 1978.

74 OA, LOL 1516 (Ladysmith, Que.), Minute book, 1893.

75 GOLBA, *Proceedings*, 1903, 54.

76 Newfoundland's own fraternity, the Society of United Fishermen, also publicly portrayed its symbolism, and today on the island there is no greater show of institutional colour and bravado than that proclaimed by the Salvation Army temples.

77 Thompson, *The making of the English working class*, 458.

CHAPTER 7

1 Morton, 'Victorian Canada,' 311–33.

2 Ibid., 314.

3 For a discussion of anti-catholic feeling in Toronto in the 1850s see Dyster, 'Toronto, 1840–1860: Making it in a British protestant town,' 404–20.

4 Berger, *The sense of power*, 103.

5 GOLBA, *Proceedings*, 1893, 37.

6 Senior, *Orangeism: the Canadian phase*, 95.

7 GOLBA, *Proceedings*, 1892, 15.

8 Smith, 'Old Ontario and the emergence of a national frame of mind,' 210.

9 Berger, *The sense of power*, 49.

10 Ibid., 217.

11 GOLBA, *Proceedings*, 1892, 15.

12 Ibid., 1900, quoted in Keyes, *The Sentinel*, 14.

13 GOLBA, *Proceedings*, 1900, 176.

14 Quoted in Keyes, *The Sentinel*, 24.

15 Quoted in ibid., 26.

16 Quoted in ibid.

17 OA, LOL 275 (Toronto), Minute book, 1917.

18 Senior, 'Ogle Gowan, Orangeism, and the immigrant question,' 205.

19 Mackenzie was also opposed by the catholic hierarchy. For once Orange and catholic interests were enmeshed and words of surprising amity passed between the two groups. In fact, Orangemen in Toronto had from 1833 refrained from marching on the Twelfth. They celebrated the occasion by private lodge dinners in order to avoid any public confrontation with catholics. For other elements of these Orange-catholic relations see Kerr, 'When Orange and Green united, 1832–9: the alliance of Macdonald and Gowan,' 34–42.

20 Sanderson, The Arthur papers, 218.

21 Lucas, ed., Lord Durham's report on the affairs of British North America, 129.

22 Quoted in Mood, 'The Orange Order in Canadian politics, 1841–1867,' 92.

23 Ibid.

24 Noted in Senior, Orangeism: the Canadian phase, 55.

25 Harcourt P. Gowan, Annual return of the Loyal Orange Institution in the County of York, Upper Canada, December, 1857.

26 Senior, Orangeism: the Canadian phase, 54.

27 Gowan, Annual return of the Loyal Orange Institution in the County of York, Upper Canada.

28 OA, Toronto Loyal Orange District Lodge, Minute book, 10 Aug. 1858–11 June 1869.

29 Ibid.

30 GOLBNA, Proceedings, 1863, 11.

31 Resolutions expressing displeasure with Cameron's defence of Patrick James Whelan were passed by Toronto lodges and the Toronto district lodge.

32 Senior, Orangeism: the Canadian phase, 95.

33 Cartwright, Reminiscences, 89.

34 Ibid., 89–90.

35 The act of incorporation arrived after a struggle of almost forty years at colonial, provincial, and national levels.

36 Hopkins, ed., Canada, an encyclopedia of the country, 320.

37 Kemp's membership in the order is noted in a letter from H.C. Hocken to Sir Robert Borden (PAC, MG 26, H (R.L. Borden papers), 13734). This information was brought to our attention by Professor Desmond Morton.

38 Hatfield, 'H.H. Pitts and race and religion in New Brunswick politics,' 46–65.

39 Ibid., 63.

40 Swainson, Oliver Mowat's Ontario, 5.

41 Ibid.

42 GOLOE, Proceedings, 1881, 14–15.

43 Prang, 'Clerics, politicians, and the bilingual schools issue in Ontario,' 85–111.

44 Ibid.; Barber, 'The Ontario bilingual schools issue: sources of conflict,' 67–84.

45 Donald C. Macdonald, Review of *G. Howard Ferguson, Ontario Tory* by Peter Oliver, *Globe and Mail* (Toronto), 24 Sept. 1977.
46 Thomas O'Hagen, *The truth, nothing but the truth* (AO pamphlets, no. 65, n.p., 1915). Cited in Pennefather, 'The Orange Order and the United Farmers of Ontario, 1919–1923,' 183.
47 *Sentinel* (Toronto), 6 Nov. 1923.
48 *Golden jubilee report of the Provincial Grand Lodge of Newfoundland*, 1914, 12.
49 GOLOE, *Proceedings*, 1940, 13.
50 Watt, 'Anti-catholic nativism in Canada: the Protestant Protective Association,' 46.
51 GOLOE, *Proceedings*, 1898, 74.
52 There are many records of PPA meetings in halls in western Ontario and two are known also for eastern Ontario. LOL 368 at Camden East and LOL 756 at Centreville, both in Lennox and Addington County, rented their halls for PPA meetings: see Brown, *Camden Township history, 1800–1968*.
53 In Essex County for example an Orange hall was rented by the PPA in the spring of 1892, but when the intent of the meeting was understood the group was ejected. Much to the expressed consternation of the Orange grand lodge, Toronto papers reported that a successful meeting had taken place. GOLOW, *Proceedings*, 1892, 21.
54 Senior, *Orangeism: the Canadian phase*, 82.
55 Watt, 'Anti-catholic nativism in Canada: the Protestant Protective Association,' 46.
56 Cited in Kyba, 'Ballots and burning crosses – the election of 1929,' 109.
57 Information obtained during field enquiries in the Kingston and Brockville areas of Ontario, 1977.
58 Calderwood, 'The rise and fall of the Ku Klux Klan in Saskatchewan,' 174–6.
59 Determined through a comparison of maps depicting the locations of Klaverns and Orange lodges. Data on the Klan from the papers of the Rt. Hon. Garfield Gardiner, reproduced in Calderwood, 'The rise and fall,' 271–3. Orange Lodge data from *Proceedings of Provincial Grand Lodge of Saskatchewan*, 1925 and 1930 (OA), with additional material from GOLBNA, *Register of warrants*.
60 Masters, *The rise of Toronto, 1850–1890*, 193.
61 Nelles and Armstrong, *The revenge of the Methodist Bicycle Company*.
62 Coined by Orangemen and employed frequently from the 1880s onward.
63 The Canadian artist and writer Wyndham Lewis described Toronto as being both 'this sanctimonious icebox' and 'this bush metropolis of the Orange lodges' (cited in Kilbourn, *The Toronto book: an anthology of writings past and present*, 48–9).
64 Mood, 'The Orange Order in Canadian politics, 1841–67,' 42.
65 City of Toronto Archives, Electoral results, City of Toronto, 1894.
66 Ibid.
67 *Evening Telegram* (Toronto), 22 Dec. 1893.

68 *Sentinel*, 21 Dec. 1893.
69 Glazebrook, *The story of Toronto*, 64.
70 G.M. Rose, ed. *A cyclopaedia of Canadian biography, being chiefly men of the time* (Toronto 1896), 186.
71 *Globe* (Toronto), 9 Oct. 1893.
72 *Evening Telegram*, 12 July 1893.

CHAPTER 8

1 *Toronto Star*, 11 July 1977.
2 *Canada Year Book*, 1971.
3 *Register and directory of the Loyal Orange Association of the City of Toronto*, 1894.
4 Berger, *The sense of power*, 264.
5 GOLOE, *Proceedings*, 1931, 10.
6 Keyes, *The Sentinel*, 33.
7 GOLOE, *Proceedings*, 1960, 9.
8 Ibid.
9 This phrase was used by A.R.M. Lower as the title for his book, *Colony to nation.*
10 Public lecture given by Northrop Frye, Victoria College, University of Toronto, 10 Nov. 1977.
11 N. Frye, 'A summary of the Options Conference,' University of Toronto *Bulletin*, 10 Nov. 1977, 6–7.
12 *Sentinel*, February 1979, 25.
13 C.K.S. Moffatt, *Canada's immigration policy?* (pamphlet, n.p., [1975?]).
14 Ibid.
15 *Sentinel* (Toronto), March 1976.
16 C.K.S. Moffatt, *The English language* (pamphlet, n.p., [1975?]).
17 T. Raymond Reside and Norman R. Ritchie, *National unity* (pamphlet, Toronto 1977).
18 *Globe and Mail* (Toronto), 9 Oct. 1976.
19 *Globe and Mail*, 6 Oct. 1977.
20 *Toronto Sun*, 6 Oct. 1977.
21 *Globe and Mail*, 13 Feb. 1978.

CONCLUSIONS

1 Description by Orange grand chaplain in GOLOW, *Proceedings*, 1886, 43.

Bibliography

The principal sources for this study are the documents of the national, provincial, county, district, and local lodges of the Loyal Orange Association of British America. Of major importance was the four-volume manuscript 'Register of Warrants, 1830–1963.' It contains a record of warrants authorizing the foundation of local lodges in all Canadian provinces except New Brunswick. These documents give the date and location of new lodges as well as the names of those to whom the warrants were issued. Comparable data for New Brunswick do not exist. The New Brunswick group, because of the province's record as an independent centre of early Orangeism, retained warrant-issuing authority but did not pay strict attention to administrative detail.

The printed documents of the association comprise another important fund of information. Rules, regulations, and basic ritual (excluding secrets) of the order are available in printed manuals. Reports of the annual sessions of the national and provincial grand lodges include, from time to time, lists of lodges and their location – critical information for reconstructing the order's geography. The annual reports also provide – through the transcribed addresses of officers, motions raised, occasional references to membership, and sundry records of fraternal business – a great deal of material on the internal operations of the order. Speeches and the odd motion contain references to general political matters relating to loyalty and the welfare of protestantism and the order. However, there was no place in the formal order of business for much discussion of party politics and electoral issues. Political passion was generally manifested outside the formal lodge session and little of it was written about in the lodge records. The same applies to the recorded affairs of local lodges.

The documents of local lodges include primarily manuscript minutes of meetings, statements of dues, and membership rolls. Minute books contain in the main a formalized set of business entries prescribed by the regulations of the organization (see above, p. 118) and occasional references to events and conditions outside the lodge. The membership rolls of the local lodges contain the names of members, generally their addresses, sometimes age or occupation, and rarely denomination. As is the case for the national and provincial records there is virtually no correspondence among the materials.

All the primary documents employed here and given the location reference OA are held in the national and regional archives under the jurisdiction of the Grand Lodge of British America. The national archive is located in Toronto; the regional repositories are kept by secretaries of the provincial lodges. Other than for the printed proceedings of the grand lodges of Ontario (1860 to present), of Canada (1830 to present), and of the other provinces (1929 to present) in the Toronto Orange archive, no central catalogue exists. The Metropolitan Toronto Library, the Public Archives of Canada, the provincial archives in Ontario, New Brunswick, and Nova Scotia, as well as a number of university libraries contain primary source material pertaining to the Orange Order. For the most part, however, the materials in those locations are fragmentary in terms of both their temporal and regional coverage. For this reason the authors approached the Canadian provincial and national grand Orange lodges and several local lodges in Ontario, Quebec, New Brunswick, Prince Edward Island, and Newfoundland. Through visits to these lodges, field excursions into Orange areas, and attendance at Twelfth parades and strawberry festivals, much was learned of Orange landscapes and local lore.

In the text, manuscript records of local and district lodges are referenced only where direct statements from them are presented. In addition, to simplify the notation of the printed annual reports of proceedings of the national grand lodge and of Ontario's two provincial grand lodges, an abbreviated form of notation is used. See the list of abbreviations under notes.

MAJOR SECONDARY SOURCES

Acheson, T.W. 'The National Policy and the industrialization of the Maritimes, 1880–1910.' *Acadiensis* I (1972): 3–28
Baker, S.E. 'Orange and Green: Belfast, 1832–1912.' In H.J. Dyos and Michael Wolff, eds., *The Victorian city: images and realities*, vol. II, 789–814. London: Routledge and Kegan Paul 1973
Barber, Marilyn. 'The Ontario bilingual schools issue: sources of conflict.' In R.C. Brown, ed., *Minorities, schools, and politics*, 67–84. Toronto: University of Toronto Press 1969
Beckett, J.C. *The Anglo-Irish tradition.* London: Faber and Faber 1976
Berger, Carl. *The sense of power.* Toronto: University of Toronto Press 1970
– *The writing of Canadian history.* Toronto: Oxford University Press 1976
Blanchard, Raoul. *Le Canada français.* Montréal: Librairie Artheme Fayard 1960
Boal, F.W. 'Territoriality on the Shankhill-Falls divide, Belfast.' *Irish Geography* 6, no. 1 (1969): 30–50
Brown, Douglas B., ed. *Camden Township history, 1800–1968.* Centreville, [Ont.] 1969

Bull, Wm. Perkins. *From the Boyne to Brampton*. Toronto 1936

Calderwood, William. 'The rise and fall of the Ku Klux Klan in Saskatchewan.' Unpublished MA thesis, University of Saskatchewan 1968

Cameron, J.M. *Pictou County's history*. Pictou Historical Society 1972

Cartwright, D.G. 'Institutions on the frontier: French-Canadian settlement in eastern Ontario in the nineteenth century.' *Canadian Geographer* 21 (1977): 1–21

Cartwright, Sir Richard J. *Reminiscences*. Toronto 1912

Clark, Andrew H. *Three centuries and the Island: a historical geography of settlement and agriculture in Prince Edward Island, Canada*. Toronto: University of Toronto Press 1959

– 'Old World origins and religious adherence in Nova Scotia.' *Geographical Review* 50 (1960): 317–441

Clark, S.D. *The developing Canadian community*. Toronto: University of Toronto Press 1962

Cowan, Helen I. *British emigration to British North America*. Toronto: University of Toronto Press 1961

Crawford, W.H., and B. Trainor, eds. *Aspects of Irish social history, 1750–1800*. Belfast: HMSO 1969

Cross, Michael S. 'Stony Monday, 1849: the rebellion losses riot in Bytown.' *Ontario History* 63 (1971): 177–90

Cullen, L.M. *An economic history of Ireland since 1660*. London: B.T. Batsford 1972

Dewar, M.W., John Brown, and S.E. Long. *Orangeism: a new historical appreciation*. Belfast: Grand Orange Lodge of Ireland 1967

Dyster, Barrie D. 'Toronto 1840–1860: Making it in a British protestant town.' Unpublished PHD thesis, University of Toronto 1970

Egan, Patrick K. *The influence of the Irish on the Catholic Church in America in the nineteenth century*. Dublin: National University of Ireland 1968

Erskine, D. 'The Atlantic region.' In J. Warkentin, ed., *Canada: a geographical interpretation*, 231–81. Toronto: Methuen 1967

Farrell, Michael. *Northern Ireland: the Orange state*. London: Pluto Press 1976

Fuller, Margaret D. *West Country Friendly Societies*. Reading: Oakwood Press 1964

Gagan, David. 'Geographical and social mobility in nineteenth century Ontario: a microstudy.' *Canadian Review of Sociology and Anthropology* 13, no. 2 (1976): 152–64

Gibbon, Peter. 'The Origins of the Orange Order and the United Irishmen: a study in the sociology of revolution and counter revolution.' *Economy and Society* 7, no. 2 (1972): 134–63

Glazebrook, G.P. de T. *Life in Ontario: a social history*. Toronto: University of Toronto Press 1971

Goheen, Peter G. *Victorian Toronto, 1850 to 1900*. University of Chicago, Department of Geography, Research paper no. 127, Chichago 1970

Gosden, P.H.J.H. *The Friendly Societies in England, 1815–1875*. Manchester: Manchester University Press 1961

Gowan, Ogle R. *Orangeism: its origin and history.* Toronto 1859

Guide book and atlas of Muskoka and Parry Sound districts. Toronto 1879

Harris, R. Cole, and John Warkentin. *Canada before confederation: a study in historical geography.* Toronto: Oxford University Press 1974

Hatfield, Michael. 'H.H. Pitts and race and religion in New Brunswick politics.' *Acadiensis* 5 (1975): 46–65

Hopkins, John C., ed. *Canada, an encyclopedia of the country.* Vol. VI. Toronto 1900

Houston, Cecil, and William J. Smyth. 'The Orange Order and the expansion of the frontier in Ontario, 1830–1900,' *Journal of Historical Geography* 4, no. 3 (1978): 251–64

– 'The Ulster Legacy,' *Multiculturalism* 1, no. 4 (1978): 9–12

Katz, Michael. *The people of Hamilton, Canada West, 1851–1861.* Cambridge, Mass.: Harvard University Press 1974

Kealey, Gregory S. 'The Orange Order in Toronto: religious riot and the working class.' In G.S. Kealey and P. Warrian, eds., *Essays in Canadian working class history,* 13–35. Toronto: McClelland and Stewart 1976

Kerr, W.B. 'When Orange and Green united, 1832–9: the alliance of Macdonnell and Gowan.' *Ontario History* 34 (1942): 34–42

Keyes, Gordon. *The Sentinel, centennial issue, 1875–1975.* Toronto: British American Publishing Co. 1975

Kilbourn, William, ed. *The Toronto book: an anthology of writings past and present.* Toronto: Macmillan 1976

Kyba, Patrick. 'Ballots and burning crosses – the election of 1929.' In Norman Ward and Duff Spafford, eds., *Politics in Saskatchewan.* Don Mills, Ont.: Longman Canada 1968

Livermore, J.D. 'The Orange Order and the election of 1861 in Kingston.' In Gerald Tulchinsky, ed. *To preserve and defend,* 245–59. Montreal: McGill-Queen's University Press 1976

Lovelock, Harry. 'Reminiscences of Toronto Orangeism.' In *Official Orange Souvenir, Toronto, July 12th, 1902.* (Pamphlet consulted at University of Toronto Library)

Lower, A.R.M. *Colony to nation.* Toronto: Longman Canada 1946

Lucas, C.P., ed. *Lord Durham's report on the affairs of British North America.* Oxford: Oxford University Press 1912

Macdonald, Norman. *Canada, immigration and colonization, 1841–1903.* Aberdeen: Aberdeen University Press 1966

Mannion, John. *Irish settlements in eastern Canada: a study of cultural transfer and adaptation.* Toronto: University of Toronto Press 1974

Moir, John S. *Church and State in Canada West: three studies in the relation of denominationalism and nationalism, 1841–1867.* Toronto: University of Toronto Press 1959

Mood, William J.S. 'The Orange Order in Canadian politics, 1841–67.' Unpublished MA thesis, University of Toronto 1950

Morton, W.L. *Manitoba, a history.* Toronto 1957

– 'Victorian Canada.' In W.L. Morton, ed., *The shield of Achilles, aspects of Canada in the Victorian age,* 311–33. Toronto 1968

Murphy, J.M. *A story of the settlement of the townships of Truro, Onslow, and Londonderry.* N.p. 1960
Nelles, H.V., and Christopher Armstrong. *The revenge of the Methodist Bicycle Company: Sunday streetcars and municipal reform in Toronto, 1888–1897.* Toronto: Peter Martin 1977
Nemec, Thomas F. 'The Irish emigration to Newfoundland.' *Newfoundland Quarterly* 4 (1972)
Noel, S.J.R. *Politics in Newfoundland.* Toronto: University of Toronto Press 1972
Oliver, Peter. *G. Howard Ferguson: Ontario Tory.* Toronto: University of Toronto Press 1977
Ontario, *Report of the inspector of insurance and registrar of friendly societies.* Annual. Issues for 1900–20 consulted.
Pennefather, R.S. 'The Orange Order and the United Farmers of Ontario, 1919–1923.' *Ontario History* 69 (1977): 169–84
Perth County historical atlas. Toronto 1879
Prang, Margaret. 'Clerics, politicians, and the bilingual schools issue in Ontario.' In R.C. Brown, ed., *Minorities, schools, and politics*, 85–111. Toronto: University of Toronto Press 1969
Rea, J.E. 'The roots of prairie society.' In David P. Gagan, ed., *Prairie perspectives.* Toronto: Holt, Rinehart and Winston 1970
'Report from the select committee appointed to enquire into the nature, character, extent, and tendency of Orange lodges, associations, or societies in Great Britain and the colonies,' with the minutes of evidence and appendix and index, *H.C. 1835 (605)*, XVII
Robertson, I.R. 'The Bible question in Prince Edward Island from 1856 to 1860.' *Acadiensis* 7 (1977): 3–25
Robin, Martin. 'The social basis of party politics in British Columbia.' In B.R. Blishen, F.E. Jones, K.D. Naegele and J. Porter, eds., *Canadian society, sociological perspectives*, vol. 3, 290–300. Toronto: Macmillan 1973
Sanderson, Charles R., ed. *The Arthur papers.* Toronto: University of Toronto Press 1957
Sanger, Chesley. 'The evolution of sealing and the spread of settlement in north-eastern Newfoundland.' In John Mannion, ed., *The peopling of Newfoundland: essays in historical geography*, 136–51. St John's: Memorial University of Newfoundland 1977
Saunders, Leslie H. *The story of Orangeism.* Toronto 1960
Sellar, Robert. *The tragedy of Quebec, the expulsion of its protestant farmers.* Reprint. Toronto: University of Toronto Press 1974
Senior, Elinor. 'The origin and political activities of the Orange Order in Newfoundland.' Unpublished MA thesis, Memorial University of Newfoundland 1960
Senior, Hereward. 'The genesis of Canadian Orangeism.' *Ontario History* 60 (1968): 13–39
– 'Orangeism in Ontario politics, 1872–1896.' In Donald Swainson, ed., *Oliver Mowat's Ontario*, 136–54. Toronto: Macmillan 1972
– *Orangeism: the Canadian phase.* Toronto: McGraw-Hill 1972

- 'Ogle Gowan, Orangeism, and the immigrant question, 1830–33.' *Ontario History* 66 (1974): 193–210
- *Orangeism in Ireland and Britain, 1795–1836.* London: Routledge and Kegan Paul 1966

Silver, A.I. 'French Canada and the prairie frontier, 1870–1890.' *Canadian Historical Review* 50 (1969): 11–36

Smallwood, Joseph R. *I chose Canada.* Vol. 1. Scarborough, Ont.: New American Library 1975

Smith, Allan. 'Metaphor and nationality in North America.' *Canadian Historical Review* 51 (1970): 247–75
- 'Old Ontario and the emergence of a national frame of mind.' In F.H. Armstrong, H.A. Stevenson, and J.D. Wilson, eds., *Aspects of nineteenth century Ontario, essays presented to James J. Talman,* 194–217. Toronto: University of Toronto Press 1974

Stanley, G.F.G. 'The Caraquet riots of 1875.' *Acadiensis* 2 (1972): 21–39

Spelt, Jacob. *Urban development in south-central Ontario.* Toronto: McClelland and Stewart 1972

Supple, Barry. 'Legislation and virtue: an essay on working class self-help and the state in the early nineteenth century.' In Neil McKendrick, ed., *Historical perspectives: studies in English thought and society in honour of J.H. Plumb.* London: Europa 1974

Talman, James J. 'Migration From Ontario to Manitoba in 1871.' *Ontario History* 43 (1951): 35–41

Thompson, E.P. *The making of the English working class.* London: Gollancz 1964

Waite, Peter B. *Arduous destiny: Canada, 1874–96.* Toronto: McClelland and Stewart 1971

Watt, James T. 'Anti-catholic nativism in Canada: the Protestant Protective Association.' *Canadian Historical Review* 48 (1967): 45–58

List of tables

List of figures

List of drawings and photographs

Index